PATIENTS' RIGHTS AND PROFESSIONAL PRACTICE

PATIENTS' RIGHTS AND PROFESSIONAL PRACTICE

James T. Ziegenfuss, Jr., Ph.D., M.P.A.

Harrisburg, Pennsylvania

VNR **VAN NOSTRAND REINHOLD COMPANY**
NEW YORK   CINCINNATI   TORONTO   LONDON   MELBOURNE

Manufactured in the United States of America

Published by Van Nostrand Reinhold Company Inc.
135 West 50th Street, New York, N.Y. 10020

Van Nostrand Reinhold Publishing
1410 Birchmount Road
Scarborough, Ontario MIP 2E7, Canada

Van Nostrand Reinhold
480 Latrobe Street
Melbourne, Victoria 3000, Australia

Van Nostrand Reinhold Company Limited
Molly Millars Lane
Wokingham, Berkshire, England

15 14 13 12 11 10 9 8 7 6 5 4 3 2 1

Library of Congress Cataloging in Publication Data

Ziegenfuss, James T.
    Patients' rights and professional practice.

    Includes index.
    1. Hospital patients. 2. Hospital patients — Legal
status, laws, etc. — United States. 3. Institutional
care. 4. Medical personnel and patient. I. Title.
[DNLM: 1. Teaching — Methods — Nursing texts.
2. Patient education — Methods — Nursing texts. W1 ST929N
no. 9 / WY 105 M665p]
RA965.6.Z53 1983   362.1'1   82-17566
ISBN 0-442-29434-4

To
Margee, Kate, and Sarah
with Love

To
Margee, Kate, and Sarah
with Love

Preface

My interest in patients' rights began in 1972 some ten years ago. At that time, I became involved as a staff member of a new unit which attempted to integrate patients' rights in a state mental hospital's residential therapeutic community program. The program was one of the earlier efforts to accommodate patients' rights by changing program designs and systems. Although open only for one year, the program did demonstrate an ability to accommodate rights by adapting existing, and creating new, organizational policies and procedures.

Since that time, I have had the good fortune to be involved in patients' rights work by helping to extend the protection of rights into evaluation designs. After all, if rights are defined as an important aspect of service, the level of compliance with rights should be evaluated along with other service system subjects. For public accountability, providing an effective service operation is necessary, but such a program cannot be sufficient without rights adherence. Services must be effective and comply with rights requirements. Evaluation of the compliance sets the stage for organizational change if necessary by defining the needs for change with respect to rights.

These experiences tied the rights issues to evaluation, and ultimately to organizational development. For me, the best way to conceptualize this fit is through the application of systems theory to organizations. I was able to continue work on both rights and organizational design through the courses I had in my training at the Social Systems Sciences Department of the Wharton School, University of Pennsylvania. There, I was able to consider whether some ways of organizing program systems are more consistent with patients' rights than are others. My advisors, Professors Eric Trist and Peter Davis were particularly supportive and helpful to the work.

During the past several years, I have been advising on the development of a patients' rights representative program for one state's welfare department. This program is focused on three activities: (1) complaint processing for patients who feel their rights have been violated; (2) education for staff and patients about what rights exist; and (3) consultation on how to develop organizational policies and procedures that are consistent with rights. Thus, the program is organizational-development oriented, not adversarial in nature. With this perspective, staff are not defined as "bad guys." They are seen as persons in need of alternative methods of behaving which are consistent with the new rights demands. Early evaluations indicate that the program is quite successful, with full acceptance and support from patients and staff.

What are the current problems and needs in the area of patients' rights? For me, it involves three core tasks derived from the organizational systems view:

Task 1 There is a need for models of human services programs which meet rights requirements.

Task 2 There is a need to assist staff in knowing how to align their behaviors with rights requirements, to provide prescriptions for ways of behaving.

Task 3 There is a need for models of complaint systems which enable organizations to use consumer and employee complaints to improve organizational structure and process.

It is in these three task areas that I place my own work as one person's first contribution to performing these considerable tasks, but certainly not as the final word. The size and complexity of the problems are well beyond a single person.

This book presents my efforts toward completing Task 2 — prescriptions for staff behavior. Two other books are to be published in the next year. The first, *Patients Rights and Organizational Models* will present a summary of my work on program designs consistent with rights (Task 1). It is based on a study at the Albany Medical College and the work at the Social Systems Sciences Department.

The second book, *Patient and Employee Grievance Programs,* is a design model for organizational complaint programs (Task 3). It is important because consumer and employee grievances are now accepted as a part of basic management data. This acceptance exists in public services such as welfare agencies and in private corporations such as IBM and American Express, both of which now have such programs. Additionally, the American Hospital Association promotes a patient representative program to achieve the same goals.

In summary, I see all of the patients' rights work as both specific to human services systems and intimately linked to the more general problem of designing and managing effective organizations.

I arrived at this point of view with the help of many persons. I particularly want to thank my dear friend psychologist Dr. David Lasky, Systems Scientists Professors Eric Trist and Peter Davis, and psychiatrists Drs. Maxwell Jones and Allan Kraft. They have all helped me to develop my thinking and to complete the work, giving freely of their time and support over the past years. I would also like to express my appreciation to three law students from Dickinson School of Law: Lawrence Kalban, Michael Wagner, and Donna Jarka. Their work in digging up the facts of the cases was most helpful. Three secretaries typed and retyped: Joanne Meinsler, Louise Morgan, and Isabel Alleman.

Finally, I would especially like to thank Susan Munger for her support and help during the development of this book.

Hopefully, this book will be of value to staff and students in the human services field who are struggling with the patients' rights problem. It will not provide ready-made mechanical answers, because the work is a constant stream of judgements based on each individual situation. The problems are complex, with social systems, philosophy, treatment technology, and law inextricably linked. The past ten years have taken me to an understanding of the problem but to too few answers. Perhaps the next ten will offer more solutions. Designing systems for people to get help and to be free is well worth the time.

Harrisburg, Pennsylvania   James T. Ziegenfuss, Jr.

Contents

PATIENTS' RIGHTS AND PROFESSIONAL PRACTICE

1
Development and Context of the Rights Problem

The purpose of this book is to assist staff in integrating patients' rights into their daily practice. First, there is a review of the nature of the rights problem, including a historical note on how it came to develop as a prominent national issue. Included in the first chapter is consideration of the developmental context of the problem with following chapters presenting a first prescription as to how rights are handled through the admission, treatment, and discharge of patients.

THE NATURE OF THE PROBLEM

The management of the *patients' rights integration problem* is defined here as a complex/simple problem. On the complex level it involves an interlocking of social philosophy, law, and mental health treatment technology. The idea of patients' rights demands that we consider how this society views its deviant individuals, how those views are represented in law, and what technologies are currently available to "treat" the individuals.[1, 2, 3, 4, 5] This complex problem requires a systematic matching of *philosophy* — *law* — and *treatment technology*. It is necessary to produce a harmony between them in order to prevent one from dominating to the exclusion of the other, e.g., treatment without rights. However, producing harmony is difficult because all three systems are in a transition phase.[6]

The complexity requires extensive theoretical and applied exploration of each of three systems' elements and their interlocking boundaries (philosophy with law with treatment technology). The ultimate solution to the rights problem — full integration — is likely only to be achieved with extensive research into constitutional law, treatment technology, and public policy issues, with evaluation of interim resolution methods over a period of years.[7]

On the simple level, the rights issue for staff is a "What do I do next problem?" Faced with decision pressures and the need to resolve a patients' rights conflict immediately, a staff person has no time for thoughts of "interlocking systems and prevailing philosophical viewpoints." Patients must be dealt with on the spot, sans theory. This work attempts to address the "simple" operational problems of what behavior comes next. Obviously, these behaviors also are complex, but the luxury of time for careful theoretical exploration by each staff person is not available.

As the concerns for patients' rights intensify, there is increasing interest in a presentation of precise prescriptions for how to respond to rights demands in widely divergent cases. The most troublesome problem is that precision is not now available either legally or clincally — the issues are too gray in nature.[8] However, it is important to begin to resolve some of the operational level conflicts even though the constitutional/theoretical answers may be some years away. One example will illustrate the reason for delay.

A woman's right to an abortion, and for government payment of its costs, is currently a hotly debated, unresolved public policy issue. How then can a mental patient's right to certain medical treatments like abortion be resolved when the question, linked with mental illness, is far more complex, intertwined with both functional and competency issues?

If the practical answers are embedded in national policy questions that are undecided, how do staff operate in treatment settings? The definitive piece cannot be written; too many issues are too uncertain, both by legal precedent and by uncertain clinical choices. Someone proposing a guide must then proceed with a working document which outlines general behaviors that will keep staff well within the law. Those general prescriptions will then rely heavily on situational interpretation by the staff — judgments in which the general prescription is matched with the characteristics of each particular case!

Through working approximations to the ideal, there is continued recognition that clinical services are still as much art as they are science, perhaps more so. There is no attempt to remove the clinical judgment aspects of a rights conflict situation. To the contrary, additional information regarding workable "generic" responses to rights conflicts is prescribed to aid the judgment, not to replace it.

There is no proposed substitute for clinical judgment. The demands of patients' rights only require that the judgment be constantly monitored and that clinicians be prepared to defend their sometimes "artistic" intuitive plans, treatment actions, and rationale. Some mistakes will be made that affect patients. Startlingly, some advocates appear surprised, forgetting that when your work task is people, mistakes (which all of us make) affect people!

A book which addresses that problem is consequently not a legal analysis but a study of the mental health task as it is affected by patients' rights. To be useful, the presentation must indicate ways to resolve rights conflicts through a study of the task. The guide cannot be loaded with legal qualifications, as some others have done, because the qualifiers confront staff with a mountain of "ifs" when quick action is often needed.

Thus, a book on how staff manage patients' rights is really a grand analysis of the primary work task of mental health staff, that is, where and how must rights be protected in all three of the essential work areas:

- admission
- treatment
- discharge

To illustrate, staff should ask themselves whether patients are protected during treatment, at points of crisis intervention, and during staff's "good faith" attempts to insure that problems are prevented. A comprehensive view of the task involves treatment, intervention, and prevention.[9]

What exactly do rights demand of the task performance? Difficult to carry out, it is nevertheless easily summarized in three statements typical of the rights advocacy position:

1. Patients' rights advocates demand that the primary tasks of the mental health system, admission, service provision, and discharge be rendered in accordance with all patients' rights.
2. Patients' rights advocates demand that these tasks be managed in ways which, for example:
   - secure the patients' environment
   - allow communication and visitation
   - maximize their freedom of movement
   - safeguard patient money and property
   - and maintain confidentiality.
3. Patients' rights advocates demand that all of the above be performed *without* violation of patient civil rights and *without* abuse, either physical or psychological.

This means that the mental health system must complete its primary tasks of admission, treatment, and discharge within a protective web of civil rights for the patients, as shown below. But how did the web come to develop?

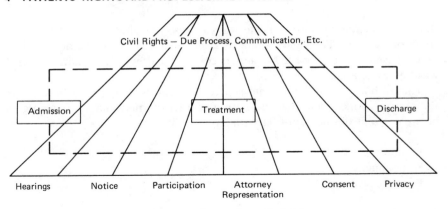

Figure 1-1. The protective web of rights.

HISTORY AND CONTEXT OF RIGHTS PROBLEM

The current concern for patients' rights did not develop overnight. It has been actively growing in the national interest since the 1960s. In that period, there was an increase in concern for the underrepresented minority groups, including blacks, the poor, women, and the mentally disabled. Widespread social concerns surfaced among students, citizen-at-large groups, and professional subgroups such as attorneys.

For the mentally disabled, a core group of attorneys led the push for patients' rights (Ennis[10], Siegal[11], Ferleger[12]), even as they were a part of a wider lawyers' group expressing a concern for the legally underrepresented.[13] These attorneys helped to push the "micro" problem of patients' rights and individual clinical interactions into the "macro" level of social system conflict and change at the levels of national and state government.[14]

It was not the first time that this "problem" of caring for the mentally disabled (with their rights intact) was identified. Indeed, reviewers examining the history of the treatment of the mentally disabled found publicity regarding rights oriented violations/conflicts in the nineteenth century.[15] There was a correct linkage of the rights of patients and the poor with a national philosophical position and resulting treatment response. Historical reviews indicate that the extent of the rights to be accorded patients shifts according to how the society views patients and how logically those views are extended into caring methodologies.[16]

Currently, there is conflict and uncertainty in the law, which in turn reflects a greater uncertainty in national philosophy, theories of problem causation, and methods of treatment. The rights problem will be resolved in the midst of intra- and interdisciplinary fights over the definition of mental disability, the methods of treatment, and the outcomes.[17]

With psychiatry, there is an ongoing debate about the extent of mental disability due to psychosocial causes as opposed to biochemical ones.[18] Recently there has been an increase in the amount of work aiming to establish the link between certain mental disorders such as depression and schizophrenia and biochemical imbalances.[19] This intradisciplinary conflict is not even near resolution. And, it is closely related to the *inter*disciplinary battles between psychiatry and the psychological/social treating professions.

Some researchers and clinicians feel that mental disability is predominantly a psychosocial problem in living and/or a series of rule violations.[20, 21] With a psychosocial cause, the logical extension suggests that treatment and outcome are psychosocial in nature and best handled by psychosocial personnel, i.e., psychologists, sociologists, and social workers. Thus, their position is radically opposed to the medical side of the psychiatry debate.

The interdisciplinary conflict when viewed as a part of the evolution of scientific thought is termed a paradigm conflict with the winner becoming the new direction of science and the model for day-to-day operational actions (as in treatment).[22] In short, if medical psychiatry wins, psychiatrists would continue to dominate the authority positions in the treatment systems, which would thus be viewed as a medical service. If social psychiatry, sociology, or psychology wins, the existing medical hierarchy would be weakened, with resulting changes in the way patients are treated and handled with regard to their rights.

Why is this conflict important to rights? Very simply, the design, development, and operation of the system of care is now inextricably related to the law which both defines and regulates it. Admissions rights, treatment rights, and such civil rights as confidentiality are currently tied to medical personnel, befitting a system that has traditionally been viewed as a medical one. However, as the debate continues, the law defining the medical view of the system comes into question concurrently with the medical-model view of causation and treatment.

The battles fought in the courts surface this conflict around such issues as confidentiality. For example, if transactions between patient and therapist are confidential, does that mean that all therapists are included or only medical personnel? Should physicians be the certifying personnel in involuntary cases? Should not psychologists or social workers serve that function? The law will be in a state of uncertainty and change until scientific positions and their logically following operational methods are settled. That is some time away from 1982 and should be determined by scientific research, not polemical debate.

Patients, quite appropriately, are not waiting for the conflict to be resolved before they ensure that their rights are protected. They are beginning to speak out for themselves.[23, 24] Patients now have a range of rights demands which potentially affect nearly all aspects of the treatment system. A listing published in 1972 still provides a good indication of the range of the rights demands:[25]

The Right To:

- be treated with dignity and respect;
- privacy;
- a safe, clean, and wholesome environment;
- be free from seclusion and restraints except on a doctor's written order, for specific reasons and for a limited time — never for punishment;
- communicate with persons outside the hospital;
- sell things you make and keep the money;
- be released as soon as hospital care is no longer necessary, or if a voluntary patient, on proper notice;
- be informed about your treatment in words you understand;
- refuse treatment;
- read and make changes in all printed forms you are asked to sign;
- refuse to be used for teaching purposes and for research purposes;
- freedom of speech;
- at a commitment hearing, to receive at least five days notice to have the help of an independent doctor on your side, to present your own witnesses and your own evidence, to have a lawyer, and to appeal.

If all these demands were instantly satisfied, both individual staff behaviors and the behavior of the service system would change considerably.[26]

To generate compliance, it is not enough to present the rights demands and the resulting change needs. As noted, they have been cited on and off for perhaps 100 years. The difficult task is creating solutions to the problems which develop when rights demands are in conflict with current system policies and procedures. Or, more important is the development of systems which will help to create the solutions. Through the history of the rights movement, there have been at least four major types of responses which have characterized the general society and the individual human service professions' responses to rights pressures.

RESPONSES

Professional service systems as a whole, along with individual service providers, have given the traditional responses to rights demands (and several new ones) as follow: (1) ignoring rights; (2) engaging in litigation to resolve rights conflicts as judicial system disputes; (3) developing formal external rights protection systems — outside the service system; and (4) developing internal systems which operate as part of the service system. The period of ignoring rights conflict is past. The litigation response has helped to stimulate sensitivities and to make systems change. In the past ten years, a number of external systems were developed, while internal service system operational efforts are more recent.[27, 28, 29, 30]

A brief review of each will bring us to the current situation, which is categorized as an eclectic combination of the forms of response.

Ignoring Rights

Many professionals perceived the rights issue to be unimportant and transient or faddish in nature. They did not reckon with the force of litigation that was to follow the initial surfacing of the problem, nor did they see the widespread base for concern. While advocates and attorneys led the interest, this "fad" has now reached the point where both staff *and* patients want patients to have rights.

The demands listed earlier demonstrate the increasing assertiveness of patients. Many staff initially chose to ignore the problem, in part because of the lack of assertiveness. Public administrators and service staff views were illustrated by the following fictional quotes:

> "Mental patients are a powerless group complaining about their conditions, which are not that bad. Besides, they really are crazy and for the most part, have a perceptual problem. That is, they perceive rights violations that are just normal complaints exaggerated by their illness."

By defining the rights problem as a part of the patient's illness, the conflict could be ignored. In effect, resolution was not possible until the patient's mental illness was "cured."

Other administrators and service staff used the resources problem as a base for ignoring the rights conflict. When asked if the rights violations were true, they would typically respond:

> "Yes, rights violations may be the case. But even if they are true, what can we do about it? For years, we have asked for money from the legislature. We do not pay enough to recruit a decent psychiatrist or any other staff for that matter. There are chronic shortages of personnel, money for special treatments, etc."

Thus ignoring the problem was an appropriate response since an increase in financial, personnel, and program resources was the real answer.[31] In the 1980s, increases are now particularly unlikely! In contrast, as is now apparent, the litigation that developed did not accept the resource excuse as a sufficient rationale for the abuse of patients' rights.[32] Litigants were joined by service professionals who considered that only a part of the rights conflict related to resources, while significant other causes were present, e.g. staff attitudes and behaviors.[33, 34] Other responses developed.

Litigation

A response that developed in part as a result of ignoring the problem was litigation. There will be no attempt here to outline the history of mental disability litigation. That has been done elsewhere.[35] It will suffice to point out that rights advocates found the courts to be as receptive to the plight of the mentally disabled as they were to other minority groups.

Wald and Friedman summarized the political-legal involvement of protection of patients:

> "Increasingly in the United States the mentally ill, the mentally retarded and the physically handicapped perceive themselves — and are politically perceived — as a minority group who have been historically denied basic civil liberties such as the right to liberty and the rights to vote, to marry, to bear children, to be employed, to go to school. Their campaigns resemble in method and legal theory those of other disadvantaged groups — racial, religious and sexual — in American politics. For their court victories, they have relied upon the same clauses of the United States Constitution, those requiring due process before liberty may be infringed and those mandating equal protection of the laws. The organized groups in the forefont of mental health law reform include the Civil Liberties Union and the Mental Health Law Project. The Civil Rights Division of the United States Department of Justice, which enforces constitutional and statutory nondescrimination rights of racial and sexual groups, has a special section to insure the rights of persons in mental institutions and in prisons and jails."[36]

Litigation for the mentally disabled thus became a part of mainstream civil rights protection.

A brief introduction to three major cases will illustrate. The *Wyatt* v. *Stickney* case was filed in Alabama in 1973. The suit contended that patient-residents of Alabama institutions have a constitutional right to receive treatment that provides each individual patient an opportunity to be cured or to improve. The court found conditions deplorable, with an unclean, unsafe physical setting, inadequate number of personnel, insufficiently trained staff, and little in the way of treatment programming. As an outcome of the case, the court mandated three fundamental conditions for the institution to qualify as a hospital:

1. a humane psychological and physical environment;
2. qualified staff in sufficient numbers; and
3. individual treatment plans.

These conditions produced litigation because the State of Alabama neglected to provide even minimal necessities appropriate to the provision of care.

In the *Halderman* v. *Pennhurst* case, the court found similar appalling conditions at a hospital for the mentally retarded in Pennsylvania.[37] Specifically:

"It was alleged, inter alia that conditions at Pennhurst were unsanitary, inhumane and dangerous, and that such conditions denied the class members various specified constitutional and statutory rights, including rights under the Act, and, in addition to seeking injunctive and monetary relief, it was urged that Pennhurst be closed and that "Community living arrangements" be established for its residents."[38]

Although the lower court ordered dispersal of the residents, on review the Supreme Court did not find a constitutional right to provide treatment in the least restrictive environment.[39]

The litigation was initiated to correct unsanitary, nontreatment conditions and ended by surfacing the problem of the degree of restriction on patients. Could they be adequately treated in the community where there are far fewer restrictions? Litigation was used to raise a specific problem with the institution and to extend it to a more general question about the way the mental health system operates, i.e. by placing residents in large very restrictive institutions instead of small community programs.[40, 41, 42]

The third case, *O'Connor* v. *Donaldson,* presented the case of a patient who argued that he was not dangerous or insane and therefore should not be involuntarily hospitalized.[43] Despite his repeated pleas for release, he was held for 15 years. As a result of the suit, the court held:

1. that dangerousness is a relevant criteria for confinement;
2. that patients should have a choice in selecting the location of treatment;
3. that the courts can get involved in what constitutes "adequate" treatment; and
4. that physicians could be held personally liable for damanges.

This case, decided in 1975, won freedom for a patient and significant precedence for patient choice and redress of grievances. It also exposed instances in which a service system imprisoned a patient without the provision of treatment. This and other cases more directly focused on the right to treatment have been cited as "agents of change" which are helping to improve the service system.[44]

In total, this brief note on three of the major cases to be fully considered in later chapters identifies the strengths of litigation. It produced major benefits for the patients involved and for their peers in other hospitals. Although as a response method, it must be remembered that the cases required years for resolution, a long period of time to solve a problem.

Formal External Advocacy Systems

In conjunction with the litigation, a third response to the patients' rights movement has been the development of external advocacy programs. These programs are exemplified by the Health Law Project, the Mental Patients Civil Liberties Projects and the projects of the American Bar Association Commission on the Mentally Disabled.[46, 47, 48] While their activities differed, they were similar in that they all attempted to explore the legal problems in providing mental health and health care services in large and small public institutions.

These programs are identified as "external" because the basis for their existence was *outside* the service systems.[49] That is, they maintained minimal relationships with providers in order to develop a non-coopted and patient-oriented perspective of the problem.

There is little question of whether these programs succeeded in meeting at least one of their goals: bringing attention to the problem. With an interest in confrontation as a primary technique, they successfully identified and publicized many shortcomings of the mental health system.

This style of response, while serving some public informational purposes, did and does work as an adversarial system. The heavy reliance on confrontation and the maintenance of pro-patient positions effectively polarized many of the problem participants. When a rights conflict emerged, the only options were to be on the patients' side. Many staff resented the either/or. Unfortunately, staff saw that many of the issues are not black or white but "gray," with implications for both staff *and* patient behaviors. Thus, external advocates became adversaries to the system and its staffs, generating much conflict that often worked to hinder solution finding.

In order to successfully negotiate solutions, there must be access to service-system decision makers and a willingness to become involved in compromises that somewhat weaken each adversarial position. Because the nature of external advocacy assumed the character of a crusade, compromise was often viewed as defeat. And because of the animosity created in the past eight to ten years, there has been an increase in the development of internal advocacy systems.

Internal Advocacy System

Partly in response to the controversy caused by external advocacy programs and partly due to a perception of the value, some organizations are developing internal grievance mechanisms.[50, 51] These programs operate within the organization and are paid for by, and report to, its chief executives. A brief review of one design indicates the nature of this kind of response to the patients' rights conflict.

In Pennsylvania, the Department of Public Welfare operates an Office of Client Rights, Patients' Rights Advisor Program, which reports directly to the Secretary

of Public Welfare.[52] This office adapted from the Michigan mod
new, but its design is illustrative of the general concept of an inte
The program is concerned with primarily one service area, mental he
centrates on three main activities:

- complaint processing
- education for staff and patients
- consultation regarding rights conflict resolution options.

The "Patients' Rights Advisors" take complaints from patients, investigate, and then develop a report which indicates substantiation of the complaint (or not) and the actions taken for resolution. As they are processing the complaints, the advisors typically educate/inform both patients and staff as to hospital treatment/administrative policies and procedures.[53] They are frequently able to offer consultation that describes possible solutions, methods other wards or units have used to solve the conflicts, or ways to avoid the problems entirely, e.g. new policies or procedures which are not in conflict with patients' rights.

Many organizations have recognized the value of soliciting consumer opinions of the quality of products or services. This Pennsylvania program operates in a manner similar to several major corporations now using consumer feedback data, in part for organizational learning.[54] Two evaluations of the Pennsylvania program indicate that it is well received by both patients and staff and that the outcomes constructively help to develop the service system.[55, 56] Both the private corporation programs (e.g. IBM, American Express) and public programs such as Pennsylvania's illustrate how organizational development can result from participant information.[56a, 56b, 56c] For advocates it means patients have a way to assert their rights.

In summary, internal advocacy, as a response to the patients' rights conflict, demonstrates that rights revealed by organizational problems can be resolved in a way which enhances the quality of service.[57] That is, the system's response is not to ignore, nor to become defensive, but to welcome the feedback as a methodology for raising the level of service — quality care delivered consistent with rights demands.[58]

Future Responses: Designs and Redesigns

The bottom line for the patients' rights movement and for the range of responses reviewed is the same. It is essentially the design of new programs and the redesign of existing ones so that they accommodate patients' rights.[59, 60, 61, 62] Few commentators on the rights movement have yet focused on this needed work, but there can be little real dispute about it as a task.

When the polemical debates are finished, the hard work of developing programs and whole systems consistent with rights will begin. There is ongoing work toward that direction. Some ten years ago, a residential program attempted to integrate patients' rights into its whole treatment regimen.[63] Although the program was only in operation for a short period, it demonstrated that certain of the rights demands could be implemented quite easily and with benefits for patients.[64]

Some continued work on program reorganization was stimulated by that experience. In the 1980s, new designs and redesigns are the most appropriate task of the patients' rights movement. One exploratory article defined the program areas needing redesign as: philosophy; clinical programs; staff roles and attitudes; physical setting; and organization and management. A working hypothesis is that the therapeutic community design (a democratic-participative one) holds the most potential, but it is by no means the only design capable of meeting rights needs.[65, 66]

In recent works, the impact of the rights demands on the mental health organization is coming to the fore, especially in terms of organization planning.[67] Viewed as impacting all aspects of the organization, rights requires a planned redesign of all aspects, if conflict is to be avoided. Work must proceed with a view of the organization and the mental health task, tracking the rights effects on each aspect from goals to resources, to policies and outcomes. The research has begun to produce some data and new ideas for redesign and new design.[68, 69, 70, 71]

This brief summary of the responses to rights then ends at the beginning of the work for the future. Who will develop the new program designs and organizations which accommodate rights? That future response is needed at two levels. It is needed at the macro level of state and national systems development and at the micro level of individual patient-staff and ward behavior. The micro level receives the attention of this current work.

PURPOSES OF THIS WORK

The purpose of this work then is to extend the responses of the last type: design and redesign. Aimed at the micro level — patient/staff behavior — the book has the following purposes:

- to identify the spectrum of patients' rights demands
- to provide information regarding the purposes of those demands
- to cite examples of the conflicts between the demands of rights and the traditional methods of the mental health system
- to offer guidance to staff in resolving those conflicts.

With regard to the purposes, several assumptions provided the base.

First, the position is taken that there are not a great many staff purposefully attempting to abuse, isolate, and psychologically harm the patients under their care. There are a few, but their numbers are often grossly overstated by well-meaning advocates. The assumption is that what is required is for staff to have more information (and resources) in order that they know *how* to treat and manage patients, here defined as consistent with their rights.

Second, this book will be construed in many instances as going well beyond the "legal mandates" of constitutional law as it currently applies. Another assumption is that that statement will be found to be absolutely accurate! It is the intent here to frame the mental health task in a set of rights which "should be." The assumption is that staff have good intentions, wish to support rights, and accomplish their primary work task; but they must be provided with some prescriptive suggestions. The suggestions aim to blend the minimal requirements of law with good thinking about the process of task completion. If according patients their rights increases the quality of care, we do not want a guide which offers a minimalist view of rights. Instead, a broader interpretation which offers an ideal or goal to strive for is appropriate.

While this may be taken to be an unrealistic expansive presentation of rights, it is not necessarily so. It is a presentation of what is (reality), what should be (ideal), and what may be (future) as litigation proceeds. Norms and guidelines are given which have strong but not exact links to constitutional law. It is a first prescription for a fair balance between law and clinical service, the task completed while accommodating rights.

Where does the national responses review lead us? In review, the findings are the following.

Ignoring the rights problem did not work in the past and will not work in the future — too much support has developed for protecting rights, with litigation successfully used to assist this support.

Litigation, while useful for identifying problems, for forcing systems-level attention, and for some major changes, will not work as a regular and quick remedy. Years are required and relatively few of the cases can go to court successfully.

External Advocacy is faster at bringing attention to the problems, but it tends to put the subjects (staff and the mental health system) on the defensive, making them less able to respond to needed changes even when constructively presented.

Internal Advocacy is able to quickly negotiate solutions to individual patient problems and is able to reach mental health system decision makers who are a part of the same overall system. Internal advocates can negotiate system-level changes relatively quickly but are in danger of being co-opted by the system and the problems of service delivery.

Actually, *all* responses are needed (except for ignoring). Litigation can be useful in major policy confrontations. External advocates can press issues which are systems-related and too sensitive for internals, while internal advocates can negotiate *daily* solutions to daily problems.

The recommendation is that staff begin to take up the cause. They have long been known as patient advocates.[72] It is staff attitudes, values, and behaviors that must accommodate rights demands. This book is intended to outline the purposes of rights to help change attitudes and provide some samples of behaviors that are consistent with rights and quality care.

SUMMARY

Patients' rights presents a complex/simple question to the mental health field. The complexity lies in the interlocking systems of philosophy, law, and treatment. The simple or direct aspect of the patients' rights question involves day-to-day operations. This book is a working document to aid the situational interpretations of patients' rights that are necessary for good clinical judgments. It does not present a strict legal analysis. Rather, it offers prescriptive suggestions for the protection of patients' civil rights in the mental health tasks of treatment, intervention, and prevention.

There is obviously a long history of concern over the conditions in mental health institutions. However, the current rights interest can be traced to the 1960s with the increased involvement of lawyers in protecting the rights of the underrepresented.

As patients' rights moved to the forefront, court battles surfaced both the need to protect patients' civil rights and the inter- and intra-disciplinary conflicts in the mental health system. The demands of patients for rights have brought about four types of responses: (1) ignoring the issues, (2) resolving specific issues by litigation, (3) external rights protection systems, and (4) internal rights protection systems. Ignoring the issues of patients' rights as a response was negated by using litigation to resolve specific issues. Cases such as *Wyatt* v. *Stickney, Halderman* v. *Pennhurst* and *O'Connor* v. *Donaldson* mandated criteria for protecting rights.

External rights protection groups such as the Mental Patients Civil Liberties Project succeeded in bringing attention to patients' rights problems. This pressure stimulated the development of internal rights protection systems which concentrate on resolving problems internally through complaint processing, educating staff, and providing resolution options. Their overall goal is to improve the quality of service provided in mental health institutions.

The bottom line response, however, is the design of new programs and the redesign of old ones in order to safeguard rights and improve patient care. For example, the therapeutic community as a democratic-participative program, may hold great promise since it incorporates rights by nature.

Redesign is important at the macro-level (state and national) as well as at the micro level (patient-staff ward behavior). This book aims at the micro level, going well beyond current legal mandates in its prescriptive suggestions. The basic question is how the mental health task can best accommodate patients' rights demands. While this work does not have all the answers, it is hoped that it will contribute to helping staff with the rights consistent with clinical judgments they must make every day.

REFERENCES

1. Vassiliou, G., "On the Rights of the Mentally Ill: A Hellenic View," *Mental Health and Society,* **3**(5–6):326 (1976).
2. Szasz, T.S., *Law, Liberty and Psychiatry* (New York: Macmillan, 1963).
3. Kittrie, N.N., *The Right to be Different* (Baltimore, Md.: Johns Hopkins Press, 1971).
4. Brakel, S. and Rock, R.S., *The Mentally Disabled and the Law* (Chicago: University of Chicago Press, 1971).
5. Arieti, A., *American Handbook of Psychiatry* (New York: Basic Books, 1959).
6. Stone, A.A., *Mental Health and Law: A system in transition* (DHEW Pubs., 1976).
7. Ziegenfuss, J.T., *Patients Rights and Organizational Models: Exploratory Research on Rights and Therapeutic Communities.* (Social Systems Sciences Dissertation, Wharton School, University of Pennsylvania, May 1980, 443 pp.).
8. Sadoff, R., Continuing Education Presentation at Harrisburg State Hospital, December 1981.
9. Kaplan, G., *Principles of Preventive Psychiatry* (New York: Basic Books, 1964).
10. Ennis, B.J., *Prisoners of Psychiatry* (New York: Avon Books, 1972).
11. Ennis, B., Siegal, L., *The Rights of Mental Patients* (New York: Avon Books, 1973).
12. Ferleger, D., "Loosing the chains: In-hospital civil liberties of mental patients," **13**, *Santa Clara Lawyer,* 447 (1973).
13. Ladinsky, J., "Careers of Lawyers, Law Practice and Legal Institutions," *American Sociological Review,* (1963) p. 53.
14. President's Commission on Mental Health. 1978. *Report to the President from the President's Commission on Mental Health,* Vols. **1–4.** (Washington, D.C.: Government Printing Office).
15. Rothman, D.J., *The Discovery of the Asylum; Social Order and Disorder in the New Republic* (Boston: Little, Brown & Co., 1971).
16. Ibid.
17. Szasz, T.S., op. cit. (item no. 2).
18. Torrey, E.F., *The Death of Psychiatry* (Radnor, Pa.: Chilton Book Company, 1974).
19. Hackett, T. "The psychiatrist: In the mainstream or on the banks of medicine?", *American Journal of Psychiatry,* **134,** 1977, p. 432–434.
20. Szasz, T.S., *The Myth of Mental Illness* (N.Y.: Harper & Row, 1961).
21. Scheff, T., *Being Mentally Ill* (Chicago: Aldine, 1964).
22. Kuhn, T., *The Structure of Scientific Revolutions* (Chicago: University of Chicago Press, 1962).
23. Allen, P., "A Consumer Speaks to Psychiatrists About Advocacy," *Bull. Amer. Acad. Psychiat. Law,* Vol. **5,** 1977, p. 275.
24. Kopolow, Louis E., "Consumer demands in mental health care," *International Journal of Law and Psychiatry.* **2**(2):263–270, 1979.
25. Mental Patients Civil Liberties Project, *Patients' Rights Manual,* (Philadelphia, Pa., 1973).
26. Ziegenfuss, J.T. "Patients' Rights Raises Questions for Psychiatry, Psychology & Law," *International Journal of Social Psychiatry,* Spring 1981.

27. Wilson, John P., Beyer, Henry A., and Yudowitz, Bernard, "Advocacy for the Mentally Disabled," in *Mental Health Advocacy,* DHEW, 1977.
28. Van Ness, Stanley C., Perlin, Michael L., "Mental Health Advocacy – The New Jersey Experience," in *Mental Health Advocacy,* DHEW, 1977.
29. Schmidt, D., "Advocacy Through Coalition – The Minnesota Experience," in *Mental Health Advocacy,* DHEW, 1977.
30. Coye, J.L., "Safeguarding Recipient Rights in Michigan's Mental Health System," in *Mental Health Advocacy,* DHEW, 1977.
31. Ziegenfuss, J.T., "Appropriations, Mental Health Services & Patients' Rights Issues," in publication review, 1982.
32. Bazelon, D., "The Right to Treatment: The Court's Role," *Hospital and Community Psychiatry,* 20(5):129 (May 1969).
33. Kahle, L. and Sales, B.D., "Attitudes of Clinical Psychologists Toward Involuntary Civil Commitment Law," *Professional Psychology,* 9(3) 1978.
34. Swoboda, J.S. Elwork, A., Sales, B.D., Levine, D., "Knowledge of and compliance with privileged communication and child abuse – reporting laws," *Professional Psychology,* 9(3), 1978.
35. Scott, Edward P., "The Mental Health Advocacy Service: A Legal Perspective," in *Mental Health Advocacy,* DHEW, 1977.
36. Wald, Patricia M., Friedman, Paul R., "The politics of mental health advocacy in the United States," *International Journal of Law and Psychiatry,* 1(2):137–152, 1978.
37. *Wyatt v. Stickney,* 334 F. Supp. 373 (M.D. Ala. 1972).
38. *Halderman v. Pennhurst State School and Hospital,* 446 F. Supp. 1295 (E.D. Pa., 1977).
39. Ibid.
40. *Halderman v. Pennhurst State School and Hospital,* 446 F. Supp. 1295 (E.D. Pa. 1977).
41. Martin, R., "Readers Forum," *Law and Human Behavior* 7, Spring 1977.
42. Switsky, H., Miller, T., "The Least Restrictive Alternative," *Mental Retardation,* 1, 52, Feb. 1978.
43. Miller, D., Miller, M., "Handicapped child's right as it relates to the least restrictive environment and appropriate mainstreaming," *54 Indiana Law Journal,* Fall 1978.
44. *O'Connor v. Donaldson,* 422 U.S. 563 (1975).
45. *Romeo v. Youngberg,* 644 F. 2d, 147 (3rd Cir. 1980).
46. Kaufman, E., "The right to treatment suit as an agent of change," *American Journal of Psychiatry,* 136:11, Nov. 1979.
47. Health Law Project, Univ. of Pennsylvania, Philadelphia, Pa.
48. Mental Patients Civil Liberties Project, Philadelphia, Pa.
49. American Bar Association Commission on the Mentally Disabled, Washington, D.C.
50. "Protecting Patients' Rights: A Comparison of Models," *Rights of the Mentally Disabled* (pamphlet), Hospital & Community Psychiatry Service, APA, Washington, D.C., 1982.
51. Coye, J.L. op. cit. (item no. 30).
52. (No author listed), "Lending An Ear: Companies Seek Complaints," *Time,* Dec. 7, 1981, p. 62.
53. Ziegenfuss, J.T., *Clients Rights Resources Manual.* Pennsylvania Dept. of Public Welfare, Office of Client Rights, Harrisburg, Pennsylvania, Jan. 1981, 317 pp.
54. Ziegenfuss, J.T., "The Varied Role of the Patients' Rights Advisor," Pennsylvania Dept. of Public Welfare, Office of Client Rights, Harrisburg, Pennsylvania, July 1981.
55. Emery, F.E., Trist, E.L., *Towards a Social Ecology* (London: Plenum Press, 1973).
56. Ziegenfuss, J.T., "Assessment of the Pilot Patients' Rights Advisor Program," Pennsylvania Dept. of Public Welfare, Office of Client Rights, Jan. 1981, 157 pp.

57. Ziegenfuss, J.T., "First Year Assessment of the Rights Advisor Program at Harrisburg State Hospital," Office of Client Rights, Dept. of Public Welfare, Harrisburg, Pa. 1982, 52 pp.
58. Ziegenfuss, J.T., Lasky, D.I., "Organizational Development As A Means of Implementing Patients' Rights," Presented at First International Conference on Psychosocial Rehabilitation, Philadelphia, Pa. 1975.
59. Ziegenfuss, J.T., Lasky, D.I., "Evaluation and Organizational Development: A Management Consulting Approach," *Evaluation Review,* 4(5), 1980.
60. Ziegenfuss, J.T., McKenna, C.K., "Process Evaluation As A Tool For Organizational Development," Presented annual meeting American Society Public Administration, Baltimore, Md., 1979.
61. American Hospital Association, "Special Issue: Quality Assurance/Risk Management Issues Are Explored," *Hospitals,* June 1, 1981.
62. Ziegenfuss, J.T., Lasky, D.I. (1974) "A Rationale for Evaluating the Quality of Services in Drug and Alcohol Programs: Purpose, Process, Outcome," *Drug Forum,* Vol. 5, No. 4, 1976.
63. Ziegenfuss, J.T., "The Resident Center of Harrisburg State Hospital (Patients' Rights Program)," Harrisburg, Pa. 1972.
64. Ziegenfuss, J.T., "The Therapeutic Community: Toward A Model for Implementing Patients' Rights in Psychiatric Treatment Programs," *Journal of Clinical Psychology,* 33(4), 1977.
65. Ziegenfuss, J.T., op. cit. (item no. 7).
66. Ziegenfuss, J.T., "Patients' Rights and Organizational Planning," in press 1982.
67. Felice, A., "Implications of the Patients' Rights Movement for Mental Health Programs," Eastern Psychological Association Convention, May 3, 1973.
68. Felice, A., "Evaluation of the Resident Center Program," Harrisburg State Hospital, 1973.
69. Ziegenfuss, J.T., op. cit. (item no. 64).
70. Ziegenfuss, J.T., *Patients' Rights and Organizational Models,* (Washington, D.C.: University Press of America, 1982).
71. Ziegenfuss, J.T., op. cit. (item no. 66).
72. Morrison, J., "An Argument for Mental Patient Advisory Boards," *Professional Psychology,* 7(2):127 (May 1976).

2
Admission

The entry point to any service program is the process and the act of admission. Admission is defined as the summation of administrative and clinical assessment procedures which result in the patients' being taken into the service system. The admissions determination is a particularly important point for patients' rights considerations because it is the start of the systems limitations on the patient. It is equally important for those patients voluntarily admitting themselves as for those who are admitted involuntarily on the certification of others (physicians, family, friends, etc.).

First, for patients voluntarily admitting themselves, the rights review process is critical because the patient is likely to be in a state in which he is not fully able to protect himself. If the patient is sufficiently convinced that there is a need for involvement in a program, he is likely to be focused on that coming process and not on the decision about time, type of program, needs, etc.[1, 2]

The patients' rights here are related to preadmission procedures, hearing procedures, and the admissions explanation process. They are important in ensuring that the patient is made as aware as possible about the upcoming event and the characteristics of their involvement in the program. Although a patient may already be convinced that he is in need of treatment, the patient's rights to adequate notice, to a hearing, and to sufficiently detailed explanations of the treatment goals and processes guarantee that he is appropriately admitted through "informed" admission. It also helps to ensure that there is little or no misunderstanding as to the process of treatment and its eventual outcome.

For those patients who are to be admitted involuntarily, these rights increase dramatically in importance. Involuntary admission to a treatment program of any type involves a deprivation of liberty. Liberty is guaranteed by the 14th Amendment to the United States Constitution and is taken as an especially fundamental right. In a free society, a core characteristic is an individual's right to maintain his freedom from the state. In many cases, however, a patient's need for involuntary commitment is apparent to friends, family, physicians and criminal justice authorities. Yet whatever the level of obviousness, it is critical to ensure that patients receive notice, a hearing, and a full explanation of the treatment process and outcome.

For involuntary patients, these steps must be taken to ensure that they are given every opportunity to argue that involuntary commitment is not needed or that other less repressive alternatives should be explored. The patient must have an opportunity to: (1) explain the situation in his own view; and/or (2) secure assistance in explaining his view (e.g. with the help of an attorney, family, friends or independent medical opinions).[3, 4, 5]

Notice, hearings, explanations of treatment, and independent opinions usually appear burdensome to staff. But staff should place themselves in the position of admission to the treatment unit. If it is the first time for a voluntary admission, the patient although convinced of the need, is quite unaware of what is to come. If an involuntary admission, the patient is fearful of the retributions for his inappropriate behavior, angry that he is about to be deprived of his liberty, and uncertain as to what lies ahead.

To ensure that both types of patients have every opportunity to secure an alternative or to demonstrate that the proposed path is incorrect, staff are required by rights guidelines to follow procedures which are sometimes perceived as a statement of the obvious. However, they are not *always* obvious, or correct.[6-13] The case examples, that will follow indicate that in addition to the admission of needy patients there are violations of patients' rights which contribute to inappropriate admissions. Involuntary commitment is a deprivation of liberty which is not the purpose of service personnel in a free society.[14, 15] The observance of guidelines for preadmission, hearings, independent medical and psychosocial examinations, and commitment procedures will help to ensure accuracy.

PRE-ADMISSION RIGHTS

Definition. Patients have the right to be present and to be assisted in presenting their version of the presenting problem *before* admission to a facility.

Persons with no relationship to a service program ("Pre-patients" if you will) have rights before the admissions process begins. That is, before being contacted by any member of the service system, patients maintain all the rights of any other citizen. As the actual admissions process begins, they have what are here called 'pre-admission rights'. A separate category identified as pre-admission rights is presented to emphasize that a patient's rights do not begin once he is in the facility. By the time a patient is officially in a treatment unit, he has already undergone certain changes in status.

If he is a voluntary patient, he is regarded as a part of the service system. His views, opinions, and explanations are regarded as coming from a person "in treatment."[16] If the patient is involuntarily committed, rights that begin after admission are granted only insofar as they belong to someone who has been certified incapable of self-management. Thus, the intent of preadmission rights is to ensure that the preventative aspect of rights is fully provided for.

The purpose of preadmission rights is twofold. First, it is to maintain objectivity about the patient's status for as long as possible. Patients at preadmission are not officially in treatment and are therefore entitled to the view that they are not in need of any service whatsoever! A second related purpose is to minimize the harm done by an inappropriate admission and the subsequent stigma resulting from that admission. This damage can be realized in two ways, either through a patient's own reinforced belief that he is in need of treatment or through the stigma generated by friends, family, and community regarding his admission to the facility.

An elaborate and extensive review of the need for admission including the rationale for matching that patient's individual situation with the characteristics of a particular treatment program is required. Without that preadmission guarantee, the "too-quick inappropriate" admission underscores the staff's and the patient's belief that the patient has the problem for which the program offers treatment.

The process by which preadmission rights are safeguarded involves three steps:

1. Allowing the patient an opportunity to present his view of the situation, which may include and/or require a "cooling off" period;
2. Allowing the patient the opportunity to contact relevant others who may not be represented at the time or place in which the admission situation is encountered;
3. Soliciting and carefully considering the views of relevant others e.g. family, friends, attorneys, independent physicians.

These three steps of the process are frequently formalized by a hearing. The patient's hearing rights are discussed in the next section. With or without a formal hearing, rights in the preadmission process should be monitored carefully.

The outcomes of monitoring preadmission are three. First, there is a diminished chance of an error of inappropriate commitments; above all, patients should not be forced to enter a hospital by mistake. Second, the process helps to inform and to educate patients. Particularly on the first occasion, the loss of freedom and the entry into a treatment facility is a dramatic and unknown event for the patient. Trauma decreases with each explanation and the support of friends or family.

Third, sufficient attention to patients' rights and to the steps required to protect them requires additional time. This is the time to begin to consider the slow process of change in which patients realize they are in need of and actually enter the first phase of treatment. The time required by pre-admission procedural rights is actually a part of the therapeutic process. Examples will illustrate.

Case 1. In *Suzuki* v. *Quisenberry,* two patients filed suit against Hawaii's mental health system including the mental illness, drug addiction, and alcoholism laws, claiming they were unconstitutional.[17] The patients, Suzuki and Alva, sought an injunction from the use of nonconsensual provision of the Mental Health Act simultaneously seeking their release from confinement. The defendant, Quisenberry, was director of the health system in the state of Hawaii.

The act in question provided for a two-day maximum confinement on the certificate of one physician and then indefinite confinement on the certification of two physicians. The patients felt that this certification process was insufficient to ensure the protection of their rights to full hearings and representation of their views prior to admission.

The patient, Sharon Suzuki, was picked up by a police officer and taken to a psychiatric facility. There she was examined by a physician who certified that she required hospitalization for a period up to 48 hours (essentially an emergency type of commitment). Subsequently, she was examined by two physicians who certified that she required further hospitalization. She objected throughout this period and was released after being confined for 26 days.

The second patient, Alva, was picked up by the police as a result of a request by her mother and taken to a psychiatric facility where she was released by the attendants. Upon her arrival at home, her mother again requested police assistance in hospitalizing her. She was again taken to the psychiatric facility where she was examined by a physician and admitted without her consent. A second physician examined her and upon her request gave her forms for a hearing and an appointment of counsel. She was released after being confined for 5 days.

A third patient, Jane Doe, was committed without her consent and told she would be confined for only 2 days. She was released after nearly two months. The court concluded that it is a violation of due process clause of the 14th Amendment to nonconsensually commit a person to a mental institution.

Notes. This case illustrates the conflict between the urgency in getting treatment and the patient's right to freedom. As the case illustrates, the patients had to fight for their rights even after they had been committed to the facility. Obviously, their standing at that point was much different than when they were free, and a certain amount of traumatic and stigmatizing harm had already been done.

There is not sufficient information in the case to determine whether the patients were in fact in need of treatment. The significant point is that both the act and the staff's interpretation of it (perhaps inappropriately) forced these patients to be committed for far longer periods of time than necessary for emergency observation.

HEARINGS

Definition. Patients have a right to a hearing before their admission to a facility.

This second part of admissions rights concerns the aforementioned hearings. The provision of a hearing is a formal opportunity for safeguarding both the rights of patients and the rights of society by ensuring that all sides are heard.

The purposes of the hearing are four. First, it is an opportunity to collect relevant information regarding a patient's need for admission to a treatment program and whether that particular treatment program matches that particular patient's current situation. Second, the hearing provides an opportunity to weigh the respective positions of the patient and the public, with regard to each one's needs, comfort and safety. Third, the conducting of a hearing promotes the idea of fairness to all present: patient, public, family, friends. Last, the hearing gathers together those persons who may be helpful through the admission process, during the treatment, and following discharge from treatment, e.g. family, friends, physicians, employers.

The process by which the hearing is organized and held differs by state. Some are very formal, some are less so. Essentially, the process requires obtaining witnesses and testimony from family, friends and authorities, and the professional opinions of physicians. Opinions include both those consistent with the patient's views and those that conflict.

One commentator identified six documents which are the focus of the involuntary commitment hearing: (1) notice of mental illness; (2) investigation report; (3) medical records; (4) prior commitment records; (5) police reports, and (6) a case history.[18] While not all will be present in a voluntary admission hearing, certainly staff should ensure the presence of medical records and assessments, prior commitment records and a case history. The review of this information is critical for determination of an accurate and appropriate admission (is the patient to be admitted and to what program unit?).

The patient has a right to legal advice during this hearing. But a word of caution. The hearings should be a dynamic balance between the formal and the informal, that is, with adequate allowance for discretion in regard to the law.[19] If the hearings are too formal, they result in a very legalistic process, which unless the patient is to be committed involuntarily, is inappropriate because it creates an adversarial atmosphere which in turn tends to interfere with the determination of appropriate needs.

If they are too informal, the hearing tends to lose some of its completeness, including the probing necessary to establish a clear picture of the facts and the situation as a whole. Thus, the most useful structure is one balanced in degree of formality between a conversationally oriented meeting of people (those "significant others" to the patient, plus complainants), and the courtroom-like process dominated by lawyers, rules of evidence, and witnesses.

The outcome of the hearing is intended to be a thorough examination of the facts of the situation. The hearing is the first attempt by patient, family, friends, authorities, and the new treatment team to balance the rights of the patient with those of family members and the general public, some of whom initiated a complaint(s).

Case 1. In *Lessard* v. *Schmidt,* the patient, Lessard, was picked up by police officers in October 1971.[20] The officers completed an "emergency detention for mental observation" form as a rationale for detaining the patient as an emergency case. Three days later the officers appeared before the judge without any notification or opportunity to appear being given to the patient. The judge issued an order permitting the confinement of the patient for 10 additional days. Three days later the psychiatrist filed an application for judicial inquiry with the judge. The doctor stated that the patient suffered from schizophrenia and recommended permanent commitment. The judge issued an order allowing 10 additional days confinement and examination by two physicians. Again, days later this detention period was extended without the patient's presence at any proceeding. At that time, the patient had been confined against her will for 13 days without any opportunity to present her case.

The patient had an interview with the judge five days into the process and was told that she would be examined and a guardian appointed for her. She retained a representative of legal services on her own initiative. A hearing was set for the 16th of November and later reset for the 24th of November to give the patient's attorney time to prepare. The patient was denied her request to be allowed to go home during the interim period.

At the hearing, the three physicians and the police officers testified, and she was committed for 30 additional days without the judge giving a reason. She was "paroled" three days later but remained an outpatient. This had been extended every month for an additional two months.

This suit was brought by Ms. Lessard alleging that the Wisconsin procedure for involuntary civil commitment denied her due process of law. Among her complaints were: (1) permitting involuntary commitment for up to 145 days without a hearing; (2) no notice requirement for hearings; and (3) failing to appoint counsel, or to allow counsel to be present at the psychiatric interview.

The court found the Wisconsin civil commitment procedure to be constitutionally defective insofar as it fails to give adequate notice of the charges against the patient and permits detention longer than 48 hours without a hearing to establish the necessity of commitment.

Notes. As found by the court in this case, the detention of patients without the provision of a hearing, and notice informing the patient that a hearing will be held is unconstitutional. Without discussion of the patient's constitutional law support, it should be apparent that a deprivation of liberty deserves at the least an opportunity for the patient to be heard and to be represented by counsel. Beyond this concept of constitutional right, this requirement would seem to be a fundamental element in any concept of fairness by treatment personnel.

Case 2. The second case is a class action suit against James Parham, Commissioner of the Department of Human Resources, Georgia.[21] The litigation sought an injunction to prevent the voluntary admission of minor children to mental hospitals by parents or guardians. The court agreed and an injunction was issued. Further commitments must first provide the child with a hearing to protect his 14th Amendment due process rights.

J.R. was born in 1962, was removed from his parents' home at age three months because of parental neglect and placed in a foster home supervised by the Georgia Department of Family and Children Services. He lived in seven different foster homes in eight years after which he was admitted to a mental hospital. Four years earlier, a juvenile court ordered the Georgia Department of Family and Children Services to place the child for adoption. Adoption did not materialize and the Department of Family and Children Services, as J.R.'s guardian, applied for and was granted admission to place J.R. in a mental hospital.

Hospital personnel found him to be mentally ill, describing his condition as "borderline mental retardation" and "unsocialized, aggressive reaction of childhood." Hospital personnel requested that the Department of Family and Children Services remove J.R., feeling he "will only regress if he does not get a suitable home placement and as soon as possible." In 1973, hospital personnel "felt that efforts to obtain permanent foster placement should be primary at this time lest J.R. become a permanent institutionalized child." No placement was made, and J.R. remained in confinement until this lawsuit was filed in October 1975. At that time, he had been confined for five years and four months by his 13th year of age.

A second child's situation was also a part of the case. J.L. was born in October of 1963 and adopted at birth. His parents divorced when he was three, and he continued to live with his mother. She remarried and with J.L.'s stepfather applied for J.L.'s admission to a mental hospital in 1970. He was found to be mentally ill with the diagnosis "hyperkinetic reaction of childhood." He was discharged to his mother in 1972, but she readmitted him 10 days later. In 1973, hospital personnel indicated to the Georgia Department of Family and Children Services that J.L. needed to be removed from confinement and placed in a foster home. He wasn't removed because funds weren't available to place him, and at the filing of this suit he had been confined for five of his 12 years.

Notes: Although these cases do not fully document what activities took place at each point of admission, the need in this case was to develop an alternative to institutional care for this child. That apparently did not happen in part because hearings to consider fully all the facts of the cases were not held.

What would be explored in the hearing for a voluntary admission of a child by his guardian? First, since the guardian is initiating the admission, the hearing should determine who will adequately represent the patient's perspective. While the assumption that guardians are *not* the advocates of their charges is not universally valid, in some cases that is true. An admissions hearing would establish the full facts of the case including the standard diagnostic work and a review of the guardian's abilities and interest in caring for the child. In this case, there was some question of the guardian's motives. The hearing should protect the patient from those guardians who do not have the patient's best interest in mind.

INDEPENDENT MEDICAL AND PSYCHOSOCIAL EXAMINATIONS

Definition. Patients have a right to an independent medical and psychosocial examination.

This right is important to the admissions process when the patient is unsure of the need for treatment and is being either persuaded or forced to enter a treatment program. If the patient has voluntarily agreed that such treatment is required, his acceptance of the existing medical or psychosocial examination does not often require outside opinions, although the number of patients who "volunteer" free of coercion is questionable.[22-25] When the patient's personal view of himself matches the existing opinion without conflict, there is no need for a second opinion. However, in cases of involuntary commitment, or in cases where there is considerable family pressure to "persuade" a patient to enter treatment, patients have a right to, and should exercise the option of, securing independent medical and psychosocial opinions.

There are two purposes for this right. The first purpose is to ensure accuracy. The existing technology and the widely varying situations relating to patient problems and professional abilities to accurately diagnose problems frequently generate errors in judgment.[26, 27] While error is common in all tasks at all times, the magnitude of the decision about deprivation of liberty requires a reduction in error and a planned increase in accuracy based on conservative and redundant methods. When in doubt, an overriding purpose of error reduction through maintenance of liberty is served by securing additional independent medical and psychosocial opinions.

The second purpose served by independent opinions is the reassurance of the patient. Although many patients and doctors are resistant to the concept of second opinions prior to their seeing how second opinions can be effective in actual clinical treatment, research on several programs has indicated that second opinions tend not to necessarily reduce surgery, but do tend to aid quality control.[28-35] The findings from the research generally indicate that patients are reassured by the fact that a second professional came to the same conclusion regarding a need for surgery. In the mental health field, a need for professional health care is reinforced by a second opinion at the point of admission.

The process of securing independent medical and psychosocial opinions is frequently troublesome. There are three points to the process which must be considered. The first is the necessity of offering this right and of informing the patients of the option to secure a second opinion. Without knowing that this option is available, few patients will elect it.

The second part of the independent opinion process is the difficulty in securing additional providers willing to give an alternative opinion. Often, other professionals within the facility or within the system are reluctant to provide differing opinions. Therefore, it is simply difficult to locate persons to provide the necessary review. A list of "alternative opinion providers" is one way to reduce the logistical difficulties.

The third troublesome aspect of the independent opinion is the covering of the costs. Who will pay — the state or the patient? If the patient's right to an independent opinion is binding, and the patient cannot otherwise pay for care, the state or a third party should pay for the independent opinion also. Since there is not yet widespread use of second opinion in mental health, the cost issue is not settled in many states.

The outcome of the independent opinion is twofold. First, it amounts to a reinforcing of the patient's interest in doing something. If the second opinion backs up the first suggesting the patient needs care, the patient has now secured two separate opinions, both recommending the same direction for action. Second, the independent opinion ensures that extreme inaccuracies are deleted, i.e. the decision to reject admission or to go ahead with admission when obviously wrong. For example, it sometimes happens that a patient is diagnosed as having acute schizophrenia when in fact it is a short term anxiety reaction resulting from acute distress in the family system, e.g. because of a recent accident. This type of error can be picked up by an alternative provider who has additional time to review the facts of the case and is sometimes fortunate in that the time elapsed permitted spontaneous recovery, or at least some significant improvement.

Case 1. This case, *Parham* v. *J.R.* extends the previous case discussion but is now focused on the independent opinion aspects and applies to the patient group J.R. and others similarly situated.[36] This group was awarded a judgment by the District Court stating that Georgia's procedures for voluntary commitment of children under 18 years of age violated the patients' due process rights. Admission according to the Georgia statute can be made through an application by a parent or guardian to a state mental hospital after which the supervisor admits the child temporarily for "observation and diagnosis." If the supervisor determines that the child is "mentally ill" and suitable for treatment in that hospital, the child is then admitted for an indefinite period.

The Supreme Court later reversed the District Court and found that the procedures for medical fact finding are consistent with constitutional guarantees. Parents retain the complete right to subject their children to proceedings for committal, subject to an independent medical judgment regarding the child's competency. The requirement of having a neutral fact-finder negates the risk of parental error or misconduct. These requirements are one and the same whether the child is in custody of his parents or a guardian.

Notes. Again the case underscores the idea of reducing the risk of error. The grave consequences associated with admission to a mental facility are thus underscored. The action of securing a second independent opinion is deemed far less troublesome and burdensome than the damage caused by an inappropriate admission to the hospital.

This discussion follows previous notes on the J.R. case regarding the requirement for a hearing. The idea that guardians are not to be tested or monitored as to their judgments in requesting commitment is rejected. While the court reaffirms the guardian's rights to make decisions, they should not be without review. Staff now must inquire whether a hearing and second opinions are provided when guardians attempt to have their charges committed.

COMMITMENT

Definition. Patients have the right to be free from involuntary commitment.

The purpose of this right is the maintenance of liberty. It is, in effect, the patients' right to liberty. Discussion at this point in the chapter is intended to be a summary of the possible results of preadmission, hearing, and independent examination rights. That is, each of the preceding rights is to ensure that admission to the treatment center occurs only after thorough and fair review of all relevant criteria. Involuntary commitment is not to be a first resort but a last one, a controlled exercise of the power of professionals.[37]

The significance of the loss of liberty is the primary force behind this position. Legal analyses of the derivation of constitutional guidelines and prohibitions are by now abundant.[38-42] The legal base seems to reinforce the legitimacy of four commitment purposes:

"Traditionally, civil commitment of the mentally ill has advanced four distinguishable social goals: (a) providing care and treatment to those who require it, (b) protecting allegedly irresponsible people from themselves, (c) protecting society from their anticipated dangerous acts, (d) relieving society — or the family — of the trouble of accommodating persons who, though not dangerous, are bothersome."[44]

How are they carried out?

"1. A petition for examination of the alleged mentally ill person is filed in the local probate court by a relative or police officer;
2. Notices of a hearing and the date are sent to the ill individual, interested relatives, and others;
3. One or more physicians are appointed by the court to examine the patient and report to the court;
4. A hearing is held at which the patient may or may not be present;
5. If the judge concludes that the person concerned is mentally ill, an "adjudication" is issued and made a matter of public record and the ill individual loses his civil rights in varying degrees;
6. A commitment to an appropriate institution is issued;
7. The sheriff's department is ordered to transport the ill person to the receiving hospital. These archaic procedures, suggestive of a criminal trial, remain in force in most States, including Ohio, despite modest efforts at renovation."[45]

The reliability and validity of the criteria and the process have now been questioned to the point that there is little debate regarding the need for revision, refinement, and whole new approaches.

There will be no attempt here to review the many new developments. Instead, one is selected which has received some discussion and which is here considered quite operational as a protective mechanism. The criteria are considered in the context of due process procedures of hearing, notice, attorney representation, etc. Stone suggested five criteria for commitment as follows:

1. reliable diagnosis of a severe mental illness
2. whether the person's immediate prognosis involves major distress
3. whether treatment is available
4. whether the diagnosable illness impaired the person's ability to communicate (cannot communicate — or cannot comprehend)
5. whether a reasonable man would reject such treatment.[46]

The use of these criteria requires a series of judgments in each. The judgments raise concern for each criteria with regard to the current level of technological development. For example, a reliable diagnosis is a good criteria, but the ability to do it is yet somewhat elusive.[47-50] But as noted in the introduction, the lack of technological capability does not stop the operational need. Therefore, the recommendation is for staff to review commitment considerations with the above criteria to the best of their ability, remembering that the judgments are always subject to review. Although staff will not always be correct, they will be as correct as a non-medical group.[51] The difficulties will arise in the borderline cases where even greater importance is attached to the procedural protection.

The outcome of the rights' protection is that commitment is used as a final resort *after* alternatives are considered and procedural protections are provided. The cases presented earlier in this chapter illustrate the nature of the difficulties.

SUMMARY

This chapter has discussed the admissions process with special reference to pre-admission rights, hearing rights, and the rights to independent medical and psycho-social examinations. Admissions as the point of entry to the care system is a most important time for ensuring that patients are provided all rights. A brief summary of the actions required to protecting those rights is as follows:

Prior to admission, patients should have:

- adequate notice of a pending hearing
- an actual hearing — formal or informal
- explanation of the purpose and process of the proposed care
- an exploration of possible alternatives which have been considered
- an explanation of the assessment of the patient including any criteria and examinations.

The hearing itself should offer a full exploration of the purpose of the hearing, the facts of the situation which have brought the patient to the hearing, and the possible outcomes.

Once the hearing is finished, the continuation of the admissions process should contain the following. The patient should be fully informed regarding:

- the nature and goals of the program
- the rules governing patients' conduct in the program including hours of services and general conduct
- the costs of the treatment and who will be liable for those costs
- a presentation of the patients' rights in total.

To ensure that staff provide these rights, the following guidelines are offered:

1. Patients should be asked to present their version of the presenting problem and should have the opportunity to secure assistance in doing so (legal and/or medical and/or psycho-social).

2. Patients to be committed involuntarily must have a hearing, while voluntary admissions should be encouraged to review with significant persons their proposed admission action.
3. Patients must always have the opportunity to secure a second medical and/or psycho-social opinion if they so desire.

REFERENCES

1. Holzman, P.S., H.J. Schlesinger., "On becoming a hospitalized psychiatric patient," *Bull. Menninger Clin.*, **36**:383 (1972).
2. Lowry, J.V., "Philosophies, not laws determine admission practices," *Hosp. & Comm. Psychiatry,* **18**:236 (1967).
3. Brunetti, J., "Right to counsel, waiver thereof, and effective assistance of counsel in civil commitment proceedings," **29** *S. W.L.J.* 684 (Fall 1975).
4. Cohen, F., "The function of the attorney and the commitment of the mentally ill," **44** *Tex. L. Rev.* 424 (1966).
5. "Constitutional law – proceedings – the right to counsel in Ohio involuntary civil commitment," **36** *Ohio St. L.J.* 436 (1975).
6. "Mental Health – validity of commitment statute," **10** *Duq L. Rev.* 674 (Summer 1972).
7. "Legal fiction, misguided paternalism, and unfounded prediction: Standards for involuntary civil commitment in Missouri," **20** *St. Louis L.J.* 120 (1975).
8. Kaplan, L., "Civil commitment as you like it," **49** *B.U.L. Rev.* 14 (1969).
9. See, J., "Insanity proceedings and black-white state hospital admission rate differences," *Int'l. J. Social Psychiat.,* **21**(3) (1975).
10. Monahan, J., "Empirical analysis of civil commitment. Critique and Context," **II** *Law & Society Review* 619 (Spring 1977).
11. Monahan, J., Cummings, I., "Social policy implications of the inability to predict violence," **31** *Journal of Social Issues* (2) 153 (1975).
12. Laves, R., "The prediction of "dangerousness" as a criterion for involuntary civil commitment: Constitutional considerations," **3** *Journal of Psychiatry and Law* (3) 291 (1975).
13. Cocozza, J., Steadman, H., "The failure of psychiatric predictions of dangerousness: Clear and convincing evidence," **29** *Rutgers Law Review* (5) 1084 (Summer 1976).
14. Ferlerger, D., *"Kremens* v. *Bartley:* The right to be free; Watkins, N., Roth, B., *Kremens* v. *Bartley:* The case for the state," **27** *Hospital and Community Psychiatry* 706 and 708 (October 1976).
15. Dybwad, G., Herr, S., "Unnecessary coercion: an end to involuntary civil commitment of retarded persons," **31** *Stanford Law Review* 753 (April 1979).
16. Rosenhan, D.L., "On Being Sane in Insane Places," *Science* Jan. 19, 1973. pp. 250–258.
17. *Suzuki* v. *Quisenberry,* 411 F. Supp. 1113 (D. Hawaii).
18. Mutnick, J. Lazar, W. "Practical guide to involuntary commitment proceedings," **11** *Willamette Law Journal* 315 (Summer 1975).
19. Schoenfeld, C., "Discretion and the law: A psycholegal overview," **5** *Journal of Psychiatry and Law* (1) 101 (Spring 1977).
20. *Lessard* v. *Schmidt,* 349 F. Supp. 1078 (E.D. Wisc. 1972).
21. *Parham* v. *J.R.,* 442 U.S. 584 (1979).
22. Owens, H., "When is a voluntary commitment really voluntary?" **47** *American Journal of Orthopsychiatry* (1) 104 (January 1977).
23. Olin, G., Olin H., "Informed consent in voluntary mental hospital admission," *American Journal of Psychiatry* **132** pp. 938–941, 1975.

24. Szasz, T.S., "Voluntary Mental Hospitalization: An Unacknowledged Practice of Medical Fraud," *New England Journal of Medicine*. **287**, pp. 277–287, 1972.
25. McGarry, A.L., "Law Medicine Notes, From Coercion to Consent," *New England Journal of Medicine* **274**, p. 39, 1966.
26. Cocozza, op. cit. (item no. 13).
27. Monahan, J., "Prediction research and the emergency commitment of dangerous mentally ill persons," **135** *American Journal of Psychiatry* (2) 198 (February 1978).
28. Gertman, Paul M., Stackpole, Debra A., Levenson, Dana Kern, Manuel, Barry M., Janko, Gary M., "Second Opinions for Elective Surgery," *New England Journal of Medicine* **302** (21) p. 1169, 1980.
29. McCarthy, E.G., Widmer, G.W., "Effects of screening by consultants on recommended elective surgical procedures," *New England Journal of Medicine* 1974, **291**:1331-5.
30. Lance, R., Haug, J.N., "An update on second surgical opinion programs," *Bulletin of American College of Surgeons* 1978; **63**:26-34.
31. McCarthy, E.G., Finkel, J.L., "Second opinion elective surgery programs: outcome status over time," *Med Care* 1978; **16**:984-94.
32. Grafe, W.R., McSherry, C.K., Finkel, M.L., McCarthy, E.G., "The Elective Surgery Second Opinion Program," *Ann Surg.* 1978; **188**:323-30.
33. Koran, L.M., "The reliability of clinical methods, data and judgments." *New England Journal of Medicine* 1975; **293**:642-6, 695-701.
34. Paris, M., Salsberg, E., Berenson, L., "An analysis of nonconfirmation rates: experiences of a surgical second opinion program," *JAMA* 1979; **242**:2424-7.
35. Rutkow, I.M., Gittelsohn, A.M., Zuidema, G.D., "Surgical decision making: the reliability of clinical judgment; *Ann Sug.* 1979; **190**:409-419.
36. *Parham v. J.R.,* 442 U.S. 584 (1979).
37. Page, S., "Power, professionals and arguments against civil commitment," **6** *Professional Psychology* (4) 381 (1975).
38. Gilboy, J.A., Schmidt, J.R., "Voluntary hospitalization of the mentally ill," **66** *N.W.U.L. Rev.* 429 (1971).
39. Chambers, D.L., "Alternatives to civil commitment of the mentally ill," **70** *Mich. L. Rev.* 1107 (1972).
40. Cohen, op. cit. (item no. 4).
41. Lockney, T., "Constitutional problems with civil commitment of the mentally ill in North Dakota," **52** *N.D.L. Rev.* 83 (Fall 1975).
42. "On the justification for civil commitment," **117** *U. Pa. L. Rev.* 74 (1968).
43. "Overt dangerous behavior as a constitutional requirement for involuntary commitment of the mentally ill," **44** *U. Chi. L. Rev.* 562 (Spring 1977).
44. Stone, A.A., *Mental health and law: A system in transition,* NIMH, DHEW, 1975.
45. Patterson, R.M., "Hospitalization Procedures for the Mentally Ill in the USSR and Other European countries," *Ohio St. Law J.* 21(1) Winter, 1960.
46. Stone, A.A., op. cit., (item no. 44).
47. Zubin, "Classification of the behavior disorders," 18 *Ann. Rev. of Psychol.* 373 (1967).
48. Hunt, W.A., Wittson, C.L., and Hunt, E.B., "The relationship between definiteness of psychiatric diagnosis and severity of disability," 8(3) *J. Clin. Psychol.* 314 (1952).
49. Babigian, et al., "Diagnostic consistency and change in a followup study of 12,015 Patients," **121** *Am. J. Psychiat.* 895, 900 (1965).
50. Kreitman, et al., "The reliability of psychiatric assessment and analysis," **107** *J. Men. Sci.* 887 (1961).
51. Badger, M., Shore, J., "Psychiatric and nonmedical decisions on commitment," **137** *American Journal of Psychiatry* 367 (March 1980).

3
Environmental Rights

The general purpose of environmental rights is to ensure that the setting in which patients are treated meets minimal standards. There are four specific purposes.

- to ensure that the physical setting is appropriate
- to ensure that the setting supports therapeutic goal intentions
- to ensure that the setting does not undermine patient dignity and respect
- to ensure that the setting promotes the safety and the humanity of patients while they are in treatment

What are the elements of the physical setting, i.e. the environment in which patients receive services?

The unit in total (its environment) includes both a physical arrangement and an atmosphere or climate. Both are increasingly recognized for their impact on the persons involved.[1-4] As research increases, there is beginning to be an accumulation of knowledge about how certain colors, room arrangements, lighting, and other architectural factors affect people.[5-9] For example, do certain colors encourage patient exuberance or depression? Do furniture arrangements aid or provide obstacles to conversation? The best aim of this work is toward the design of facilities that account for these concerns when construction begins. Unfortunately, many old mental health institutions have architectural arrangements which are not supportive of patient care. Changing them is both costly and difficult in design.[10-12] Interest in environmental conditions has been high for some years but the results are slow in emerging, although there is and has been support for the collaboration of psychiatrists and architects.[13, 14, 15, 16, 17]

This chapter addresses some of the major issues in a patient's right to appropriate environmental conditions, but it is not a review of all the significant architectural design elements. Essentially, these concerns involve discussion of the following:

- dining areas
- grounds
- the level of restrictions in the setting
- lighting
- personal effects and private space
- adequate ventilation, etc.

The maintenace of minimal standards requires both establishment of standards and continuing inspection of those areas and items defined in the standards.

The inspections are conducted through continuous monitoring, which asks what is acceptable to people on the outside. Essentially, the above purposes are converted to questions.

- Does the physical environment support therapeutic goals?
- Does the setting preserve and enhance (if possible) dignity, respect and humanity?
- Is the environment safe for patients?

The patient's right to an appropriate environment is one which is designed to preserve dignity, respect, safety, and the general humanity of the patient. In reviewing this right, the following lead subjects will be considered: clothing, health and nutrition, safety, and humanity.

CLOTHING

Definition. Patients have the right to clothing that is appropriate for the season and is suitable to minimum standards of dignity.

Clothing is the first of the environmental rights consideration. The *Wyatt* v. *Stickney* case defines the purpose and the specific topics of this right quite clearly as follows:[18]

"Patients have a right to wear their own clothes and to keep and use their own personal possessions except insofar as such clothes or personal possessions may be determined by a qualified mental health professional to be dangerous or otherwise inappropriate to the treatment regimen. . . .

The hospital has an obligation to supply an adequate allowance of clothing to any patients who do not have suitable clothing of their own. Patients shall have the opportunity to select from various types of neat, clean and seasonable clothing. Such clothing shall be considered the patient's throughout his stay in the hospital. . . .

The hospital shall make provision for the laundering of patient clothing."

The purposes of this right are first to provide clothing suitable to the season, and then to ensure that the personal appearance of each patient maintains or enhances the treatment effort. Patient dignity outside the treatment facility is frequently associated with the type and manner of dress. When patients enter treatment, the loss of both appropriate clothing and the ability to choose what to wear is demeaning. The inability of patients to define certain clothing as their own has a negative impact on patient self-image and general welfare.

The process by which this right is maintained is one of adhering to a standard established in *Wyatt* v. *Stickney*.[19] The case produced the following standards which are still applicable:

"a. Each resident shall have an adequate allowance of neat, clean, suitably fitting and seasonable clothing. Each resident shall have his own clothing, which is properly and inconspicuously marked with his name and he shall be kept dressed in this clothing. The institution has an obligation to supply an adequate allowance of clothing to any residents who do not have suitable clothing of their own. Residents shall have the opportunity to select from various types of neat, clean, and seasonable clothing. Such clothing shall be considered the residents throughout his stay in the institution.

b. Clothing both in amount and type shall make it possible for residents to go out-of-doors in inclement weather, to go for trips or visits appropriately dressed, and to make a normal appearance in the community.

c. Nonambulatory residents shall be dressed daily in their own clothing, including shoes, unless contra-indicated in written medical orders.

d. Washable clothing shall be designed for multi-handicapped residents being trained in self-help skills, in accordance with individual needs.

e. Clothing for incontinent residents shall be designed to foster comfortable sitting, crawling, and/or walking, and toilet training.

f. A current inventory shall be kept of each resident's personal and clothing items.

g. The institution shall make provision for the adequate and regular laundering of the residents clothing."

Since the standard is established, it remains only for each organization to adhere to that standard as closely as possible.

The outcomes of adherence to the *Wyatt* standards are: (1) patients are clothed in the manner which supports maintenance of normal appearance and which enhances or works toward normal appearance; and (2) patients have clothing suitable to individual needs as related to their treatment situation, e.g., whether ambulatory or incontinent. In total, the concern with clothing is in the interest of maintaining normality for the patients in what is a very personal part of their daily living.

Case 1. Mrs. Doe was hospitalized at Green State Mental Hospital in the summer of 1972.* As she had no friends or family and had been living in a boarding home for two years, she brought little in the way of clothing. As winter approached, she requested that the hospital purchase for her a winter dress. Her only dress was a short-sleeved cotton one. The hospital provided her with one which was stolen from her the first night she had it in her room. She requested a second dress. Citing a low budget and the fact that she had a dress (to be worn with sweaters) the hospital refused to supply a second. Mrs. Doe filed a complaint citing her right to be provided with a dress suitable to the season. The court agreed, stating that it was a minimum requirement for maintenance of dignity.

Notes. Theft on the ward in this case clearly cost the hospital additional money to provide a second dress, the loss is not a sufficient rationale for denying the patient the dress. Along with the issue of dignity, there is a question of whether or not a summer dress with sweaters is suitable winter wear. Thus, on two levels, the hospital was in a questionable position in denying clothing. Although the dress incident may seem insignificant to some persons, others attach great value to the manner of dress. Patients often become particularly conscious of their appearance.

HEALTH AND NUTRITION

Definition. Patients have the right to appropriate health and nutrition including diet, exercise, and hygiene.

The purpose of this right is to ensure that the treatment setting makes minimal provisions for maintaining the patient's health and nutrition status. The *Wyatt* case offers standards for diet:[20]

"34. A nourishing, well balanced diet shall be provided to each resident.
  a. The diet for residents shall provide at a minimum the recommended daily dietary allowance as developed by the National Academy of Sciences. Menus shall be satisfying and shall provide the recommended daily dietary allowances. In developing such menus, the institution shall utilize the moderate cost food plan of the U.S. Department of Agriculture. The institution shall not spend less per patient for raw food, including the value of donated food, than the most recent per person costs of the moderate cost food plan for the Southern Region (the region of the units location) of the U.S., as compiled by the U.S. Department of Agriculture, for appropriate groups of residents, discounted for any savings which might result from institutional procurement of such food.

*Fictitious case.

b. Provision shall be made for special therapeutic diets and for substitutes at the request of the resident or his guardian or next of kin in accordance with the religious requirements of any resident's faith.
c. Denial of a nutritionally adequate diet shall not be used as punishment.
d. Residents, except for the non-mobile, shall eat or be fed in dining rooms."

As this quotation illustrates the *Wyatt* case attempted to identify standards for diet which would develop a minimum baseline for measuring compliance.

Continuing a concern for the patient's environment, the case identifies personal care standards:

"37. Each resident shall be assisted in learning normal grooming practices with individual toilet articles, including soap and toothpaste, that are available to each resident.
b. Teeth shall be brushed daily with an effective dentrifice. Individual brushes shall be properly marked, used, and stored.
c. Each resident shall have a shower or tub bath, at least daily, unless medically contra-indicated.
d. Residents shall be regularly scheduled for hair cutting and styling, in an individualized manner, by trained personnel.
e. Residents who require such assistance, cutting of toenails and fingernails, shall be scheduled at regular intervals."

It is difficult to prescribe standards for all of the possible areas and the process that would be used to monitor the treatment setting's adherence to them. Procedurally, each of the above standards are converted to questions for review with staff. In general, what is the level at which these settings should be maintained?

The environmental standard is essentially to provide a safe sanitary facility that offers an appropriate diet, meeting daily nutritional requirements; provision for exercise including out-of-doors time; recreational opportunities; and personal care training assistance if required. While some criteria are unclear and somewhat arbitrary, extreme violations are apparent.

The outcome of the health and nutrition rights can be no less than the protection of a patient's physical health. The right helps to ensure that patients will be able to maintain current health and nutrition levels, although for some patients it is acknowledged that the hospital setting will signify an improvement.

Case 1. In *Eckerhart* v. *Hensley* the plaintiffs represented all patients involuntarily confined to the forensic unit of Fulton State Hospital, Missouri, at the time of the decision.[21] The forensic unit consists of two residential units, one for the more dangerously insane inmates which is maximum security in nature, and another which is less restrictive. In addition to recognizing the patients' general right to treatment, the court addressed some specific complaints brought by the inmates.

First, there was overwhelming evidence that a combination of extreme temperature and high humidity caused the patient living areas to be almost unlivable during late spring and summer. Testimony indicated that the heat and humidity produced lethargy in the patients. The court ruled that those conditions were not minimally adequate.

Second, the lavatory facilities were found not to be minimally adequate with respect to patient privacy. Shower stalls were without curtains, toilet stalls were without doors and were not completely enclosed by partitions.

Third, evidence indicated that the patients did not have enough privacy in their sleeping dormitories. The dormitories are divided into cubicles usually containing two beds in close proximity to one another. The court found the conditions inadequate due to lack of privacy which created the possibility of assault, sexual or otherwise. Also, the cubicles in the maximum security ward contained only beds. All personal belongings were stored in a clothing room or were in a small locker in the ward day room. The court felt that these surroundings were abnormal and suggested a more individualized approach.

Notes. In this case a range of environmental issues was considered but only a few addressed health and nutrition. The most significant were those of extreme temperatures and high humidity. These conditions are detrimental to the health of all patients, but especially to the elderly. Some research has indicated that combination of high temperature and high humidity can result in hospitalization and/or death, particularly when patients are taking drugs. The court moved to prevent the hospital from maintaining the life threatening environment in which treatment was purportedly rendered. The case also illustrates the ease with which a violation of this extreme can be identified.

Case 2. In *U.S.* v. *Kahane* a federal prisoner brought an action to establish his right to obtain food in prison which meets Orthodox Jewish dietary requirements.[22] The prisoner, a Jewish radical activist, was sentenced to one year in prison for violating his probation requirement that he not associate with people engaged in storing and smuggling firearms for Israel. His violation occurred after the murder of the Israeli athletes in Munich and various attacks on Jewish settlements by Palestinian guerillas. The court after a lengthy discussion on the importance of kosher food, ruled that for the prison to deny him access to kosher food would be a denial of his constitutional rights.

Notes. As indicated in the *Wyatt* standards, a prisoner or a hospitalized patient has a right to a diet which supports his religious preference. The hospital must accommodate this need. While the court upheld the right, it is necessary to consider whether a patient's views are enduring. That is, a brief history of the patient will be used to determine whether the religious views are newly adopted for the purpose of causing a disturbance. Some patients do adopt new religious beliefs (or beliefs for the first time) when hospitalized. It is not too difficult to assess the sincerity. But, when in doubt, allowing the special diet does not cause extraordinary problems.

SAFETY

Definition. Patients have the right to a safe environment which protects them from physical injury.

The purpose of this right is to ensure that the treatment setting's environment does not contribute to physical injury. The risks are not to be the patient's alone. The treatment center's administrative and clinical staff have an obligation to ensure that patients receive treatment in an environment with a minimum of, or with no risks at all, to their personal safety.

The process for ensuring that this right is intact involves a continuing review of the physical setting, including the level of safety precautions. These precautions would include:

1. Review of the level of monitoring of aggressive, assaultive patients (sufficient staffing).
2. Review of the placement of assaultive patients (e.g., which wards, sleeping arrangements).
3. Review of the availability of sharp instruments.
4. Examination of the unit for "jumping" places.

These four topics are common problems. In general, the intention here is to achieve purposeful arrangement of the environment to minimize the risk of physical injury, or to eliminate it if possible. Safety requires a structured attention to the arrangement of both objects and people as indicated by the four topics highlighted above. In some cases an adjustment of ward staffing patterns may be needed as recommended after one study of unusual incidents.[23]

The outcome of scrutinizing the safety aspects of the system is that the treatment setting itself does not become an instrument of injury. A person coming in for treatment has a right to treatment in a safe environment.

Case 1. Lucy Webb Hayes National Training School v. *Perotti* was a wrongful death action against a hospital affiliated with Lucy Webb by the widow of a patient who committed suicide by jumping through a hospital window.[24] At the time of the suicide, the patient was under observation in a closed ward, a ward reserved for the more seriously disturbed patients. Shortly before the incident, the patient asked permission to go to the open side. Since hospital regulation prohibited this unless the doctor gave orders to the contrary, his request was denied.

A short while later, a nurse spotted the patient standing in a corrider of the open section. No one knew precisely how he got there. The nurse asked a psychiatric technician to return the patient to the closed section. At first the patient cooperated, but after walking ten steps he suddenly turned and ran back toward the living room where he just was and jumped through the window.

The court ruled that enough evidence was presented to establish the hospital's negligence in allowing the patient to leave the closed ward and in not having a sufficiently strong window installed.

Notes. The case illustrates the necessity of the above reviews regarding the precautions to be taken to ensure the safety of the patient. Here the arrangement, or the lack of arrangement, for an open ward and easily breakable windows was used as a suicide mechanism. The staff failed to "examine the unit for jumping places." Admittedly, an inspection of the physical plant each week, or month is not the most thrilling clinical work. But as this case illustrates, its absence can be a life-threatening or life-ending mistake.

Patients have a right to an environment that is free from situations that present opportunities for physical injury. When the situations are not removed, staff are exposed to negligence and malpractice actions.

HUMANE ENVIRONMENT

Definition. Patients have the right to treatment in a humane environment.

Essentially, a continuation of the earlier environmental rights, the right to a human environment goes beyond the more directly determined areas of safety, health, and nutrition. In general, the purpose of the right is to ensure that the treatment unit does not violate minimum standards required for meeting a "humanity test." There is, of course, no such test, only a monitoring of certain conditions. Through the reviews, the question of humane conditions is considered via individual judgments, mostly using the norms of "outside the center existence."

Currently, there is considerable work toward the redesign of hospital settings to increase their "humanity."[25-27] Some efforts address specific factors.[28-29] While others have completely redesigned the setting to be, for example, a village or a mall.[30, 31] The architectural factor is real and can be taken into consideration in design to increase the degree of "humaneness."[32-34]

As in the safety discussion just presented, the monitoring of humanity levels is for the most part an informal process of continuous inspection of both physical and psychological settings of the hospital (the architectural and psychological climate). One sensitizing process for the review is to let each staff member ask if he or she would consider exchanging places with the patients. Is the patient's position sufficiently inhumane for the staff member to feel trepidation at the thought of the exchange?

What are the elements of an inhumane environment? Overcrowding is one; the denial of patient decision-making is another.[35] An exhaustive review of all architectural and psychological characteristics is not intended here. The following is only an illustrative listing. A treatment center is architecturally and psychologically inhumane if it:

1. is overcrowded
2. unfurnished
3. dirty
4. allows no private space
5. does not permit patients to alter its furnishings or arrangements
6. is constantly noisy (e.g., continual loud television)
7. has bare blank walls
8. does not permit patient questioning
9. shows no compassion or flexibility

The list can be made much longer perhaps by each unit's staff joining with the patients to fill out the list as it pertains to their unit. Some items are measurable — many are not — all are relative. How dirty? How much decision making?

The concept is troublesome, but many staff would likely answer by saying, "I know inhumane when I see it." Extreme violations are not easily overlooked — patients will know too!

The outcome of the right is a protection of the patient's humanity, however it is defined for each patient and staff person. The right is intended to reduce the abuses such as patients sleeping in hallways and the callous indifference of staff to patient concerns, whether large or small.

Case 1. In *Padgett* v. *Stein* three inmates at the York County Prison sought to remedy alleged unconstitutional conditions at the prison.[36] Originally, both parties entered into a consent decree with agreement to the following conditions: (1) that prison officials would comply with the state minimum requirements for county prisons; (2) that there would be no discrimination with respect to race, color, etc., and (3) that the prison would provide adequate visitation time with families with the appropriate amount of privacy. Plaintiffs contend that conditions (1) and (3) have not been fully complied with. Do the prisoners have a right to humane treatment?

One of the specific issues concerned the prison's policy of denying visitation privileges to those inmates placed on the segregation tier for various misconducts. The court said prisoners could only be denied visits if there was a serious violation of visitation rules or, if there had been an obvious security threat.

The final issue dealt with overcrowding. To accommodate an overflow of prisoners, the prison had been housing inmates on cots in walkways outside the cells. This constituted unlawful overcrowding. The court mandated that no more than two can be housed in a cell and that every prisoner had to be in a cell. The court also required the prison to segregate habitual criminals and mentally weak prisoners from the general population.

Notes. Although this case includes a range of concerns, two significant issues were overcrowding and visitation. A point to be made is that both the denial of visitation and extreme overcrowding diminish the patient's humanity by first denying other person contact and then increasing prisoner contact. Certainly most definitions of humanity would allow for visitation and would put certain limits on overcrowding. The warehousing of prisoners in hallways on cots would not appear to be a humane method of dealing with either prisoners or mental patients.

Case 2. Laaman v. *Helgemore* concerns living conditions in programs available at the New Hampshire State Prison.[37] The original suit brought by Laaman involved an emergency lockup of the prison. Later, the case grew to include the medical care, working conditions, education and rehabilitation opportunities, visitation and mail privileges, and a general attack on the conditions of confinement at the prison.

The physical structure of the prison needs improvement. Problems involve the plumbing, heating, and lighting facilities of the inmates' living quarters. Kitchen facilities are filthy. The court described the recreational building as so unappealing that many inmates prefer to remain in their cells rather than spend time there.

Three types of isolation cells were found at the prison. The court noted that the combination of total isolation, inadequate lighting, ventilation and plumbing, the size and the uncontrollable temperatures coupled with the practice of stripping the offending inmate and providing a simple canvas mattress created a scene found only in medieval dungeons. The cells were often used for mentally disturbed prisoners, a procedure which violates all modern treatment practice.

Visitation facilities are dingy and uninviting. The gym located directly above the visitors room is used sparingly so as not to disturb the people visiting below. Serious fire hazards exist throughout the building; no emergency exits, evacuation plans, or fire prevention equipment exists in the facility. Medical facilities are equally poor.

The court ordered that plans for improvement in sanitation, physical facilities, isolation policy, food service, fire safety equipment, staff size, medical care, mental health care, record keeping, safety of prisoners, work opportunities, vocational training, opportunity to join programs, and visitation rights be submitted within 90 days.

Notes. The above description, in particular the linking of the image of the inmates isolation cells to medieval dungeons, pretty much defines the converse of the condition of humanity claimed as a right for patients in any kind of institution. Staff in many facilities would find one or two items on the check list to be troublesome in a humanity test. Here mentally disturbed offenders are confronted by a consistent pattern of environmental characteristics leading to a conclusion of environmental inhumanity. The description presented above is unfortunately more frequently found than most officials would prefer to believe. By upholding the issue of a right to humanity, the courts provide patients and prisoners with a path for redress of their grievance. It also opens a staff liability question with regard to the conditions – for which the staff are responsible.

SUMMARY

The purpose of environmental rights is to ensure that the physical setting meets the minimum standards for appropriateness, supports therapeutic goals, does not undermine dignity and respect, and promotes both safety and humanity. This involves establishing standards for each of these areas and continually monitoring the physical setting to see that the standards are met. Environmental rights cover the specific areas of clothing, health and nutrition, safety, and humane conditions.

Patients have a right to clothing that is appropriate for the season and meets minimal standards of dignity. That is, clothing should be neat, clean and seasonable, and should maintain or enhance the treatment effort. The standards from *Wyatt* v. *Stickney* indicate that all patients should look as normal as possible and the individual needs of non-ambulatory and incontinent patients should be met.

Patients have the right to have health and nutrition needs met in the areas of diet, exercise, and hygiene. Dietary standards should follow the recommended daily allowances of the National Academy of Sciences. Exercise must be provided, including out-of-doors time and recreational activities. Patients' hygiene should be monitored and help provided for learning normal grooming skills.

The aim is to protect and possibly improve patients' physical health.

The right to a safe environment means that the hospital and staff are responsible for protecting the patient from injury – inflicted by self or others. This requires a continuing review of the setting for safety precautions, e.g., sharp instruments, jumping places, and the placement of assaultive patients.

A humane environment goes beyond the issues of safety to guard each patient's personal dignity. Obvious abuses include overcrowding, unfurnished dirty wards, and lack of private space. As with other environmental areas, extreme violations are easy to see. It is the more subtle abuses of these rights that require the constant informal monitoring of a sensitive, compassionate staff.

REFERENCES

1. Belknap, I., *Human Problems of a State Mental Hospital*, N.Y.: McGraw-Hill, 1956.
2. Cumming, J. and Cumming, E., *Ego & Milieu: Theory and Practice of Environmental Therapy*, Aldine, Chicago, 1966.
3. Moos, R.H., *Evaluating Treatment Environments*, N.Y.: John Wiley & Sons, 1974.
4. Proshansky, H.M., Ittelson, Wm. H., Rivlin, L.G., *Environmental Psychology*, New York: Holt, Rinehart & Winston, 1970.
5. Ittleson, W.H., Proshansky, H.M., Rivlin, L.G., "The Environmental Psychology of the Psychiatric Ward," in *Environmental Psychology*, N.Y.: Holt, Rinehart, & Winston, 1970.
6. Sivadon, P., "Space as Experienced: Therapeutic Implications," in Proshansky, op. cit., pp. 409–419.
7. Smith, C.W., "Architectural Research and the Construction of Mental Hospitals," *Mental Hospitals*, vol. 9, June 1958, pp. 39–45.
8. Ozerengin, M.F. and Cowen, M.A., "Environmental Noise Leads as a Factor in the Treatment of Hospitalized Schizophrenics," *Diseases of the Nervous System*, vol. 35, May 1974, pp. 241–243.
9. Spivack, M., "Sensory Distortion in Tunnels and Corridors," *Hospital & Community Psychiatry*, vol. 18, January 1967, pp. 12–18.
10. Izumi, K., "An Analysis for the Design of Hospital Quarters for the Neuropsychiatric Patient," *Mental Hospitals*, vol. 8, April 1957, pp. 31–32.
11. Whitehead, C., et al., "The Aging Psychiatric Hospital: An Approach to Humanistic Redesign," *Hospital & Community Psychiatry* 27(11), Nov. 1976, p. 781.
12. Good, L.R., Siegel, S.M., and Bay, A.P., *Therapy by Design Implications of Architecture for Human Behavior*, Thomas, Springfield, Illinois, 1965.
13. Ziegenfuss, James T., *Patients' Rights and Organizational Models*, Social Systems Sciences Dissertation, Wharton School, Univ. of Pennsylvania, in book publication, Washington: University Press of America, 1982.
14. Goshen, C.E., ed., *Psychiatric Architecture*, Washington, D.C.: American Psychiatric Assoc., 1959.
15. Latenser, J., "The Nebraska Psychiatric Institute: Some Architectural Considerations," in *Psychiatric Architecture*, Goshen, C.E., ed., Washington, D.C.: American Psychiatric Association, 1959.
16. McLean, C.C. "Furnishing a Psychiatric Hospital," in *Psychiatric Architecture*, Goshen, C.E., ed., Washington, D.C.: American Psychiatric Association, 1959.
17. Foley, A.R. and Lacy, B.N., "On the Need for Interprofessional Collaboration: Psychiatry and Architecture," *American Journal of Psychiatry*, vol. 123, February 1967, pp. 1013–1018.
18. *Wyatt* v. *Stickney*, 344 F. Supp. 387, 1972.
19. *Wyatt* v. *Stickney*, Ibid, p. 403.
20. *Wyatt* v. *Stickney*, Ibid, p. 403.
21. *Eckerhart* v. *Hensley*, 475 F. Supp. 908 (W.D. Mo. 1979).

22. *U.S.* v. *Kahane,* 396 F. Supp. 687 (E.D. N.Y. 1975).
23. Damijonaitis, V., "A Six Month Study of Incidents Involving Patients at a State Psychiatric Center," *Hospital and Community Psychiatry* **29**(9), September 1978, p. 571.
24. *Lucy Webb Hayes Natl. Training School* v. *Perotti,* 419 F^{2d} 704 (D.C. Cir. 1969).
25. Whitehead, C., et al., op. cit. (item no. 11).
26. Bayes, K., *The Therapeutic Effect of Environment on Emotionally Disturbed and Mentally Subnormal Children,* Kaufmann International Design and Award Study, 1964-1966.
27. Edwards, J. and Hults, M.S., "Open Nursing Stations on Psychiatric Wards," *Perspectives in Psychiatric Care,* vol. **8,** September-October 1970, pp. 209–217.
28. Levy, E., "Designing Environments for Mentally Retarded Clients," *Hospital & Community Psychiatry* **27**(11), Nov. 1976, p. 793.
29. Levy, E., *Effects of Environmental Enrichment on the Behavior of Institutionalized Mentally Retarded Adolescents,* Developmental Disability Office, Department of Health, Education, and Welfare, Washington, D.C., 1974.
30. Means, G.C., Ackerman, R.E., "South Carolina's Village System," *Hospital & Community Psychiatry* **27**(11), Nov. 1976, p. 789.
31. Capital District Psychiatric Center – Albany, New York, personal visit – invitation and tour – Alan Kraft, M.D., 1979.
32. Izumi, K., "Architectural Considerations for Mental Health Facilities," section 10, Part II, *Canadian Building Standards and Guide Material for Hospital and Health Facilities,* Department of National Health and Welfare, Ottawa, Canada, 1965, pp. 39–44.
33. Izumi, K., "Architectural Considerations in the Design of Places and Facilities for the Care and Treatment of the Mentally Ill," *Journal of Schizophrenia,* vol. **2,** no. 1, 1968, pp. 42–52.
34. Jones, C.L., ed., *Architecture for the Community Mental Health Center,* Mental Health Materials Center, New York City, 1967.
35. Proshansky, H.M., Ittleson, W.H., Rivlin, L.G., "Freedom of Choice and Behavior in a Physical Setting," in *Environmental Psychology,* N.Y.: Holt, Rinehart, and Winston, 1970, p. 173.
36. *Padgett* v. *Stein,* 406 F. Supp. 287 (M.D. Pa. 1975).
37. *Laaman* v. *Helgemore,* 437 F. Supp. 269 (D.N.H. 1977).

4
Treatment

OVERVIEW — THE RIGHT TO TREATMENT

The centerpiece of the patients' rights movement is a dual interest in the right to treatment and the right to refuse treatment. Other topics have high visibility with regard to patients and the service system, e.g., admissions or discharge; but what happens to patients when they are in the treatment process is of primary importance.

The concept as noted is acutally dual. There are two rights: (1) patients have the right to treatment, and (2) patients have the right to refuse treatment; that is, treatment cannot be forced and/or continued without concerted efforts to provide treatment that meets minimal standards of quality. The right to refuse treatment is the right to reject those types of treatment which do not meet minimal standards and/or those which provide high risk of harm or negative side effects.

To some extent the issues are two sides of the same task. The right to treatment problem requires that some minimum level of care be offered to all patients within the treatment setting. The other side of the issue is that the care to be provided must involve a generally accepted level of risk. Any unusual procedure or procedures which have a high potential for negative side effects must be open to rejection by the patients.

In the rights to treatment and to refuse treatment, the conflict surfaces the three subjects noted in the Introduction as the context of the problem — philosophy, treatment technology, and law. Three questions will illustrate the core conflict.

1. *Philosophy.* Does the American social system intend to provide patients with treatment absolutely, or will the American society allow some patients to be held in facilities of various kinds without treatment? This is a philosophical question which concerns the country's desire to treat its unfortunates and the subsequent level of support to do so. Philosophy is a significant determinant of the system's behavior.[1] Rights must be considered within the context of the milieu which on a large scale is national policy.[2,3]

2. *Treatment Technology*. Does the human services system have sufficient knowledge at this time to determine what constitutes treatment? If the society philosophically determines that treatment for all is appropriate, is there sufficient knowledge of what *is* being provided and what *should be* provided? Can standards of care be defined based on our current knowledge?

3. *Law*. Is the legal system of rules consistent with the directions of philosophy and law; i.e., does the law constitutionally mandate a right to treatment and to refuse that treatment if that is the desired direction? Some of the questions are shortly to be addressed by the Supreme Court.[4] It is unclear now.

The overall question then is this: Are there currently consistent positions on mental patients' rights to treatment and to refuse treatment with regard to philosophy, treatment technology, and law? The answer appears to be no. Philosophically, it is uncertain whether patients are to be given liberty or treatment, even according to a leading promotor of freedom.[5, 6, 7] The national public policy which is an operational statement of philosophical position is uncertain, shifting, and in need of new definition.[8, 9]

Second, the right to treatment can actually be considered the right to effective treatment.[10] To secure effective treatment, there must be knowledge of what treatments work for what kinds of problems with which patients. While significant progress is being made, the level of knowledge is not yet sufficient.

Last, the law itself reflects the diversity of positions in philosophy. And it suggests in its case reviews that the treatment system and its technologies are not yet able to withstand rigorous judicial review. This has been particularly demonstrated in the problems of involuntary commitment where an assessment of dangerousness is required.[11-14]

These problems of developing consistency within and between philosophy, treatment, and law do not obviate the need to do something. With the prevailing uncertainty, there is a greater necessity to establish working positions in each area and some beginning guidelines for both the right to treatment and the right to refuse.

The right to treatment involves problems of warehousing, problems of custodial care, and problems of inadequate personnel, financial, and programmatic resources to provide a minimal level of treatment. The conflict over the right to treatment arose because "patients" were locked up without even minimal attempts to treat them.[15] After a number of exposés in newspapers and magazines dating back several centuries, concerned citizens have helped to expose the many cases of inadequate and antiquated systems of care, both private and public.

Thus from the public exposure, there emerged two distinct pressures. First, the absence of any care produced pressure to provide at least some minimal level of care through mandates for the presence of the basic elements. Second, the poor performance of the system produced pressure to provide those mandated elements of care at minimal quality levels. Their mere existence was necessary but not sufficient.

As a result, the right to treatment question became a dual one: 1. Are the appropriate services and treatment elements provided in the care setting? 2. Are those elements of minimal quality provided by appropriate staff? As discussed later in this chapter, lack of detailed knowledge of conditions was widespread. However, in the last decade a series of cases identified treatment settings in which no care was provided while other cases illustrated that the standard of care provided was inadequate. It was necessary, therefore, to begin by defining the elements of care.

What is treatment? The following list is one view of the primary elements of treatment, which if followed will enable a program to propose that it provides the elements of a quality care program:

- examinations
- habilitation and treatment plans
- informed consent
- case records — accurate and up-to-date
- normalization philosophy and setting
- education and training plans and programs
- accurate and appropriate placement
- qualified staff
- generally accepted treatment practices
- support services
- clinical status and progress review reports

These elements required for quality care became the guideposts for the right to treatment. An elaboration of each will demonstrate.

The presence of the elements in the treatment program means that the right to treatment requires:

1. Examinations on entrance and as necessary throughout the course of treatment.
2. Habilitation and treatment plans with the expected purpose, process, and outcome of treatment defined.
3. Informed consent to the treatment plan and to treatment procedures, particularly unusual ones.
4. Case records accurate and up-to-date from admission through planning, treatment, and discharge of the patient.
5. A plan for and actions to normalize existence within the treatment unit.
6. Staff who are trained, experienced, and in sufficient numbers to provide quality care.

7. Quality treatment practices which meet residents' needs as defined in the care plan.
8. Support services as needed, e.g., dental, speech, physical, and rehabilitation therapy.
9. Constant clinical status reviews with ongoing progress reviews and reports.
10. Education and training to develop skills necessary for future independent living.
11. Placement in a unit or community setting which matches the resident's needs.

The fact that these must be present does not guarantee that each will be provided in a quality way, i.e., performance will be high and appropriate. But their absence means that significant elements of the basic requirements of treatment are missing. If the elements are absent, any comment regarding performance is irrelevant.

Once these elements are generally accepted as a baseline for defining treatment (and they are quite close to general acceptance now), courts when reviewing a case, will investigate to determine if the elements are present. If not, the absence may form the basis for a violation of the right to treatment. If all elements are present, the case will focus on performance — *how well* each of the elements was provided. And once the right to treatment is satisfied, the second part of the conflict emerges.

The right to refuse treatment is the second aspect of the treatment issue. The right is based on the fact that certain treatments are either directly harmful, or they risk harm to patients. Although all treatments have hypothesized benefits, there are cases in which treatments do more harm than good. Additionally, many treatments are quite intrusive.

Do patients have the right to limit treatment?[16] The purpose of the right to refuse treatment is to help the patient maintain control of his own fate with respect to the risk of harm. It is also to involve him in the value-loaded decisions about risk by giving him the option of refusing to take a given risk at a given time.

The critical issue with the right to refuse is that some patients do not have the capacity to decide what is in their best interest. They are incompetent to give consent or to refuse.[17-20] Some authors have suggested that the judicial incompetence procedure should be used to manage those instances.[21] Once adjudicated incompetent with all due process, the right to consent and to refuse are officially and fairly lost. Otherwise, with the rights pressure to maintain the civil right to refuse, some clinicians feel that patients' refusals will mean they are "rotting with their rights on."[22] The problem applies to all patients but is exaggerated in cases where patients are prone to violence, which some treatment helps to control.[23] Consensus on solutions to the conflict is not yet apparent.

Problems have emerged with regard to the right to refuse treatment. Several of the significant questions currently under debate are as follows:

- Who should make the decision if the patient is temporarily or permanently unable to determine his own best treatment process?
- What should be done about the lack of alternatives problem — patients reject certain treatments in favor of alternatives which are not available?
- Do patients retain any treatment decision making if they are involuntarily committed?
- How is the right to refuse treatment operationalized, particularly the choice among alternatives?
- Do patients have the right to participate in planning and treatment process decisions (self-determination on value-loaded decisions)?
- Can patients refuse medication?
- Can patients refuse unusual treatment procedures when those procedures require a high degree of technical competence to determine usefulness?

Answers to the questions with general clinical consensus are some years off.

Two cases will illustrate the range of these concerns in the right to treatment and the right to refuse treatment. The specific issues which relate to each of these broad areas will then be individually addressed throughout the remainder of the chapter.

Case 1. A direct quotation from *Wyatt* v. *Stickney* opens the area:[24] "This class action originally was filed on October 23, 1970, on behalf of patients involuntarily confined for mental treatment purposes at Brice Hospital, Tuskaloosa, Alabama. On March 12, 1971, in a formal opinion and decree, this court held that these involuntarily committed patients "unquestionably have a constitutional right to receive such individual treatment as will give each of them a realistic opportunity to be cured or to improve his or her mental condition."

The court further held that patients at Brice were being denied their right to treatment and that defendants, per their request, would be allowed six months in which to raise the level of care at Brice to the constitutionally required minimum.

In this decree, the court ordered defendants to file reports defining the mission and functions of Brice Hospital, specifying the objective and subjective standards required to furnish adequate care to the treatable mentally ill and detailing the hospital's progress toward the implementation of minimum constitutional standards. . . .

"On September 23, 1971, defendants filed their final report, from which this court concluded on December 10, 1971 that defendants had failed to promulgate and implement a treatment program satisfying minimum medical and constitutional requisites."[25] Generally, the court found that the defendants treatment program was deficient in three fundamental areas. It failed to provide: (1) a humane psychological and physical environment; (2) qualified staff in numbers sufficient to administer adequate treatment; and (3) individualized treatment plans. More specifically, the court found that many conditions, such as nontherapeutic, uncompensated work assignments, and the absence of any semblance of privacy, constituted dehumanizing factors contributing to the degeneration of the patient's self-esteem. Physical facilities at Brice were overcrowded and plagued by fire and other emergency hazards. The court found also that most staff members were poorly trained and that staffing ratios were so inadequate as to render the administration of effective treatment impossible. The court concluded, therefore, that whatever treatment was provided at Brice was grossly deficient and failed to satisfy minimum medical and constitutional standards.

Notes. This was the first major case to open the right to treatment in which the lack of minimal standards are at issue. As noted, there was no semblance of either the elements of treatment, or the high level performance of them. Given an opportunity to make the required corrections, the service system was unable to do so, although some significant improvements were made.[26-27]

Consequently, the court was forced for the first time to address the question of what are the minimum medical and constitutional elements of treatment. The court presented a set of standards which have become a model for, or a part of, standards in many states. Additionally, they are used as part of its standards by the Joint Commission on the Accreditation of Hospitals, which reviews organizations throughout the United States.[28]

The standards are included as part of the eleven elements listed above, which are subject headings for this chapter. In *Wyatt* v. *Stickney* they were summarized by the court under three main headings: (1) a humane psychological and physical environment; (2) qualified staff in numbers sufficient to administer adequate treatment; and (3) individualized treatment plans.

A second case will further outline the broad range of problems which have surfaced under the right to treatment topic.

Case 2. This second case will be extensively presented because it immediately offers a graphic illustration of the breadth and depth of treatment problems. Little explanation is needed — the situations are all too clear. The *Rone* v. *Fireman* case opinion outlines six distinct issues in three separate time settings:[29]

1. Living Conditions
2. Staff
3. Medical Care
4. Administration of Drugs
5. Therapeutic Treatment
6. Alternative Settings

The issues are analyzed by a pre-April 1975 view (when the present Director of the Ohio Department of Mental Health and Mental Retardation assumed his position); an April 1975–May 1976 period when a preliminary injunction was issued; and in May 1976 to the present. The time periods are the boundaries for the change efforts:

Living Conditions. Prior to April 1975, living conditions at Western Reserve were both substandard and dangerous to both the mental and the physical health of patients. Housekeeping and maintenance were extremely poor; many fire and safety hazards existed, and the patient areas were generally filthy and malodorous. The patient quarters were crowded and privacy and quiet were nonexistent.

The defendants attempted to eradicate these conditions upon their appointment in 1975. However, budget constraints and inadequate staff levels forced the conditions to become insufficient for custodial care. The issuance of the preliminary injunction required defendants to hire a substantial number of staff members and housekeepers. They were also forced to improve the safety conditions and sanitary facilities. The number of patients to each cottage was limited to prevent overcrowding.

These conditions improved Western Reserve to the point that it is no longer considered an inhumane and dangerous place. However, cottage 21 was an exception — security was poor; there were ventilation problems; the patient rooms did not meet fire and safety code requirements; and there was no therapeutic environment.

The preliminary injunction remedied most of the problems with the living conditions at Western Reserve. However, there still was a serious problem of physical and sexual abuse of the patients by staff members. An investigation by the Ohio Police resulted in 100 staff members being removed because of patient exploitation. The current Director has established a patient abuse committee which substantively reduced the incidents of physical and sexual abuse.

Staff. The problem before April 1975 with staff shortages was severe. Patient care and treatment was impossible. The defendants were aware of this problem but were financially unable to remedy it. The preliminary injunction forced Western Reserve to hire 25% more staff members. Western Reserve complied with this requirement by hiring 253 more staff members.

The staff to patient ratio went from .9 to 1.43. This enabled the institution to more adequately treat the patients by placing Western Reserve at slightly above the national average for a facility having similar patients.

The numbers above are not directly proportionate to the quality of care. The qualifications of the personnel are also vital. Before the injunction, the staff was generally inexperienced and incompetent. The preliminary injunction required strict hiring credentials and a continuous education and training program for the staff members.

Medical Care. Western Reserve uses three different means of medical care. Initially, each patient is assigned to a unit and treated by the physician assigned thereto. Patients requiring more extensive care are transferred to a medical surgical service — essentially a hospital within a hospital. Finally, those patients requiring continuous care are treated at the infirmary. Most of these patients are nonambulatory.

The medical care at Western Reserve was deficient in several areas. Unlicensed physicians were employed by the hospital and had direct and unsupervised contact with the patients. Some had difficulty speaking English, and others were lacking in training and/or experience dealing with problems of particular importance to institutionalized chronically ill patients. There was no continuing medical education. The oxygen and resuscitation equipment was antiquated and often nonoperational. Routine medical examinations were irregularly, if ever, conducted.

Since the issuance of the preliminary injunction, most of these problems have been solved. More physicians were hired and the unlicensed physicians dismissed. A substantial effort has been made to conduct regular and complete physical examinations. A new medical coordinator was appointed. He encouraged ongoing medical education and participation in seminars. A biweekly mandatory meeting of all physicians is now held to ensure proper organization and cooperation. The court found the medical care since the preliminary injunction to be consistent with minimally acceptable community standards.

Administration of Drugs. Another major issue raised was the manner in which psychotropic drugs were administered to patients at Western Reserve. Many patients were treated with more than one psychotropic drug simultaneously. Additionally, patients were treated with drugs for which they exhibited no symptoms. The administration of drugs often continued for more than six months without either a change in the symptions or an alternative medication tried. The preliminary injunction spurred the publication of a guidebook on the use of psychotropic drugs, which was issued to the patients and their families. Also, a drug monitoring system was initiated to allow review of prescribed drugs by a pharmacist to detect any synergistic or adverse interaction between prescribed drugs. It also allowed for the determination of whether the drug was appropriate for the symptoms. A training course in psychotropic medicines and psychopharmacology was given to all the medical personnel. The court found the improvement to be sufficient.

Therapeutic Treatment. This area includes nonmedical treatment such as educational and vocational rehabilitation. Prior to the preliminary injunction, patients received no programming or constructive activity. They spent the day milling around and watching TV. There was virtually no staff/patient interaction.

The preliminary injunction required the hiring of many social workers and social program specialists, vocational counselors, and staff trainers. Improvements in the physical plant also facilitated patient rehabilitation programs. The study of the nonmedical treatment at Western Reserve revealed that the therapeutic units were still inadequate. The consensus was that intensive staff training would provide the necessary improvements to remedy the therapeutic programs.

However, since the study was conducted, many therapeutic programs have been implemented including relaxation programs, behavior modification, family involvement, one-on-one counseling, and social reeducation. In addition, there are music, cooking, sewing, and other manual dexterity activities.

The court found these programs promising, but the overall therapeutic programming was still inadequate because of the lack of personnel. Vocational training was a major area the court found to be inadequate. A plan to ameliorate the situation was presented by the court as a remedy for the vocational shortcomings.

Alternative Settings. It is widely accepted that nonhospital treatment, such as treatment in the community, is beneficial to the patients. However, most patients at Western Reserve would not benefit from these alternative settings because: (1) they have forensic and dangerous propensities; (2) they are nonambulatory; and (3) there is a large group of organically mentally ill patients. Various other patients required different levels of supervision and structured settings. Few discharges were made because of the lack of appropriate community services and residential facilities.

Western Reserve has developed some outside settings. It acquired a girl scout camp which it uses for community training. Patients there are given entire responsibility for all daily chores. Other purchases for use as halfway houses have been thwarted by area residents seeking injunctions. One successful program, however, was conducted in an area college dormitory with college students as supervisors. The court found these efforts to be commendable.

Notes. In this case the areas of concern expanded and highlighted as they were, touch nearly all aspects of hospital care. The six areas: living conditions, staff, medical care, administration of drugs, therapeutic treatment, and alternative settings have emerged as central issues of concern in the rights movement. The case details the kinds of conditions that exist in some hospitals, demonstrating why such litigation arises in the first place. It is clear that the problems are not easily corrected.

SUMMARY

The philosophical direction, technological links, and legal status of both the "right to treatment" and "the right to refuse treatment" are uncertain and shifting. Those who desire a yes/no response will need to wait until the developments decrease the "grayness" of current positions. What is clear is that there needs to be a balance between the two.[30]

Patients have the right to some level of treatment, constrained only by the resources available and the technological know-how of staff. Unfortunately, there are very real constraints at this time. Patients have the right to refuse and to choose alternatives. But in reality the refusal and choice are constrained by growing interest in contracting for certain services in treatment plans. There is also recognition at the point of treatment entrance that options are limited.

Both the right to treatment and the right to refuse treatment involve the presence and performance of the following elements: examination, habilitation and treatment plans; informed consent; case records; normalization; education and training; placement; staff; treatment practices; support services; and status and review reports. They are individually discussed.

EXAMINATIONS (PHYSICAL, SOCIAL, MENTAL)

Definition. Patients have the right to an examination containing physical, social, and psychological components at admission to the treatment unit and as necessary throughout their stay.

The purpose of this right is to ensure that a patient's needs are assessed at the start of his relationship with the treatment center. No treatment activity is to begin prior to examination unless there is an emergency. The patient's right to an examination is a fundamental one because the examination is used to develop a base for treatment planning. How can plans and subsequent treatment proceed without the assessment base for understanding the problem?

Additionally, the purpose of the right is to underscore the importance of developing a measure for later accountability. If assessments define the problem (diagnosis), treatment should logically follow. Initial examination and assessment then becomes a yardstick for measurement of the success of the treatment. That is, the diagnostic outline and the plan for treatment should be followed by the actual treatment activities according to timing and sequence, which should in turn solve the patient's problem, at least within the limits of current technological expertise.

There are several actions for protecting the patient's right to an examination. The Joint Commission on the Accredidation of Hospitals uses a set of standards which include a very rigorous and comprehensive assessment process as follows:

"The program shall be responsible for a complete patient assessment that includes clinical consideration of each of the fundamental needs.

— this shall include, but is not limited to, an assessment of the physical, psychological, chronological age, developmental, family, educational, social, cultural, environmental, recreational, and vocational needs of the patient.

— clinical consideration of each area of the fundamental needs of the patient shall include the determination of the type and extent of special clinical examinations, tests, and evaluations necessary for complete assessment. The assessment of the patient's physical health shall be the responsibility of a qualified physician.

— the physical health assessment shall include a complete medical and drug history.

— in in-patient programs, the physical health assessment shall include a complete physical examination and, when indicated, a neurological assessment."[31]

The above standard suggests that an assessment according to JCAH is a holistic process including the physical, social, psychological, cultural, and other aspects of the patient. Furthermore, the standard indicates that the different assessment components should be conducted by different personnel; for example, a physician must do the physical health component, while a psychologist conducts the intellectual development reviews.

In addition to the JCAH guidelines, each professional group has ethical standards. One group's standards include the following statement applicable to all staff:

"In the development, publication, and utilization of psychological assessment techniques, psychologists make every effort to promote the welfare and best interests of the client. They guard against the misuse of assessment results. They respect the client's right to know the results, the interpretations made, and the bases for their conclusions and recommendations."[32]

Staff must ensure that assessments are responsibly used and that patients are fully informed.

What are the outcomes of a rigorous and complete assessment demanded by the standard? The right and the supporting standard ensure:

- that the patient's priority needs are addressed first;
- that the assessments provide actual data for the treatment plan;

- that clusters of medical and psycho-social needs are identified;
- that all possible needs of the patient (including complex interacting needs) are identified as early in the treatment process as possible.

With those outcomes, the right helps to establish a base for both effective treatment and effective accountability.

Case 1. Mary Doe, a 16-year-old high school student arrived at an emergency unit of the community general hospital on a Saturday evening.* She was in an acute state of anxiety but was incapable of defining the problem. She was given a medical examination which did not surface a physical problem. As her condition continued, the staff chose not to release her but to refer her to the emergency unit at the state mental hospital. A summary of her records were passed along.

The state hospital staff noted that she had received a medical examination and that no physical problems were identified. They admitted her for observation. An interview by a social worker did not reveal the source of the problem, although it did record a decrease in anxiety and fear. Since her symptoms were subsiding and no other problems were identified, she was processed for release.

At the discharge interview, the patient began sobbing and refused to return to her home. With continual probing about the source of the problem, the girl related that her stepfather beat and raped her.

Notes. The case illustrates the difficulty in problem identification and the necessity for a multiple topic assessment. In this case, medical reviewers did not detect evidence of assault. Additionally, the disturbed mental state was actually an acute reaction to assault and sickness/criminality in the family system. It is unlikely that there are many cases in which two reviews do not identify the primary problem. However, without both assessments, critical areas of patient need are overlooked. If the three areas of need in this case — medical attention, family systems help, psychological fear — are not identified in the examination, they are not likely to surface in the patient's treatment plan and subsequent treatment. Thus, the patient's right to appropriate, effective treatment is denied.

CASE RECORDS

Definition. Patients have the right to accurate and up-to-date case records.

The purpose of the case records right is to ensure that the treatment center fully records plans, progress toward achievement, and unusual incidents which

---

*Fictitious case.

occurred during the service. A second purpose is to provide a baseline for the measurement of services delivered. The services are provided, in theory, according to a plan. The case record documents how the "theory" of the treatment plan matches the reality of the situation. It is not always consistent since there is often some degree of difference between a person's theory of behavior and theory in use.[33] The important point is that a matching of theory and practice should occur so that the intended goals are reached.

What is the process for protecting the patient's right in this area and what are some of the elements of the right as it relates to service? Required elements include the following:

- regular monitoring of the case records
- patient inspection with clinician assistance as needed
- patient/attorney review when required by the patient
- details sufficient to indicate what treatment is being provided by whom, for what reason, and when.

Wyatt v. *Stickney* again prescribed the standards for case records as follows:

"Complete records for each resident shall be maintained and shall be readily available to qualified mental retardation and mental health professionals and to the resident care workers who are directly involved with the particular resident. All information contained in a resident's records shall be considered privileged and confidential. The guardian, next of kin, and any person properly authorized in writing by the resident, if such resident is capable of giving informed consent, or by his guardian or next of kin, shall be permitted access to the resident's records. These records shall include:

a. identification data, including the resident's legal status;
b. the resident's history, including but not limited to:
   1. family data, educational background, and employment record.
   2. prior medical history, both physical and mental, including prior institutionalization;
c. the resident's grievances, if any;
d. an inventory of the resident's life skills;
e. a record of each physical examination which describes the results of the examination;
f. a copy of the individual habilitation plan and any modifications thereto and an appropriate summary which will guide and assist the resident care workers in implementing the resident's program;
g. the findings made in periodic reviews of the habilitation plan which findings shall include an analysis of the successes and failures of the habilitation program and shall direct whatever modifications are necessary;

h. a copy of the post-institutionalization plan and any modifications thereto, and the summary of the steps that have been taken to implement that plan;

i. a medication history and status;

j. a summary of each significant contact by a qualified mental retardation professional with the resident;

k. a summary of the resident's response to his program, prepared by a qualified mental retardation professional involved in the resident's habilitation and recorded at least monthly. Such response, whenever possible, shall be scientifically documented.

l. a monthly summary of the extent and nature of the resident's work activities and the effect of such activity upon the resident's progress along the habilitation plan;

m. a signed order by a qualified mental retardation professional for any physical restraints;

n. a description of any extraordinary incident or accident in the institution involving the resident, to be entered by a staff member noting personal knowledge of the incident or accident or other source of information, including any reports of investigations or resident mistreatment;

o. a summary of family visits and contacts;

p. a summary of attendance and leaves from the institution;

q. a record of any seizures, illnesses, treatments thereof and immunizations."[34]

The above elements of the case records and the stringent use of them ensures that there are:

- plans which include rationale and expected outcomes
- documentation of the treatment provided including when, where, and what
- results and definable progress on the way to results
- unusual incidents recorded and explained.

The case record is to be the mechanism for documenting the intended outcomes and the basis for matching them with the actual outcomes of the planned treatment. The patient has a right to accurate and up-to-date case records because records are the foundation for review of both the intentions of treatment and the actual accomplishments.

Case 1. In *Gotkin* v. *Miller,* Janet Gotkin was a mental patient voluntarily hospitalized on several occasions between 1962 and 1970, mainly because of a series of suicide attempts.[35] She had not received treatment since 1970. In 1973, the Gotkins contracted to write a book about Janet's experiences. To verify her recollections of various incidents, she wrote to three hospitals where she had been a patient and requested copies of her records. Two refused and a third did not respond.

This suit filed by Mrs. Gotkin claims that the refusal to forward her records is a deprivation of property without due process of the law and thereby a violation of the 14th Amendment. The court rejected this argument saying that property rights were not absolute and that patients do not have an unrestricted right to directly inspect a copy of their hospital records.

Notes. The court did not uphold this right to examine the records. Presumably, the court reviewed the usefulness of her proposed review, perhaps including: (1) the therapeutic value of the information; and (2) the public value gained by a public presentation of the process of her treatment. After conducting the review, the court determined that in this particular case no useful personal or public purpose was served by her gaining access to her case records. The case indicates that patient access does not include all case records and does not include all situations in which patients would request the review.

TREATMENT AND HABILITATION PLAN

Definition. Patients have the right to an individualized treatment and habilitation plan.

The purposes of the individual treatment and habilitation plan are:

- to demonstrate a plan of attack on the patient's problem.
- to demonstrate the staff's understanding of the problem and their expertise in matching the patient's problem with a proposed solution.
- to establish guideposts for measuring the success of the plan at the beginning, at the middle, and at the end of the treatment.
- to provide the patient an opportunity to participate in the definition of his future as it will be shaped by his treatment plan. In general, the patient's right to an individualized treatment plan guarantees that the treatment system is taking into account the patient's individual characteristics and that it has attempted to match those characteristics with the best treatment solution drawn from a wide array of possible solutions.

The process by which this right is protected involves standards for individualized treatment plans. In a review of several mental health professionals' responses to the *O'Connor* v. *Donaldson* case,[36] Clayton, a writer in the mental health field, quoted one professional as identifying five basic guidelines for individual treatment plans:

- "the patient should be included in the development of the plan and goals;
- short term and long term goals that are achievable and reasonable should be set;

- the goals should be stated in behavioral and in observable and measurable terms;
- the patient's strengths should be considered as well as his problems and needs;
- who will do what and when should be clearly stated and every goal should have an anticipated time frame."[37]

Additionally, the Joint Commission on the Accreditation of Hospitals identifies a list of items that must be included in the development of an individualized treatment plan: consistency with treatment philosophy; multidisciplinary input; specific staff person responsible; specification of services to be provided; referrals if appropriate; supplemental services needed (speech, hearing, etc.); goals — long-term, short-term and measurable; evidence of patient participation; locations and frequency of treatments; methods for measuring outcomes; and plan for family involvement.[38]

While some of the criteria affect the degree of flexibility for clinicians, work is constantly continuing to develop new formats for planning.[39]

The formulation of goals are of critical importance, and it is at the point of treatment plan development that they are defined. Martin summarizes the establishment of the goal and related legal issues quite well:

"The goal of a behavior change project should be related to the behavior which justified the intervention of the state in the first place [or family, friends, employer]. The goal should thus be to change that behavior so that the state involvement can be terminated [and anyone else's concerns]. The change should basically benefit the individual and should not look for its justification too far outward into society's needs or too far inward into institutional convenience. An individual's behavior should not be the focus of change when changing something else in the environment can solve the problems. It should never be your goal to change behavior which is constitutionally protected."[40] (Bracketed words are author's.)

The outcome of the patient's right to an individualized treatment and habilitation plan is that the rights pressure is directed at ensuring the development of an overall strategy and a plan of attack, which includes specific measurable activities. The treatment plan establishes a baseline by which both the patient's progress and the staff's provision of service can be measured. Without the treatment plan, there is no way to determine where the staff is taking the patient and/or the degree of the patient's progress toward that future position.

INFORMED CONSENT FOR TREATMENT

Definition. Patients have the right to consent to treatment after being informed of the treatment's intended benefits and potential negative side effects.

The purpose of the right is first to include patients in the decision making concerning the process and outcome of treatment. Second, the right helps to involve a patient in values and choices which affect his social/physical health and perhaps his life. The third purpose is to ensure that a patient knows the potential risks and benefits of the treatment he is about to undergo.

The informed consent principle is derived from the "patient's right to exercise control over his or her own body," and the fact that the "patient depends completely on the physician for information on which he or she (the patient) makes decisions."[41-43]

Informed consent is the means by which patients approve their involvement in a treatment practice or a whole program. Whether it can exist at all in certain coercive treatment settings is an open question.[44, 45] There are arguments that it is a workable concept and that it is not.[46, 47, 48]

The process by which the right is protected is through an enhanced involvement of the patient in decision making at every step of the treatment process. Traditionally, treatment was provided to the patient by a provider. He was the determiner of the treatment process as well as the outcome because he held the required expertise. Only technical experts were believed capable of making the decisions. However, there is now increasingly more involvement of patients in this process because providers recognize the value of having patients know the intended goal of treatment and the methods they use to get there. That is, informed, educated patients are likely to increase the results of therapy.[49-51]

This right can be narrowly prescribed to focus on consent for certain procedures, or it can be broadly prescribed to focus on the treatment plan as a whole. In an expansive view, it can be interpreted to mean that patients must give informed consent to every aspect of their involvement with the treatment regimen. At the minimum, patients should give informed consent (by signing) to any unusual procedures which deviate significantly from the plan or which generate unusual risk. Patients should be involved in any of the major decisions of the plan at various points in the treatment process, e.g. new therapeutic drugs, change of unit, participation in a new encounter group. Each of the changes must document the patient's involvement in, and understanding of, the decision.

Two tests are used to determine whether staff provide enough information to patients.[52] One test requires that staff (physicians plus other staff) provide the same amount of information as provided by other competent staff in the community. The second test requires that enough information be provided to enable the patient to make an intelligent decision regarding the proposed procedure. The right is best protected by doing both, i.e. provide the expected amount of information according to local practice *and* with enough explanation to ensure that the patient fully understands.

Importantly, when unusual procedures are attempted which have a certain level of risk or a very high risk, the patient or the patient's guardian should be fully informed of the costs and benefits and have a say in determining whether that procedure should go ahead.

Certainly the broader view is the preferred position for rights advocates. Inclusion of patients in all phases of the treatment decision making (to the best of their ability) will ensure that informed consent is given in every instance possible. The highest level of "informed consent" is generated by a constant patient awareness of the patient's position in the treatment process. The "wherepossible" and the "best of their ability" are qualifiers to the right. But these qualifiers do not ask for more than the careful "best judgement" by clinicians in each individual case. Clinicians will be held accountable for their judgments so "where possible" and "to the best of the patient's ability" must be well reasoned.

The greatest problem with consent involves the patient who is not competent to give consent. One emerging view is that voluntary patients *always* have the right of informed consent. Involuntary patients do not if they are involuntarily committed by a court — but involuntary patients retain the consent right with regard to unusual procedures. By one statute, involuntary patients are only those who are also incompetent.[53] In states where those codes do not exist, staff must continue to make judgments about the levels of competency for consent and the degree of "informed."

The outcome of this right is that patients are involved in the decision making regarding what is to happen to them. Significant negative effects are derived from mental disability when the patient's involvement in decision making decreases. Requiring staff to secure informed consent at major decision points in the patient's path through the system in turn requires involvement of patients in those choices. Persuading instead of mandating may be necessary, and certainly explaining the basics of the treatment process and outcome are prerequisites.

Case 1. In *Knecht* v. *Gillman* a patient/inmate was given a drug which is used to induce vomiting.[54] The case is presented in detail later in this chapter. It involved giving the drug apomorphine to prisoners who acted out in a variety of ways (e.g., swearing, talking, lying, not getting up). The "treatment" which induced vomiting was to convince the inmate not to do it again. The patients were to have initially given consent to be involved in this treatment.

Notes. In this case, the court's opinion was that the purpose of the "treatment" was not rehabilitation but administrative efficiency. Providing a drug to alter inmate behavior regarding ward and unit rules was not a part of the patient's "treatment plan." Thus, the patient did not *consent* to treatment since it was not treatment. Although some patients might agree to this even with full understanding, there is a serious question about whether the coercive environment would allow a truly "voluntary choice."[55]

EDUCATION AND TRAINING

Definition. Patients have the right to education and training while in the treatment setting.

The purposes of this right are to ensure that patients maintain their educational levels and that they are provided with activities which help them progress to higher levels. The right also ensures that they receive training to maintain and enhance their personal living skills.

The right provides two directional pressures: (1) to maintain academic and personal living skills at their current levels, and (2) to increase academic and personal living skills to "normal" levels, or to advanced levels if patients are already minimally capable. For example, a low level of academic skill might be a third grade education, while low personal skills would include not knowing how to shop or to use a public transportation system.

The process by which education and training is provided is through an organized system of academic and personal care programs. The academic programs are targeted at children or adults who have not finished the equivalent of a high school education. The personal living programs are aimed at all clients who do not have the personal living skills necessary to maintain life on the outside, e.g., personal hygiene, transportation, shopping, cooking.

Rights protection for education and training is provided by affirmative responses to the following monitoring questions:

1. Has an education and training needs assessment of the patient been conducted?
2. Are education and training needs matched with appropriate programming and presented in the treatment plan?
3. Has the patient participated in the education and training planning, and does he consent to the planned activities?
4. Are the programs defined clearly as to type, frequency, expected outcome, and evaluation measures?
5. Are the programs offered in the unit or by outside contract, and is attendance arranged and supervised?
6. Are the education and training programs periodically reviewed as to patient progress, continued appropriateness and performance?

The outcome of this right should match its initial purpose: to ensure that current education and training skills are maintained and deficiencies corrected. A second outcome is that the possibility of progress toward a higher level of sophistication is opened. Meanwhile, the minimum level of capability needed to maintain life outside the treatment setting is established.

Case 1. In *Halderman* v. *Pennhurst State School and Hospital* the issue involved whether or not the residents at Pennhurst had been victims of violations of their statutory and constitutional rights.[56] Specifically, the case considered whether Pennhurst as an institution had been violating the rights of its retarded residents in failing to provide them with minimally adequate education, training, and care. The court recognized mental retardation as an educational problem. It stressed the need for proper training to give retarded individuals the opportunity to increase their capabilities.

The court's outline of the history and conditions at Pennhurst is informative. Since the institution's founding in 1908, it has been overcrowded and understaffed. Although Pennhurst had undergone tremendous improvements since the 1950s when approximately 4000 people resided at the facility, the defendants admitted that minimum standards for adequate training of the residents had not been met. There was little contact between residents and the outside world. Psychological and vocational testing results evidenced a decline in skills, particularly social skills. The institution afforded the individual no privacies. The residents slept, lived, and ate in group settings. All had to conform to the schedule dictated by the institution.

Staffing problems were enormous. Professionals who left were not replaced. No psychologists were on duty at night or on the weekends. Nor were routine housekeeping services available during those times. More importantly, the education and training programs needed to aid the residents were not available due to staff shortages. And, those available had long lists of residents waiting to be included. Not only were programs inadequate to meet minimum professional standards, but evaluations of residents to determine their rehabilitation needs were both infrequent and shoddily performed.

No formal plans existed to return residents to the community or to provide support services in those communities which would receive out-patients. Restraints were used as control measures in lieu of adequate staffing. Seclusion rooms, physical restraints, and drugs were frequently used. Reports found the physical environment at Pennhurst to be hazardous to residents both physically and psychologically. Often skills learned, such as toilet training, could not be practiced due to inadequate facilities. Physical injury by another patient or through self-abuse was a prevalent problem. Staff abuse of residents was responsible for a minimum amount of injuries.

Patients "voluntarily" admitted or those admitted by their parents technically were free to leave when they reached 18. But the notion of voluntariness in connection with the right to leave was an illusory concept, since those who deserved to leave had no place to go and were frequently recommitted through a court process initiated by the staff. Furthermore, those residents who either did not understand their alternatives, or were physically unable to indicate that they desired to leave, were deemed to have consented to their continued placement at the institution.

The court noted the general acceptance of the theory of normalization by professionals and state officials. The goal of normalization was to treat the retarded individual as much like the non-retarded individual as possible. The basic principle involved is that a person responds according to the way he or she is treated. The thrust of the normalization programming aims at remediation of the delayed learning process so as to develop maximum growth potential by the acquisition of self-help, language, personal, social, educational, vocational, and recreational skills. Obviously, Pennhurst could not hope to implement such a program. A primary barrier to implementing such a program is the lack of state funding for community facilities, which are actually less expensive to maintain than institutions such as Pennhurst.

Both the plaintiffs and the defendants agree that changes must be made. Defendants contend, however, that they are neither constitutionally nor statutorily mandated to make these transfers or to upgrade the care, education, and training provided at Pennhurst. It is their position that no constitutional or statutory rights have been violated. The court emphatically disagreed.

The court made several distinct conclusions: A patient either "voluntarily" admitted or committed to a state mental health facility has a constitutional right to minimally adequate rehabilitation under the least restrictive conditions consistent with the purpose of the commitment; residents of state institutions for the retarded have a constitutional right to freedom from harm; the retarded have a constitutional right to receive at least as much education and training as afforded by the state to others (i.e. equal protection under the law); retarded citizens of Pennsylvania have a statutory right to minimally adequate rehabilitation under the Mental Health and Mental Retardation Act of Pennsylvania; retarded citizens have a federal statutory right under the Rehabilitation Act of 1973 to a private right of action and to be protected from unnecessarily separate and minimally inadequate services . . . .

Injunctive relief ordered: (1) that community facilities be established to provide minimum adequate rehabilitation; (2) that individualized programs be created and that periodic revisions of these programs be made; (3) that monitoring of community facilities be established; (4) that a special master be appointed to implement these orders who will report to the court; (5) that no further patients are to be committed to Pennhurst or to be urged to "voluntarily" admit themselves; (6) that Pennhurst be closely supervised until community facilities are available; (7) that physical abuse or restraint be prevented; (8) that the abuse of drugs shall cease; (9) that increased medical care and evaluation be provided to all present Pennhurst residents.

Notes. The case is the lead case which tests education, training, and normalization issues. The operation of the Pennhurst State School and Hospital was such that any defense stating that the programs and procedures there assisted in the normalization activity was without credibility. The list of difficulties highlighted by the final nine items again presents an example of the broad range of violations which do exist in certain large institutions.

With specific reference to normalization, it was clear that in terms of both the physical setting and the psychological climate, patients of the Pennhurst School were not in a setting modeling the "normal." Additionally, they were not receiving care which would assist them in either maintaining their education and training levels or developing beyond existing levels. When the setting is such that the current education and training levels of patients are undercut as was apparent in this case, there is absolutely no standing for the position that the program is increasing levels of sophistication. A further discussion of normalization is helpful.

NORMALIZATION

Definition. Patients have a right to be treated in a way and in a setting which mirrors life outside the treatment center.

The purpose of this right is to assist patients in preparing for the outside by providing a practice area for some patients and a continuation of outside behaviors for other patients. The concept of normalization has developed in human services in the last ten years. This right derives from the fact that the treatment setting is often an artificial environment which does not operate in a way similar to the outside. Extended stays in the treatment setting in a "non-real" atmosphere can actually decrease the patient's ability to function on the outside.[61] Thus, the concept of normalization demands that patients have a right to be treated in as normal an environment as possible.

The process by which this right is protected is a combination of ongoing monitoring of two dimensions: (1) the physical setting; and (2) the psychosocial climate of the treatment center. The variables can include physical design, behaviors, organizational structure, psychological and sociological aspects, and reinforcement rules (rewards).[62]

Wolfensberger outlined the two areas with sub-topics as follows:[63]

Physical integration
    Location — e.g., community or institution
    Physical context — e.g., consistency with service type
    Access — e.g., availability and convenience
    Size or dispersal — e.g., services sites are dispersed across a region
Social integration
    Program — e.g., handicapped children in regular classrooms
    Labeling — e.g., what clients are called, names of the facilities
    Building perception — e.g., does it look like a prison?

Monitoring of both physical and social normalizing influences will ensure that patients are served in a way which matches other persons to as great an extent as possible.

The outcome of the patient's right to a normalized setting is dual. First, with normalization policies and procedures, patients do not become accustomed to artificial environments that neither look nor behave like the environments from which they came. In a normalized treatment setting, the physical environment and the psychological climate acts very much like the situation patients will be likely to experience on the outside. If there is distress in their own physical setting or psychological climate (e.g. an alcoholic father and family in poverty), the treatment setting becomes a positive influence operating very much like an appropriate setting on the outside (i.e. non-alcoholic, non-poverty).

Second, patients with a normalized setting are less likely to lose skills they possess for living outside the unit. The purpose of the patient's right to normalization is to ensure that one negative outcome of some treatment units is missing, that is that patients do not lose skills they have already learned. The normalization right demands that treatment units help patients to maintain personal living skills they have and to learn others they do not have. Particularly for patients with low skill and intelligence levels, learning to adapt to a non-normal physical and psychological setting is counterproductive.

Case 1. The *Halderman* v. *Pennhurst State School and Hospital* case was the lead one in developing support for a normalized environment.[64] Since it has already been reviewed, it will not be repeated. The case relates to the normalization right because the total impact of the offensive conditions (both physical and psychological) were a definition of non-normality. Patients do not live on the outside in conditions that were present at Pennhurst. The continuation of those conditions would have forced patients to adapt to a living situation unlike anything they would encounter on release. Training in that institution under original conditions resulted in the unlearning of modes of civilized behavior.

PLACEMENT

Definition. Patients have a right to a treatment program placement which matches their clinical needs.

The purpose of this right is to ensure that patients are *purposefully* placed in settings which meet their clinical needs as defined by an assessment of social, physical, and psychological characteristics. The patient's right to appropriate treatment implies accuracy in matching the patient with a program where the individual patient's needs will be met.

The process by which this right is ensured is a matching of assessed patient needs in the physical, psychological, and social dimensions with the characteristics of the available treatment program. The "best fit" of needs and program charac-teristics should determine placement. The problem arises because this matching process is far from exact. Although clinicians are now able to make some gross determinations about what patients do well in what kinds of treatment programs, they are not specifically able to continuously identify the treatment models which successfully treat certain types of patients. Both the characteristics of the patient's problem and the characteristics of the program models are often ill defined.[65-67]

Thus, while the right is an appropriate one for patients, the process by which it is protected depends on a technological sophistication which is not yet avail-able. Increased sensitivity to the purpose of the matching process and the rights element can be useful in screening out extreme errors. For example, a young first-time acute patient is placed in a treatment setting which deals primarily with long-term chronic patients hospitalized for 10 to 25 years. The patient is likely to experience trauma and not to experience the type of emergency short-term treatment he needs.

Protecting the patient's placement rights is effected by a review of the follow-ing questions:

1. Is the placement the "best fit" between patient needs and treatment pro-gram characteristics, and does it fit the patients overall treatment plan?
2. Does the placement offer any risk to the patient due to its program char-acteristics or location? If so, were a hearing and attorney representation provided?
3. Has the patient given informed consent to the placement?
4. Is the transition into and out of the placement fully planned?
5. Is the placement permanent or temporary? If temporary, are the review time and change criteria defined?

The documentation of the above responses must be detailed enough to allow for a post-placement review.

The outcome of this right is ensuring that patients needing one type of care are not placed where that care is not available. It also protects patients from placements which offer a care program that could be harmful; for example, a patient with low ego strength is placed in a confrontation-oriented setting. The right protects against a placement outcome which does nothing for the patient or a placement which could harm him.

Case 1. In *Garry* v. *the State of Louisiana,* the case involved the state's place-ment of Louisiana children in Texas mental institutions.[68] Visits by parents are rare and by Louisiana caseworkers non-existent. The plaintiffs were Louisiana residents placed in other states' hospitals. They contended that such placement denies them the opportunity for reintegration into their home communities. They demanded instate placement as a "least restrictive alternative," or their freedom.

The court ruled that interstate placement could not be made without therapeutic considerations for the deprivation which resulted. It rejected the plaintiffs contention that they have a constitutional right to instate treatment as long as the state considers the needs of the individual and does not automatically consign some patients to out-of-state institutions.

The court promulgated the following minimum requirements for placement of juvenile mentally deficient patients in any institution.

1. A semi-annual review of the treatment plan by an independent expert.
2. A semi-annual program report.
3. Unrestricted visitation rights.
4. Free access to the outside world via communications through the mails.
5. Interaction with the opposite sex or at least non-segregation.
6. Rigid regulations in using psychotropic drugs.
7. Elimination of locked room deterrents.

Notes. This case illustrates the temporary solutions that can be developed to accommodate patients when beds are not available. The essential question here is whether or not placement of patients in another state's mental hospitals is in the best interests of the patient. The court does not agree that placement in another state in and of itself constitutes a problem. The essential issue for the court is whether or not the patients' clinical needs have been considered prior to that placement. That is, does the placement address the five questions cited, particularly the quality of match between the program characteristics and the patient's treatment plan?

Although the detail of the case does not provide information as to whether the State of Louisiana was automatically referring patients out of state, the court in following up this question would focus on that issue. An out-of state institution could be a beneficial placement for certain patients requiring certain services. In other cases, such a placement would be detrimental, for example, if there is strong family support and willingness to become involved in helping the patient solve his problem. Geographical separation reduces that possibility. Placement of poor children in out-of-state facilities would virtually eliminate family visitation.

The court chose to go beyond the placement issue, suggesting criteria for institutional selection regardless of location. As in previous cases, the court cited the criteria of treatment reviews, progress reports, visitations, mailing rights, and strict control of drugs. With all the cases, the problem of defining adequate treatment is surfaced again and again with similar criteria repeatedly reiterated by the courts.

STAFF

Definition. Patients have the right to receive treatment by qualified treatment staff.

The purpose of this right is to ensure that patients receive treatment from staff who are trained and experienced to render that care. Although it seems inconceivable that organizations would be run by and depend on staff not qualified to perform their activities, that in fact has been the situation. Several cases have produced documentation that some institutions are operating with too few staff and without staff of appropriate qualifications, including both training and experience. The severity of the problem is uncertain but there is both awareness and some recent studies that will help increase the knowledge of the manpower deficiency.[69-71]

The assumption by some commentators is that the rights problem derives from inadequate numbers of staff and from the presence of unqualified staff. Others suggest staff behaviors are a problem.[72] The assumptions that appropriate staff will solve all rights problems is disputed by both the complexity of the rights topic and the fact that others, patients for example, have an impact on rights protection.[73] Additionally, staff attitudes toward rights and knowledge of them has increasingly been a topic of interest.[74-78]

The *Wyatt* v. *Stickney* case was the first major one to highlight the staff problem. In the *Wyatt* case standards were prescribed which began to define the staffing requirements for a state mental retardation or a state mental health institution. The following quote from the case identifies those standards:

"1. Each qualified mental retardation professional and each physician shall meet all licensing and certification requirements promulgated by the state of Alabama for persons engaged in private practice of the same profession elsewhere in Alabama. Other staff members shall meet the same licensing and certification requirements as persons who engage in private practice of their specialty elsewhere in Alabama.

A. All resident care workers who have not had prior clinical experience in a mental retardation institution shall have suitable orientation training. . . .

B. Staff members on all levels shall have suitable regularly scheduled in-service training.

40. Each resident care worker shall be under the direct professional supervision of a qualified mental retardation professional.

41. Qualified staff in numbers sufficient to administer adequate habilitation shall be provided. Such staffing shall include but not be limited to the following full-time professional and special services. Qualified mental retardation professionals trained in particular disciplines may in appropriate situations perform services or functions traditionally performed by members of other disciplines. Substantial changes in staff deployment may be made with the prior approval of this court upon a clear and convincing demonstration that the proposed deviation from this staffing structure would enhance the habilitation of the residents. Professional staff shall possess the qualifications of

of qualified mental retardation professionals as defined herein unless expressly stated otherwise.

C. Qualified medical specialists of recognized professional ability shall be available for specialized care and consultation. Such specialists services shall include a psychiatrist on a one-day-per-week basis. A physiatrist on a two-day-per-week basis, and any other medical or health related speciality available in the community."[79]

The above standards are not unusual or surprising in their nature or their breadth of concern. What is surprising is that they must be reiterated by a court. The traditional matching of qualified staff for certain positions did not occur in that hospital setting and does not occur in other institutions across the country.

Meeting this rights demand for treatment by qualified staff requires matching the demands of the position with appropriate staff training and experience. It requires the obvious review of credentials and employment, ensuring that, for example, a psychologist just out of graduate school is not hired as a supervising head of a psychology department. Seemingly a ludicrous example, the combination of shortages of qualified staff and limited financial resources for recruiting result in surprisingly inequitable matches of personnel and positions. Psychiatrists in particular appear to be troublesome to recruit with shortages in many states.[80]

The outcome of this right is that patients are more likely to receive treatment by persons who are qualified to provide that treatment. They will be more likely to receive psychological care by trained and experienced psychologists, medical care by trained, experienced, and licensed physicians.

Case 1. In *Wyatt* v. *Stickney* the court found that staff shortages were so severe that the provision of treatment was impossible. Those staff who were in the institution in many cases had inadequate training and experience for their positions. The court in response defined both the type of staff and their number (ratios).

Notes. The well known Wyatt case was the first to attempt to define a staffing requirement for mental institutions. While there may be some debate on the exactness of this ratio it does provide a yardstick for identifying extreme shortages. The Alabama organization's staffing levels were so low as to make defense of the levels useless. It also indicated that the court would not accept the lack of financial resources and the difficulty of recruiting as sufficient cause for inappropriate staff levels.

TREATMENT — THE RIGHT TO TREATMENT

Definition. Patients have the right to treatment in an appropriate setting with appropriate therapies and other methods.

The context of the debate around this right was highlighted in the chapter opening. The right has received considerable attention in the legal literature.[81-85] And the debate on its purposes, value, threat, and operational conflicts has not been overlooked by clinicians.[86-91]

This right includes items such as assessment, placement, normalization, philosophy, and so forth. Very simply, the purpose of the right is to ensure that patients are not in treatment settings for custodial purposes only. The right stems from the philosophical point of view that the deprivation of liberty, whether voluntary or involuntary, must have an overriding purpose. That purpose in the mental health system is treatment. The right specifically attempts to protect the patient from an illogical process whereby the assessment, diagnosis, and treatment provided do not follow one from the other.

One process by which the right can be protected is a careful review of the degree of logic in the treating process. For example, does the treatment unit use the following six steps with each patient?

1. Determine the *type of problem* which exists — assessment plus diagnosis.
2. Determine the *type of care* to be provided.
3. Determine the *amount of care* to be provided and develop type and amount into a *treatment plan.*
4. *Document* both the assessment and the diagnostic procedures.
5. Describe the *matching process* by which the assessment provides data for diagnosis which leads logically to the treatment and, document the *types* and *amounts* of treatment provided over a period of time.
6. Periodically *review* the patient's progress.

While the above list is a simplistic presentation of the treatment path, it does outline the critical elements of treatment. For example, the importance of a physical/medical examination mentioned elsewhere is again stressed in order to ensure that in the medical hospital the prescription of mental disability needs does not overwhelm the need to review the physical status of the patient. A physically sick patient would obviously be receiving *inappropriate illogical* treatment if all he received were psychoanalysis.

The outcome of the right to treatment is on one level very straightforward. It ensures that patients receive treatment, not just custodial care; and it ensures that they receive appropriate treatment, that is, treatment that follows the logical process from assessment through diagnosis, treatment, and discharge.

Since this is an important area, several cases will be used to exemplify the right to treatment problem.

Case 1. In *Whitree* v. *State* a patient, Mr. Whitree was arrested in 1945 for stabbing another man.[92] He was charged with assault, second degree, and pleaded guilty. He appeared in court on 18 different dates and finally withdrew his plea, pleading guilty to assault third degree. At the time, he justified his change of mind as a way to save lawyers expenses and because he couldn't afford the time off from work. He was given three years probation which he violated. He was subsequently taken to Bellevue Hospital for psychiatric evaluation. The maximum penalty for his criminal acts was three years.

He was reported after examination to have been incapable of understanding the charge or of making a defense by reason of his chronic alcoholism. As a result, he was committed to a state mental hospital for an indefinite period.

The court found the hospital records to be grossly inadequate. There was no indication that the plaintiff received any psychiatric care during his 14-year incarceration.

An examination in 1954 revealed that Whitree had no personality deterioration and that his intellectual functions were "intact."

Throughout his incarceration, Whitree was moved from ward to ward. There are indications that he was physically abused by both patients and hospital staff. He spent the last 7 years of his confinement in the maximum security ward of the hospital. Finally in 1971, he was declared competent to stand trial for the charges brought against him in 1947. He had already served 11 years longer than the maximum sentence for the crime he may or may not have committed.

Mr. Whitree was in reasonably good condition when he was admitted in 1947 at age 48. While incarcerated he received first degree burns on his face and chest, lost or fractured 6 teeth, a fracture of the nose, a laceration requiring 4 stitches to close, severe headaches from repeated beatings, a fractured hand which healed improperly and is permanently deformed, a fracture of his right shoulder which was also set improperly and various broken ribs and injuries to his spinal cord.

The court found the state to be derelict in its duty to provide treatment and rehabilitation programs. It also found the hospital to be inadequate as "holding pens" for people found to be offensive to "normal society." The court awarded Mr. Whitree $300,000 in damages as a result of his mistreatment.

Notes. Little needs to be said about the damage and harm that was done to Mr. Whitree during his "convalescence" in the hospital for treatment. The court clearly found that not only did Mr. Whitree not receive treatment of appropriate amounts and quality, he in fact received no treatment at all. What he did receive was a series of physical and psychological abuses.

Exacting academic and theoretical definitions of what constitutes treatment may be unavailable. But the above list of treatment requirements can easily be matched against Mr. Whitree's service record. It is obvious that the treatment and the documentation of it were woefully lacking.

Case 2. In *Welsh* v. *Likens,* the patients were 6 mentally retarded residents in Minnesota State Hospitals ranging in degree of retardation from moderate to severe. All were judicially committed. They sought relief claiming the defendants were violating their due process right by not providing an adequate program of "habilitation" consisting of individualized treatment, education, and training for the residents of the institution. The court found that since the plaintiffs have not been found guilty of any criminal offenses against society, treatment is the only constitutionally permissible purpose for their confinement.

Notes. The important point of this case is that patients committed involuntarily must be committed for treatment. That is, in the absence of any criminal offense there is no reason for committing patients to a hospital other than for treatment. In cases like this, the court will focus on the six treatment requirements cited above (or some other suitable list) to determine whether patients are receiving treatment. If they are not receiving treatment, they must be immediately released, for that is the only justification for confinement.

TREATMENT — THE RIGHT TO REFUSE

Definition. Patients have the right to refuse treatment.

This right was discussed in the opening, and it will overlap with some of the others. The basic purpose of the right is to ensure that patients, whose very life may be affected by the method of treatment and/or the outcome, are given the option of rejecting both the treatment and the process. The right provides the basis on which patients can act on their own behalf to avoid harmful side effects, or even direct effects. This right, too, is being extensively reviewed in the legal and clinical periodicals.[94-100]

The purpose of the right to refuse is to assist and to encourage patients to engage in the values choices. The patient has a right to refuse treatment because the treating members of the staff are here viewed as part society's advocates and part patients' advocates. Staff advocate treatment that is theoretically balanced for both society and patient, but the balance is a dynamic one, shifting from one side to the other. When the society side is emphasized to the detriment of the patient, the patient should have the right to refuse that particular treatment at that particular time.

The right to refuse treatment can operate at the following points in the treatment process:

- in planning for the treatment;
- at the time the treatment is to be administered;
- at the time of obtaining consent for unusual procedures;
- at the time in which certain procedures are to be repeated.

Each point of refusal provides the patient with an opportunity to be involved in the decisions about his treatment process.

Many clinicians are comfortable with the theory of the patient's right to refuse treatment. However, their concern becomes apparent when a patient who is severely disabled exercises his right to refuse treatment that would help him. The patient is in effect "incompetent" to make the refusal decision. Thus in this instance, an informed consent to treatment or an informed refusal is inadequate because of the presence of incompetency.

A solution to the problem that limits a patient's right to refuse appears to be gaining some level of acceptance in both legal and clinical circles. For example, under Utah statutes a patient that is civilly committed has no right to refuse treatment for the mental illness that led to his commitment.[101, 102] The court determined that the patient's right to a fair hearing was considered at commitment. Since commitment was justified, the right to refuse treatment is, therefore, limited. This plan appears to work but is here considered only appropriate for the loss of refusal of "generally accepted treatments." Any unusual treatment procedures which include high risk (e.g., electroconvulsive therapy) and/or irreversible change (e.g., sterilization) still should include the patient's right to refuse.

What is the outcome of the right to refuse treatment? Primarily, it provides a second check by patients on potentially harmful procedures. Second, it involves patients in the choice of treatment process and treatment outcome. And third, the right to refuse treatment increases the sheer number of informed choices by patients, since to be able to refuse treatment means patients will be likely to receive a greater number of alternatives.

Several cases have already been discussed which involve the right to refuse treatment. One will be considered in some detail here.

Case 1. In *Winters* v. *Miller,* the patient Mrs. Winters is a 59-year-old spinster who has been supported under public assistance for over 10 years.[103] For several years she lived in a hotel in Brooklyn, creating some difficulty there because of constant demands that she be given a room with a private bath and because of her alleged failure to maintain a proper state of personal cleanliness.

In 1967, she was told by her welfare caseworker that she would have a private bath if she moved to another hotel in Manhattan which she agreed to do. She had lived there a year when the manager told her she would have to move to another room in that hotel. She refused and the police were called. She was taken to Bellevue Mental Hospital where she was involuntarily admitted by certificates from two staff psychiatrists.

For 10 years prior to her admission, she had been a practicing Christian Scientist. At the hospital she refused to allow her blood pressure to be taken or to allow injections of medication. Despite her refusal, she was subjected to heavy doses of tranquilizers.

Throughout her confinement she had never been adjudicated "mentally ill." No effort was made to get a judicial declaration regarding Mrs. Winter's competency. The court found this to be a violation of the basic premise in our society that recognizes the right to be heard before being subjected to loss of liberty or loss of any kind.

Notes. This case is an illustration of the need to develop a rationale for treatment suited to each individual patient in the hospital unit. The rationale for treatment called for the use of forced medication on a patient who was a practicing Christian Scientist. Theoretically, the patient's characteristics (religion) would be considered at the time the treatment plan was developed. In this case, the patient's rejection of the medication was derived from her religious positions which were held for some 10 years prior to the time of the treatment. It would seem in this case that the patient had every right to refuse to take medication. While the exercise of that right would have made it difficult for staff to create an alternative treatment, that in fact is their task.

Should staff have felt that she was not competent to make that refusal decision, they could have taken her to court where she would have been adjudicated mentally ill and incompetent. In that case her refusal to take medication would have been a decision made by an incompetent person who was not able to make decisions. The staff's position, that forced medication was in her best interest, then would have held more weight. It still would have required the rationale and consistency with the treatment plan.

MEDICATION REFUSAL

Definition. Patients have the right to refuse medication.

This right is essentially a continuation of the broader concerns about the right to refuse treatment. Medication is now considered one of the primary means of treatment. The right to refuse medication is a sub-right within the overall right to refuse treatment. However, the importance of medication in modern mental health care programming suggests that an individual discussion of this right is appropriate.

The purpose of the right to refuse medication follows on those previously stated for the right to refuse treatment. That is, it offers the patient an opportunity to refuse medication both as a method of treatment and as to its outcome. It provides the patient with a means to reject the harmful side affects that sometimes result from medication. And it provides a way for the patient to engage in the values choices about methods of treatment, as with the Christian Scientist noted above.

The purpose of the right generates the most conflict around the issue of refusing *forced* medication. What is the question? Should patients who need and who do well on medication be forced to take it against their wishes? Additionally, the question requires consideration of what alternatives are available to the patient as treatment methods if medication is not to be used.

This latter problem is particularly troublesome since medication has been cited as a revolutionary agent in the field of mental health care. That is, it allows many more patients to control their harmful behaviors and function outside a treatment setting much quicker than if medication had not been used.

The problem of the right to refuse medication quickly converts to a dual one of both treating the individual and managing the treatment unit. The right to refuse medication is thought to increase the incidence and prevalence of violent outbursts on the wards noted in at least one study.[104]

A second related problem concerns the use of medication as a restraint on behavior. This is the essence of the "treatment unit management" problem discussed above. Medication can be used to lower the incidence of violence on the wards. At the same time it can have the effect of severe reduction of the patient's behavior and thought processes, i.e. through overmedication or through an individual patient's physiological response to the medication.

The medication refusal question is further clouded by the voluntary/involuntary commitment option. Should all patients be given this right? Some feel that if patients are voluntary they can refuse medication. In turn, they can be asked to leave if they refuse, since they are not "participating" in the therapeutic regimen of the treatment setting. Some commentators feel that involuntary patients lose their right of medication refusal. By definition, these patients are court committed because they are no longer capable of making decisions and should not be able to decide about medication.

Under the above reasoning, the right to refuse medication remains with voluntary patients. Along with that right, however, is the staff's right to ask voluntary patients to leave the treatment setting if they are not participating in the prescribed treatment (medication). The right to refuse medication for involuntary patients does not exist because they have given up their decision-making power in the court process.

The process by which the right would be protected, however, would require a review of each patient's status at the point of their refusal to take medication. Unless an emergency situation exists, the medication would not be forcibly given until alternatives to medication were explored and the question of voluntary/involuntary status was settled.

The issue is controversial and to date unsettled, with a Supreme Court test of the conflict to be addressed in mid 1982. There is some opinion that even though certain patients are involuntarily committed and incompetent such as the Christian Scientist believer, their wishes to refuse medication should be respected.

Controversy swirls around the broader issue of the right to refuse treatment, as well as the specific concerns about the type and levels of medication, the effects, and the interaction between several medications taken simultaneously.

In a recent New Jersey Court opinion, the judge in considering the right to refuse medication outlined the following rules for giving forced medication:[105]

- Both involuntary and voluntary patients may be forcibly medicated in a psychiatric emergency, defined as a "sudden, significant change in the patient's condition which creates danger to the patient or to others in the hospital."
- In nonemergency situations, involuntary patients may be forcibly medicated only after their case has been reviewed by a state-appointed independent psychiatrist.
- Legally incompetent involuntary patients may be medicated without written consent if proper consent from relatives or guardians is obtained in accordance with state law and once a patient advocate has been called in to review the case and assist the patient.
- A treating physician may declare an involuntary patient "functionally incompetent" if the patient is unable to give a knowledgeable consent, but such cases must also be referred to a patient advocate.[106]

This is as of now not binding, but it does indicate the degree of complexity of the issue and one attempt to find a solution. As indicated, it utilized independent opinions and much "information" to support the consent or refusal decision. For staff considering what to do, an attempt to implement the above to the best of their ability is likely to be acceptable behavior.

The outcome of the right to refuse medication is parallel to the outcomes for the right to refuse treatment. It provides patients with a way to participate in the process of treatment and the outcome of the treatment. It is a means for patients to be involved in the decision to take a chance on harmful side effects. Finally, it is another case in which the patient is forced to make an informed choice about taking or not taking a treatment methodology. As patients continue to be involved in decision making, they can continue to be involved in critical aspects of living outside the treatment setting.

Case 1. Rennie v. *Klein* involved a patient, discribed as a "highly intelligent" 30-year-old white divorced male.[107] John Rennie was a pilot and flight instructor before his psychiatric difficulties began. He began having symptoms of mental illness in 1971 which were magnified by his two brothers' deaths in an airplane accident in 1973.

He was admitted to a psychiatric hospital on 4-1-73 and diagnosed as a paranoid schizophrenic. He was given an anti-psychotic drug and released. He subsequently went through a sequence of readmissions and discharges with trials of different medications. He developed "aggressive and abusive symptoms." During this time he had religious delusions and believed he was Christ.

His 8th admission from August 26, 1974 to September 10, 1974 was initiated when the Secret Service brought him to state authorities after he threatened to kill President Ford. This "assaultive behavior" influenced the hospital staff to place him on homicidal precautions.

His 11th admission was November 16, 1978 until June 9, 1979. His behavior was erratic, alternating between being depressed and suicidal to manic and homicidal. During this period he attempted to commit suicide by taking an overdose of a psychotropic drug.

This suit occurred during the patient's 12th admission and involuntary commitment. He refused to take medication and frequently fought with other patients and attendants. Prior to the suit, the patient reported that evening shift attendants beat him with sticks while he was tied to a bed. The investigation that followed resulted in one employee being suspended. Following his reinstatement, the attendant and the patient remained on the same ward.

At the trial the experts disagreed over the patient's diagnosis and appropriate treatment. The writing of the opinion occurred more than 4 months after the trial. The court therefore refused the patient's request for an injunction to prevent forced medication since it wasn't known what had occurred in those four months. The court did mention that should Mr. Rennie now refuse any medication, a temporary injunction would be issued until a hearing is held.

The patient subsequently renewed his motion for a preliminary injunction. He utilized the court's statements to the effect that should he refuse any further forced medication, a temporary injunction would be issued until the hearing could be scheduled. The patient's condition deteriorated and the hospital administered drugs without his consent. An injunction was issued and a hearing held the next day.

The finding of facts during this period was that the patient refused medication and as a result became increasingly abusive and assaultive. He also suffered from dehydration, abnormal fluctuations of temperature, and infections. The court considered four factors in its decision on the efficacy of issuing an injunction.

1. The patient's physical threat to other patients.
2. The patient's capacity to decide on a particular treatment.
3. Whether any less restrictive treatment exists.
4. The risk of permanent side effects from the proposed treatment.

Since the patient has had to be restrained in the past and his capacity to reason is limited, the drugs proposed have only minor side affects and can be very helpful. The court concluded that no injunction should be issued.

Notes. As in many of the other cases, the litigation focuses on the right to refuse treatment, but in the course of investigating the facts regarding medication, several other issues surfaced. The case illustrates the difficulties encountered by a patient obviously struggling with mental disability who exercises his right to refuse the medication which had helped him.

Importantly, the court here proposes a four point test to assist the determination of whether to allow the patient to refuse medication: (1) Is the patient physically threatening to other patients? (2) Does the patient have the capacity to decide whether alternative treatments are available? (3) Does any less restrictive treatment exist? and (4) Is there a risk of permanent side effects? These are the considerations for patient use of his right to refuse any kind of treatment, not just medication. If those criteria are sufficiently considered, and the documentation of the rationale for medication is provided in the case record, patients can be best served by forced medication at certain times. However, staff should keep in mind that at any point they can be asked to justify their denial of the patient's right to refuse medication, including their decision precedence over the patient's.

UNUSUAL TREATMENT PROCEDURES

Definition. Patients have the right to refuse unusual treatment procedures.

The purpose of this right is to highlight the consent component in relation to procedures which are outside normal professional treatment activity.[108, 109] What are some examples of the kinds of procedures that would be considered unusual? Certainly, lobotomy, abortions, and sterilization are treatment procedures which are not standard in a normal course of mental health care. They are above and beyond the primary mental health activities.

How is this right protected? Special consideration for unusual procedures must be reviewed by each staff person individually at the time an unusual procedure is considered. There must be an assessment of whether the potential benefits outweigh the costs and whether there are alternatives which are more in line with standard practice. Additionally, special ward or institutional level procedures should be developed which in effect become an unusual procedures check and balance system. Finally, there should be retrospective review of the special procedures to evaluate their usefulness and determine if their repetition in this or other similar cases is warranted.

In effect, the process by which this right is protected relies on both staff and patients. Patients have the right to refuse unusual treatment procedures while staff have the responsibility to not propose them when alternative means are available. Additionally, staff must consult other staff for second opinions on the use of unusual procedures, certainly in the case of the three listed above (lobotomy, abortions, and sterilization). These procedures would require second and possibly third opinions, as well as ward and institutional level discussion. They would not become a part of any patient's treatment unless they were literally a last resort.

The outcome of the patient's right to refuse unusual procedures is that unusual procedures are viewed as a last resort subject to possible veto by the patient. A second outcome is that individual staff review is emphasized by the fact that staff will need a justifiable rationale to explain to patients who have the right to refuse. Third, a systems level outcome is developed which requires that unusual procedures be viewed both before and after use.

Staff should review the appropriateness of unusual procedures because the court can always become the final arbitrator of that appropriateness. To the extent that the procedures deviate substantially from the accepted norm *and* the results are costly, the probability of legal intervention increases as do costs and negative impacts on the staff.[110-112]

Case 1. In *Knect* v. *Gillman,* the patients in custody brought suit against officials of the state of Iowa. They claim that injections of the drug apomorphine at the Iowa Security Medical Facility without their consent constituted cruel and unusual punishment.

The use of apomorphine at the Iowa State Medical Facility was an "aversive stimuli" in the treatment of inmates with behavior problems. Any breach of protocol, such as not getting up or giving cigarettes against orders, talking, swearing, or lying, would result in an intramuscular injection by a nurse, following an unconfirmed report by another inmate.

The decision to administer the drug was followed by its injection in a small room containing only a toilet. The patient was exercised for 15 minutes and then began vomiting. This wretching spell lasts anywhere from 15 minutes to an hour.

The drug was often used without the consent of the inmate and often once consent was obtained, it could not be withdrawn. Medical behavior experts testified that this treatment is highly questionable. It was called worse than controlled beatings since the one administering it cannot control its effects after it is administered.

The court dismissed the defendants contention that treatment is not subject to an 8th Amendment security since the 8th Amendment deals with cruel and unusual punishment. The court said that it is the substance of the act not its semantic classification which subjects the act to constitutional requirements. The court stated that forcing someone to vomit 15 minutes to an hour is to be regarded as cruel and unusual unless the inmate consents in writing. The use of apomorphine was enjoined unless: (1) a fully recognizable written consent form is signed by the inmate and read by a physician; (2) it may be revoked at any time; (3) a doctor or nurse personally observes the inmate's misconduct; it is not sufficient that a violation of protocol be reported by another inmate.

Notes. This is a clear and definite presentation of an unusual treatment procedure. While the defendants attempted to present some rationale, it is clear that the patients experienced considerable distress when going through the "treatment." This could possibly be defended as a "last resort" when full and complete documentation of the failure of alternatives is provided. However, it is unlikely that this is an easily accepted procedure at many treatment units. The court did not think so.

SUPPORT SERVICES

Definition. Patients have the right to support services.

The purpose of this right is to ensure that the treatment setting offers care which will meet all needs of the patient, not just mental disability needs. It is in philosophy a holistic approach. The treatment center does not need to provide all services itself but must ensure through referrals and agreements with other centers that such services are available.

The process by which this right is preserved differs according to the size of the treatment center. Large units generally have on staff some of the support service professionals, including speech therapists, dentists, physical therapists, etc. Smaller units have a combination of formal and informal referral arrangements which in effect "provide" those services to patients. The process of protecting the right is a matter of ensuring that the formal and informal arrangements do exist and continue to exist.

The outcome of the right is to ensure that patients receive all the services needed whether they are physical, social, psychological, recreational, dental, or other.

Case 1.* John Doe, a patient in a state hospital was partially crippled from a suicide attempt by jumping through a window. Broken bones did not mend properly, resulting in severe difficulty in walking. John was receiving treatment for depression but no assistance in regaining proper use of his legs. A caseworker inquiring on his behalf about physical therapy was informed that it was not available as a part of the treatment program. No assistance was offered to John in obtaining physical therapy. Since he was not mobile, he was denied social interactions that would have helped his depression.

Notes. If the patient would file a complaint citing a denial of support services, he would have cause. Although the hospital is not mandated to have physical therapy, referral and linkage assistance is a necessary part of the patient's needed treatment. Not providing the physical therapy service itself or at least a referral is considered neglect based on inadequate treatment.

---

*Fictitious case.

CLINICAL STATUS, PROGRESS REPORTS, AND PERIODIC REVIEW

Definition. Patients have the right to an initial assessment of clinical status, to regular assessments which detail progress or the lack thereof, and to formal periodic review of the assessments and the progress.

This right derives from the necessity of establishing the groundwork for treatment. If there is a right to treatment, it follows that there must be assessments of treatment need and direction and regular evaluation to ensure that treatment is on course. The purpose of this right is to ensure that the clinical status is initially and regularly assessed, that specific achievements indicating progress toward discharge goals are noted, and that there is regular formal review of the progress which either reinforces the appropriateness of the clinical treatment plan or surfaces inadequacies which lead to a revision of the plan.

The process by which the right is protected again shifts the emphasis to documentation. The documentation tends to force or at least require the actual behaviors. That is, the nature and findings of the clinical status assessments must be outlined in full. These behaviors which are required for documentation (actually few staff make them up) in turn form the basis for the periodic reviews. The reviews are expected at varying periods according to differing state and organizational regulations and policies. The reasonable time period which finds some consensus is every 30 days.

At the time of review, the patient's clinical status should again be reviewed, in relation now to the treatment plan. The progress notes/reports should detail progress in terms of the stated goals and treatment plan. Thus there is a convergence of the progress of treatment documentation at the periodic reviews: clinical status and progress notes lead to periodic review, which leads to the treatment plan, which leads to clinical status and progress notes, which leads to periodic review.

The outcome of this right is assurance that each of these occurs individually (clinical status, progress note-taking, and periodic review). It should also help to ensure that they receive a linked consideration — that is that they do actually converge.

*Case 1.** Mary Smith was a patient at the Alpha Treatment Center for three months. A core component of her treatment plan was attainment of part-time employment and renewed contact with her family. In treatment for a severe anxiety reaction, she was reunited with her family and gained employment in the first month. Although she needed continued treatment, there was no review of her status nor was she informed of any new treatment plans. A clinical review team sent by the funding state agency cited the program for

*Fictitious case.

violating the patient's right to regular review. They refused to approve reimbursement until a clinical review was completed.

Notes. In this case the treatment team appeared to be neglecting the recognition of changes in the patient. Since initial treatment plan goals were substantially achieved, a review team could ask what then was the treatment purpose. Without evidence of a regular review, the treatment team has no way to document that they are current. And, in the absence of the documentation it can appear that treatment (and billing) is continuing without reason.

LOCALE

Definition. Patients have the right to be treated in a locale that is appropriate to their former and future living arrangements.

The purpose of this right is to ensure that patients are not placed in hospitals when they could be treated in community settings close to where they live. This right is secondarily to ensure that patients are treated as close to their home setting as possible except when clinically contraindicated.

The process by which this right is protected is again a review process ensuring that adequate matching has been attempted between the patient's individual living situation and the treatment plan which arranges a future living situation. The right puts considerable pressure on the question of judgements about living situation, about values regarding certain living arrangements, and about the selection of living arrangements from a limited array of possibilities. For example, what male-female arrangements are acceptable?

The outcome of this right is that patients can stay in touch with former living situations including friends, family, and significant surroundings (when helpful to their treatment progress). A second outcome is that patients will be returning to an area of which they have some knowledge.

Case 1. In the Doe case, the patient Doe was involuntarily committed to a state mental hospital located 100 miles from his home.* He filed suit claiming that he was forced to receive service outside his home community. Since his family had limited financial resources, they were unable to visit him and unable to participate in his care decisions. They could not afford to pay for transportation. The superintendent of the nearby state hospital stated that no beds were available, although some patients were from Doe's home community and others from out-of-state. Patients in the hospital where Doe was being treated received all community reorientation and aftercare in that area only.

---

*Fictitious case.

Notes. The case illustrates the combined treatment/administrative problem of placement. For the patient Doe, it is more beneficial to have him treated in his home community where family visits, family assistance in decision-making, after-care, and reorientation are easier and feasible. However, if no beds are available, he must receive treatment where beds exist. The court could force transfer of other patients, but the decision would rest on whether there was sufficient necessity to require transfer of other patients to meet the needs of the patient demanding local treatment. In the placement decision there should be attempt to match the patient with preferred geographic location.

SUMMARY

Rights and treatment involve two issues. The issues are the right to appropriate habilitation and the right to refuse treatment. The problem has philosophical, legal, and treatment technology components which are not clearly defined but which require good working relationships in order to avoid conflict.

The right to treatment focuses, for example, on appropriate services, treatments, and the education and numbers of staff. *Wyatt* v. *Stickney* provided mandates for a humane environment, quality and appropriate numbers of staff, and individualized treatment plans. This does not include the full breadth and depth of treatment issues involved. The necessary elements to treatment are listed and defined below.

The patient must have an *examination* which results in a proper and complete needs assessment and that sets priorities and helps define the treatment plan. The patient must have private and confidential *case records.* These must include complete and objective progress reports to assess the effectiveness of treatment and to include other aspects of patient history, etc., as outlined in the *Wyatt* v. *Stickney* decision.

An individualized *treatment/habilitation plan* must be provided which shows an understanding of the problem, a match with solutions, and a means of assessing the proposed solution's effectiveness. The patient must give *informed consent* to this treatment plan and any other procedures that are to be used. This necessitates the provision of enough information for the patient to make intelligent choices. Adjudicated incompetents would be the only patients deemed unable to make decisions or participate in the planning process.

Education and training must be provided to maintain patients' current capability levels and to aid their development. This should be accomplished through a system of academic and personal care programs. *Normalization* requires that the patient's environment and interactions be as close to normal daily living as possible. This deters institutionalization and transition problems at the time of discharge. A patient's *placement* must match his clinical needs in physical, psychological, and social areas. *Staff* quality and staff/patient ratios must be maintained at the best level possible for effective service delivery. The patient is guaranteed the provision of *treatment* that works toward improving his condition, not just custodial care. In addition, *support services,* e.g. recreational or dental, must be provided in accordance with patient needs. *Clinical status, progress reports,* and *periodic reviews* must be formal and ongoing procedures to maintain treatment direction and progress, and to provide up-to-date information about the patient and the program.

The other side of the right to treatment issue, the *right to refuse treatment,* focuses on the risk/harm factors involved in various treatments. It also concerns the availability of alternatives. The critical point here is the ability to make the decision to refuse treatment. This obviously involves information about the proposed treatments, informed consent issues, and determinations of competency. Patients can refuse "regular" treatments, medication, and "unusual" treatments based on their desire to avoid the harmful side effects or the direct effects of any given procedure.

REFERENCES

1. Lowry, J.V., "Philosophies, not laws determine admission practices," *Hosp. & Comm. Psychiatry,* **18,** 236 (1967).
2. Vassiliou, G., "On the Rights of the Mentally Ill: A Helenic View," *Ment. Hlth. Soc.,* 3:326–328 (1976).
3. President's Commission on Mental Health, Report Vols. **1–4,** Washington, D.C., Government Printing Office.
4. *Romeo* v. *Youngberg* 644 F. 2d 147 (1980).
   Mills v. *Rogers* 49 U.S.L.W. 3779 (U.S. April 21, 1981).
5. Vassiliou, G., op. cit., (item no. 2).
6. Monahan, J., "Was Mill for freedom for all," *American Journal Psychiatry,* 1978.
7. Mill, J.S., *On Liberty,* N.Y.: Appleton Century Crofts, 1947.
8. Stone, A.A., *Mental Health and Law: A System in Transition,* NIMH – Dept. HEW, 1975, G.P.O.
9. Talbott, J.A., "Toward a Public Policy on the Chronically Mentally Ill Patient," *Am. J. Orthopsychiatry,* **50**(1):43–53, 1980.
10. Schwitzgebel, R.K., "The Right to Effective Treatment," *Calif. L. Rev.* **936,** May 1974.
10A. Schwitzgebel, R.K., "Implementing a Right to Effective Treatment," 1 *Law and Psychology Review,* 117, Spring 1975.
11. Shah, S.A., "Dangerousness: A Paradigm for Exploring Some Issues in Law and Psychology," *American Psychologist,* **33,** 224, 1978.
12. Cocozza, J.J., and Steadman, H.J., "The Failure of Psychiatric Predictions of Dangerousness: Clear and Convincing Evidence," *Rutgers Law Review,* 1976, **29,** 1084–1101.
13. Monahan, J., "The prediction of violence," in *Violence and Criminal Justice,* D. Chappell & J. Monahan, eds., Lexington, Mass.: Lexington Books, 1975.
14. Shah, S., op. cit., (item no. 11).
15. *Wyatt* v. *Stickney,* 325 F. Supp. 781 (M.D., Ala. 1971).
16. Plotkin, R., "Limiting the Therapeutic Orgy: Mental Patients' Right to Refuse Treatment," **72** *Northwestern University Law Review,* (4) 461 (September–October 1977).

17. Olin, G.B., Olin, H.S., "Informed Consent in Voluntary Mental Hospital Admissions," *Am. J. Psychiatry*, **132**:938–941, 1975.
18. Palmer, A.B., Wohl, J., "Voluntary-Admission Forms: Does The Patient Know What He's Signing?" *Hosp. Community Psychiatry*, **23**:250–252, 1972.
19. Grossman, L., Summers, F., "A Study of the Capacity of Schizophrenic Patients to Give Informed Consent," *Hosp. Community Psychiatry*, **31**:205–206, 1980.
20. Berg, A., Hammitt, K.B., "Assessing the Psychiatric Patient's Ability to Meet the Literacy Demands of Hospitalization," *Hosp. Community Psychiatry*, **31**:266–268, 1980.
21. Stone, M., "The Right of the Psychiatric Patient to Refuse Treatment," 4 *The Journal of Psychiatry and Law*, (4) 515, Winter 1976.
22. Gutheil, T.G., "In Search of True Freedom: Drug Refusal, Involuntary Medication, and Rotting With Your Rights On," *Amer. J. Psychiat*, **137** (3), 327–328, 1980.
23. Roth, L.H., "Clinical and Legal Considerations in the Therapy of Violence Prone Patients," *Current Psychiatric Therapies*, **18**, 55–63, 1978.
24. *Wyatt* v. *Stickney*, op. cit., (item no. 15).
25. *Wyatt*, Ibid.
26. Leaf, P., "*Wyatt* v. *Stickney:* Assessing the Impact in Alabama," *Hospital & Community Psychiatry*, **25**(5), 1977.
27. Leaf, P., Holt, M., "How Wyatt affected Patients" in *Wyatt* v. *Stickney Retrospect and Prospect*, Jones, R.J., Palour, R.R., eds., New York: Grune and Stratton, 1981.
28. Joint Commission on the Accreditation of Hospitals.
29. *Rone* v. *Fireman*, 473 F. Supp. 92 (N.D., Ohio 1979).
30. Greenblatt, M., "The need for balancing the right to treatment and the right to treat," *Hosp. & Comm. Psychiatry*, **28**(5), 1977, p. 382.
31. Joint Commission on the Accreditation of Hospitals, *Consolidated Standards*, Chicago: JCAH, 1979.
32. American Psychological Assn., "Ethical Principles of Psychologists," *American Psychologist*, **36**(6), June 1981, p. 633.
33. Argyris, C., Schon, D.A., *Theory in Practice: Increasing Professional Effectiveness*, Washington: Jossey Bass, 1975.
34. *Wyatt* v. *Stickney*, 325 F. Supp. 781 (M.D., Ala. 1971).
35. *Gotkin* v. *Miller*, 514 F. 2d 125 (2nd Cir. 1975).
36. *O'Connor* v. *Donaldson*, 422 U.S. 563 (1975).
37. Clayton, T., "*O'Connor* v. *Donaldson:* Impact in the States," *Hosp. & Comm. Psychiatry*, **27**(4), 1976, p. 272.
38. Joint Commission on Accreditation of Hospitals, op. cit., (item no. 31).
39. Knesper, D. and Miller, D., "Treatment Plans for Mental Health Care," **133** *American Journal of Psychiatry*, (1) 45 (1976).
40. Martin, R., *Legal Challenges to Behavior Modification*, Champaign, Illinois: Research Press, 1975, p. 57.
41. Cataldo, M.F., Ventura, M.G., "Patient Rights in Acute Care Hospitals," in *Preservation of Client Rights*, G.T. Hannah, W.P. Christian, H.B. Clark, eds., N.Y.: Free Press, 1981, p. 301.
42. *Cobbs* v. *Grant*, 8 Cal. 3d 229, 104 Cal. Rpter. 505, 502 P. 2d. 1, 9 (1972).
43. *Schloendorff* v. *Society of New York Hospital*, 211 N.Y. 125, 105 N.E. 92, 93 (1914).
44. Murphy, J., "Total Institutions and the Possibility of Consent to Organic Therapies," **5** *Human Rights*, 25 (Fall 1975).
45. Ziegenfuss, J., Gaughan-Fickes, J., "Alternatives to Prison Programs and Client Civil Rights: A question," *Contemporary Drug Problems*, Summer 1976.

46. Meisel, A., "The 'Exceptions' to the Informed Consent Doctrine: Striking a Balance Between Competing Values in Medical Decisionmaking," 2 *Wisconsin Law Review*, 413 (1979) (504, 913).

47. Peek, C., "Current Legislative Issues Concerning the Right to Refuse versus the Right to Choose Hospitalization and Treatment," 38 *Psychiatry*, (4) 303 (1975).

48. Miles, D., "Informed Consent – The Rejoinder," 234 *Journal of the American Medical Association*, (6) 616 (1975).

49. Aiken, L.H., "Patient Problems are Problems in Learning," *American Journal of Nursing*, Sept. 1970, 70 (9), 1916–18.

50. Cox, C.J., "Time Saver for M.D.'s," *Medical Economics*, Sept. 18, 1967, 44, 101–104.

51. Robinson, L.A., "Patients' Information Base: A Key to Care," *Canadian Nurse*, Dec. 1974, 70 (12), 34–36.

52. Health Law Center, *Problems in Hospital Law*, Rockville, Md.: Aspen Systems Corp. 1974, p. 68.

53. Lebeque, B., Clark, L.D., "Incompetence to Refuse Treatment: A Necessary Condition for Civil Commitment," *Amer. J. Psychiat.*, 138:8, August 1981.

54. *Knecht* v. *Gillman*, 488 F. 2d 1136 (8th Cir. 1973).

55. Ziegenfuss, J. and Gaughan-Fickes, J., op. cit., (item no. 45).

56. *Halderman* v. *Pennhurst*, 446 F. Supp. 1209 (ED., La. 1976).

57. Bank-Mikkelsen, N.E., "A Metropolitan Area in Denmark: Copenhagen," in *Changing Patterns in Residential Services for the Mentally Retarded*, R. Kugel and W. Wolfensberger eds., Washington: President's Committee for the Mentally Retarded, 1969.

58. Nirje, B., "The Normalization Principle and its Human Management Implications," in *Changing Patterns in Residential Services for the Mentally Retarded*, R. Kugel and W. Wolfesberger, eds., 1969.

59. Kugel, R. and Wolfensberger, W., eds., *Changing Patterns in Residential Services for the Mentally Retarded*, Washington: President's Committee for the Mentally Retarded, 1969.

60. Wolfensberger, W. *The Principle of Normalization in Human Services*, Toronto: National Institute on Mental Retardation, 1972.

61. Goffman, E. *Asylums*, New York: Anchor Books, 1961.

62. Moos, R.H., *Evaluating Treatment Environments*, New York: John Wiley & Sons, 1974.

63. Wolfensberger, op. cit., (item no. 60).

64. *Halderman* v. *Pennhurst*, op cit., (item no. 56).

65. Blaney, P.H., "Implications of the Medical Model and its Alternatives," *American Journal of Psychiatry*, 132(9), September 1975.

66. Goldstein, M.S., "The Sociology of Mental Health and Illness," *Annual Review of Sociology*, 5, 1979.

67. Adler, D.A., "The Medical Model and Psychiatry's Task," *Hospital & Community Psychiatry*, 32(6), June 1981.

68. *Gary* v. *State of Louisiana*, 437 F. Supp. 1209 (E.D., La. 1976).

69. Perls, S.R., et al., "Staffing Patterns in Community Mental Health Centers," *Hosp. & Community Psychiatry*, 31(2) Feb. 1980, p. 119.

70. Langsley, D.G., Robinowitz, C.B., "Psychiatric Manpower: An Overview," *Hosp. & Comm. Psychiatry*, 30(11), 1979, p. 749.

71. Albee, G.W., "Psychiatry's Human Resources: 20 Years Later," *Hosp. & Community Psychiatry*, 30(11), 1979, p. 783.

72. Thorner, N., "Nurses Violate Their Patients' Rights," 14 *Journal of Psychiatric Nursing and Mental Services*, (6) 7 (1976).

73. Greenblatt, Milton, "The Need for Balancing the Right to Treatment and the Right to Treat," *Hosp. & Community Psychiatry*, 28(5), p. 382 (1977).

74. Laves, R., Cohen, A., "A Preliminary Investigation into the Knowledge of and Attitudes Toward the Legal Rights of Mental Patients," *Journal of Psychiatry and Law,* Spring, 1973.

75. Ziegenfuss, J.T., "Drug and Alcohol Addiction Personnel: An Exploratory Study of Attitudes and Knowledge of Legal Rights of Patients," Dauphin County Executive Commission on Drugs and Alcohol, Harrisburg, PA, 1976.

76. Kahle, L.R., Sales, B.D., "Attitudes of Clinical Psychologists Toward Involuntary Civil Commitment Law," *Professional Psychology,* 9(3), 1978.

77. Swoboda, J.S., et al., "Knowledge of and Compliance with Privileged Communication and Child-abuse-reporting Laws," *Professional Psychology* 9(3), 1978.

78. Jagin, R., et al., "Mental Health Professionals' Attitudes Toward Confidentiality, Privilege, and Third Party Disclosure," *Professional Psychology,* 9(3), 1978.

79. *Wyatt v. Stickney,* 325 F. Supp. 781 (M.D., Ala. 1971).

80. Knesper, D., "Psychiatric Manpower for State Mental Hospitals," *Arch. Gen. Psychia.,* (1) 19, Jan. 1978.

81. Birnbaum, M., "Civil Restraint, Mental Illness, and the Right to Treatment," 77 *Yale L. J.,* 87 (1967).

82. Birnbaum, M., "The Right to Treatment," 46 *A.B.A.J.* 499 (1960).

83. "Civil Restraint, Mental Illness and the Right to Treatment," 77 *Yale L.J.,* 87 (1967).

84. Halpern, C.R., "A Practicing Lawyer Views the Right to Treatment," 57 *Geo. L.J.,* 782 (1969).

85. Katz, J., "The Right to Treatment — An Enchanting Legal Fiction," 36 *U. Chi. L. Rev.,* 755 (1969).

86. Morris, G.H., "Legal Problems Involved in Implementing the Right to Treatment," *Bull. Am. Acad. Psychiat. & Law,* 1:1 (1973).

86a. Curran, W., "Public Health and the Law; the Right to Psychiatric Treatment," *Am. J. Pub. Health,* 58:2156 (Nov. 1968).

86b. Currie, Edward J., Jr., "Constitutional Law — Due Process — Right to Treatment for Nondangerous Involuntarily Civilly Committed Persons," 46 *Miss. L.J.,* 345 (1975).

87. McGough, Lucy S. and William C. Carmichael, II, "The Right to Treatment and the Right to Refuse Treatment," *Am. J. Orthopsychiatry,* 47(2):307 (1977).

88. Burris, Donald S., *The Right to Treatment; A Symposium,* N.Y.: Springer (1969).

89. Holder, A.R., "The Right to Treatment," *J.A.M.A., 220*:1165 (May 1972).

90. Hoffman, P. Browning and Robert C. Dunn, "Guaranteeing the Right to Treatment," *Psychiatric Annals,* 6(6):7 (1976).

91. Stone, A., "Right to Treatment," in *Mental Health and Law: A System in Transition,* by Stone A., Rockville, Md.: NIMH, 1976.

92. *Whitree v. State,* 56 Misc. 2d. 693, 290 N.Y.S. 2d 486 (Ct. Cl. 1968).

93. *Welsh v. Likens,* 373 F. Supp. 487 (D. Minn. 1974).

94. Peck, E., "Current Legislative Issues Concerning the Right to Refuse versus the Right to Choose Hospitalization and Treatment," *Psychiatry,* 38(4):303 (1975).

95. Brooks, A., "Mental Health Law: The Right to Refuse Treatment," *Administration in Mental Health,* 14(2):90 (1977).

96. Scott, E., "The Right to Refuse Treatment: A Developing Legal Concept," *Hosp. & Comm. Psychiatry,* 28(5):372 (May 1977).

97. Bandman, E.L., "The Mentally Disabled Person's Right to Receive and to Refuse Treatment," *Issues in Mental Health Nursing,* 1 (Winter), 31–43, 1979.

98. Symonds, E., "Mental Patients' Rights to Refuse Drugs: Involuntary Medication as Cruel and Unusual Punishment," 7 *Hastings Const. L.Q.,* 701 (Spring 1980).

99. Stone, A.A., *Mental Health and Law: A System in Transition,* Washington: DHEW, 1975.

100. Glass, E.S., "Restructuring Informed Consent: Legal Therapy for the Doctor Patient Relationship," 79 *Yale Law Journal,* 1533 (1970).

101. Lebeque, B., Clark, L., "Incompetence to Refuse Treatment: A Necessary Condition for Civil Commitment," *Am. J. Psychiatry,* **138**:8 Aug. 1981, p. 1075.
102. *A.E. and R.R.* v. *Mitchell.*
103. *Winters* v. *Miller,* 446 F. 2nd 65 (2d. Cir. 1971).
104. Ziegenfuss, J.T., *"Patients' Rights and Organizational Models: Sociotechnical Systems Research on Mental Health Programs,* Washington: University Press of America, 1982.
105. *Rennie* v. *Klein,* 462 F. Supp. 1121 (D. N.J. 1978).
106. Editors, "New Jersey District Court says patients have qualified right to refuse psychotropic drugs," *Hospital & Community Psychiatry,* **31**(1) 1980.
107. *Rennie* v. *Klein,* op. cit., (item no. 105).
108. Cook, J., et al., "Consent for Aversive Treatment: A Model Form," *Mental Retardation,* **16**(1):47 (February, 1978).
109. "Constitutional Law – Eighth Amendment – Aversion Therapy as Cruel and Unusual Punishment," 13 *Duq. L. Rev.* 621 (Spring 1975).
110. Wexler, D., "Behavior Modification and Other Behavior Change Procedures: The Emerging Law and the Proposed Florida Guidelines," *Crim. L. Bull,* **11**(5):600 (1975).
111. Wexler, D., "Token and Taboo: Behavior Modification, Token Economics, and the Law," **61** *Calif. L. Rev.* 81 (1973).
112. Wexler, D., et al., "Symposium: The Control of Behavior, Legal, Scientific, and Moral Dilemmas – Part 1," *Crim. L. Bull.* 598 (September–October 1975).

5
Medical Rights

OVERVIEW

Patients have the same medical-care rights other citizens do, including access to care, minimum qualities of treatment, and special services as needed. The mentally disabled have the right to medical care without discrimination.[1] In general this set of rights is designed to ensure that the patient, while in the treatment system, is able to have his physical medical needs met. The patient does not have a right to a greater range of care or to a higher quality than is comparatively available locally outside the treatment system. That is, no citizen has a right to medical care better than generally available.

The rights problem stems from findings that, for example, many institutional populations (including patients, prisoners, and prisoners with mental problems) receive dramatically substandard care in antiquated medical facilities often with substandard staff and equipment.[2-4] In providing mental health care, there is no intention to penalize the patient by providing him with poor medical services.

The process by which quality standards are maintained involves combined monitoring and matching. The medical services are monitored to ensure quality of care, broadly defined to include the type of service, the staff providing the care, and the facilities and equipment.

The matching process centers on a comparison between the type and quality of services rendered in the mental health treatment setting and the general standards of care available in the local community. Those who are assessing the nature and availability of medical care in a treatment unit do so by a matching process.

Outside the mental health treatment system, citizens have access to care by a physician they select. The rights emphasis on medical care is designed to extend the access and quality standards of the local community into the treatment setting. In that way, patients are assured that the outcome of their care for mentally disability does not also include as a side effect the provision of substandard general medical care.

There is no need here to overemphasize the patient's right to arrange medical care. For the most part, patients with access to initial examinations have access to follow-up care addressing the findings of the examinations. However, two areas of general medical services appear to present more than their share of difficulty for the mentally disabled — medication and speciality services such as dentistry. They will be specifically addressed.

This chapter reviews the following four areas: access; examinations; selection of physicians; and treatment, including two specific types, medication and special services. The focus here is on medical care that is an adjunct to the primary care received in a mental health unit. Some units define care for the mentally disabled as medical care provided by physician-psychiatrists. Here there is a discrimination between general physical medical care, e.g. examinations, surgery, etc., and psychiatric medical care, e.g., counseling, drug therapy, analysis.

ACCESS TO MEDICAL CARE

Definition. Patients have the right to access to medical care.

The right establishes the base for matching what is available to persons inside and outside the treatment system. All citizens generally have the right to a minimum level of care through a governmental medical program even if personal funds are not available.

In general the "access" right serves two purposes. First, it is to provide patients in a treatment setting with equivalent care, care no better or worse than generally available. Second, the right ensures that involvement in mental health treatment does not result in punishing the patient by depriving him or her of medical care. These purposes then define the two core elements of this right to have access to medical care and to have that medical care be of "reasonable, equivalent" quality.

The process by which this right is protected involves a series of five standard questions. They are led by the stipulation that the patient must be informed of the available care in total. When specific situations or needs arise, the questions for protection of the right and meeting the need are:

- What type of care is provided?
- Where is it provided?
- By whom is it provided?
- When is it available?
- What is the cost to the patient?

By scrutinizing these five questions, monitors can be assured that patients know the full range of care that is available. They will know whether, in fact, it is available and key information such as when to get it, where to get it, and how much it costs. These are not unreasonable questions for patients and advocates to ask. And, they are the kinds of questions received by medical service providers outside the treatment center.

The outcome of this right, and also the protective guideline, is that general medical services provided in a mental health unit are equivalent to those on the outside according to the prevailing level of quality. Essentially, the patient must be informed of the availability of general medical care and must receive that care when necessary. To be informed and to receive care is the essence of the access question.

Case 1. A patient, John Smith, was in a treatment unit which employed a part-time physician for approximately 20 hours per week.* The service complex provided extended care to approximately 350 patients in a series of independent units. It was generally difficult for the physician to see all patients for general checkups or even when specific complaints were made.

Smith complained of a broken ankle which was not examined until four days after the complaint. Additionally, at the time of the examination no x-rays were taken. Following an examination, the physician's judgment was that the ankle was not broken. X-rays were not readily available at the unit since the patients had to be referred to a community facility to have them taken at special cost.

The patient complained that his access to medical care was insufficient. He initiated litigation complaining of two problems: (1) the care response was delayed — the physician took an extended period of time to see the patient; and (2) the care was then not available in the full range that was needed and available elsewhere (no x-ray technologist or referral to one).

Notes. Here the organizational problem of sufficient medical staff in large institutional settings was surfaced. An outcome of "thin" staffing was demonstrated by the slow response to treatment and the lack of availability of other treatments. The patient certainly had a right to the care, although not necessarily in that center. However, if full care is not available in the patient service center, the patient should be referred and accompanied by staff to a community medical facility. At the very least, the center should have on-call a series of private practitioners who could supplement the in-house physician as special needs arise.

The difficulties in securing medical professionals for work in psychiatric facilities is well known. Some community hospitals have additional difficulties in hiring psychiatrists. But a few have solved the problem by recruiting physicians to serve two institutions. Others have physicians serve psychiatric units as only a part of their service territory.

---

*Fictitious case.

MEDICAL EXAMINATIONS

Definition. Patients have the right to a medical examination at the onset of their involvement with the treatment system.

The right means exactly that — at a minimum, patients entering a health care facility should receive a physical examination within hours of their arrival.[5] Although the hour requirements differ by facility, there is little question of the need for this review within time constraints.

In general, the purpose of the review is to ensure that physical medical needs are identified at the onset of involvement with the treatment system. In some patients, psychological and/or psychiatric difficulties will derive from, or be associated with, physical medical problems.[6] At the very least, these should be identified at the start of the patient's treatment. Additionally, there are times when the physical medical problems are acute and in need of immediate treatment. They must be dealt with first or simultaneously with the initiation of other treatment focused on the mental disability.

The process for safeguarding this right involves development of a checking procedure that ensures that medical examinations are given on entrance to the system within so many hours (the exact hours are prescribed by each state, e.g., 12, 24, 72, etc.). Each patient's file should be checked to make sure that the examination was given at or right after admission within the time requirements. For example, the requirements here can be defined quite specifically by each center. Medical examinations are performed at admission by the physician in charge, paid for by the patient or a third party payer. This organizational policy should become a standard operating procedure, and one which should not be neglected. While some of the other rights allow for interpretive differences, this one is direct and specific, providing strong accountability should a review be necessary.

The outcome of this right is the protection of patients from physical harm due to pressing physical medical needs. As noted above, psychiatric and psychological distress may derive from certain medical needs. Delay in addressing priority physical ailments may result in greater immediate harm than the psychiatric or psychological.

Case 1. Patient Jane Doe was in and out of psychiatric hospitals for nearly 10 years during her early 20s and up to age 30.* However, she had not received psychiatric treatment for some 5 years. One evening while visiting with family and friends, the patient went into what appeared to be hallucinations after feeling sick for most of the day. Emergency service was called — she was taken immediately to the emergency room of the local hospital.

---

*Fictitious case.

She was there examined briefly, and without any tests taken to the psychiatric ward.

It was assumed by staff on duty who happened to know her that because of her hallucinations, she was having another psychiatric episode. Her hallucinations were the main symptoms of the problem. She died two hours after admission to the hospital.

Because it is rare to die of hallucinations, there was a review of her status at death, although not a formal autopsy. At the review, it was discovered that she was suffering from an ailment which produced high fever and delirium. With quick action and an appropriate prescription of drugs to reduce the fever, she might have survived.

Notes. Although this type of case is rare in medical settings, it does identify an example of the difficulty with medical and mental problems. Mental patients with a history of bizarre behaviors can entangle their medical needs with previous psychiatric situations. Without a close medical examination for each and every patient each time one enters the hospital, there is no way to be sure that such historical entanglements will not endanger the life of the patient.

Medical staff are trained to consider all causative factors at the point of emergency diagnosis. But the patient history and present bizarre behaviors tend to be quite seductive, influencing the diagnostic finding to the psychosocial area. Even when medical problems are an expressed complaint, there is a tendency to see them as hypochondrial in origin.

USE OF PRIVATE PHYSICIAN

Definition. Patients have the right to use a private physician for their medical care.

This right is limited to medical care which is a secondary service to primary mental health care provided by the treatment unit. In general, the purpose of this right is twofold. First, it is to ensure that patients have the opportunity to continue treatment with their own physician if they so desire. This is a basic right available to people outside the mental health treatment system. There is no reason why patients may not exercise that choice within the mental health system. Additionally, it has the effect of reducing the overload demand for medical care within the organization.

Second, the purpose is to allow for and to encourage maintenance of the physician/patient relationship, if at all possible. If patients are being treated over a long period of years for a certain ailment, there is an advantage in having those physicians continue treatment. They are familiar with the case and have established a trust and rapport with the patient that will also be beneficial to the helping relationship.

For the protection of this right, there are several requirements. First, the process requires an availability of physicians who are willing to continue treatment once their patient enters a center for mental health care. Second, there must be a formal agreement by the physician that he will be responsible for the care. Third, there is the question of payment by the client for these extra arrangements. Dependent on the organization, it is likely that the medical care will not be included as a part of their per diem expenses at the center if it is provided by a personal physician.

Once these requirements are satisfied, the use of the private physician can be an excellent supplement and continuous contributor to mental health care. In cases where there are medical complications linked to the mental health problems, the patient's use of a private physician on the outside may aid the solution of the emotional problem. Additionally, the private physician provides a form of continuing follow-up care when the patient finishes involvement with the treatment setting.

The outcome of this right is the support of continuity of care that happens if a private physician provides services to the patient over a period of years. The opportunity to continue that care is beneficial to both physician and patient. A second outcome is affording patients the freedom of physician choice — a freedom they have outside the treatment system.

Case 1. A patient, Robert Doe, was in treatment for a period of 10 years for two difficulties.* The first was a condition of diabetes which was then linked to a depression problem. The patient had been hospitalized on a number of occasions both for depression and for the complicating diabetes.

On a recent admission to the treatment setting, the patient requested the retention of his private physician to handle the diabetic side of his joint physical/psychological illness. The treatment staff refused to do so, stating that they wanted to be the primary directors of the care provided to the patient whether psychological or medical. The patient objected to the rejection of his private physician and left treatment. He stated that he felt the center was not allowing him the right to choose his own private physician to administer to his physical medical needs which were not the primary presenting problem — depression.

Notes. It is unclear whether mental health treatment staff can be forced to allow a patient who is receiving service for mental health care to choose his own medical physician. The choice can be beneficial to the patient in terms of continuity of care. And it does diminish the pressure for medical services on the center, allowing other patients more service. There may be cases in which

---

*Fictitious case.

the relationship between the patient and his medical physician is contributing to the problem. Certainly, this possibility must be screened for, and if present would lead to rejection of the arrangement.

MEDICATION

Definition. Patients have the right to an appropriate rationale for and use of medication.

This right assumes that in some cases medication is used inappropriately. The general purposes of the right are three. First, it is to ensure that the patient receives appropriate types of medication, administered in the right dosage at the right time. Second, the right is to ensure that there is an adequate and timely response to unexpected adverse reactions of medication. Third, the purpose is to ensure that patients are free from abuse, for example, by the use of medication for restraint purposes or for the purpose of punishment.

The process by which this right is protected is by focusing on three areas identified by the Joint Commission on the Accreditation of Hospitals:

1. the development of drug treatment plans
2. the careful scrutiny of medication orders
3. the special care handling of drugs with abuse potential

The concentration on these three areas results from the view that they are the sources of the most difficulty in the use of medication. The checks and balances for the areas are as follows:

1. thorough training
2. careful management of amounts and supplies
3. proper administration of the drugs
4. careful and continued monitoring of results

In the *Wyatt* v. *Stickney* case, medication standards were prescribed. Due to their continuing acceptance and their clarity, these standards will be quoted here in full:

"A. No medication shall be administered unless at the written order of a physician.

B. Notation of each individual's medication shall be kept in his medical records. . . . At least weekly the attending physician shall review the drug regimen of each resident under his care. All prescriptions shall be written with the termination date, which shall not exceed 30 days.

C. Residents shall have a right to be free from unnecessary or excessive medication. The resident's record shall state the effects of psycho active medication on the resident. When dosages of such are changed or other psycho active medications are prescribed, a notation shall be made in the resident's record concerning the effect of the new medication for new dosages and the behavior changes, if any, which occur.

D. Medication shall be not used as punishment, for the convenience of staff, as a substitute for a habilitation program or in quantities that interfere with the resident's habilitation program.

E. Pharmacy services at the institution shall be directed by a professionally competent pharmacist licensed to practice in the State of Alabama. Such pharmacist shall be a graduate of a school of pharmacy accredited by the American Council on Pharmaceutical Education. Appropriate officials of the institution, at their option, may hire such a pharmacist or pharmacists full-time or, in lieu thereof, contract for an outside pharmacist.

F. Whether employed full-time or on a contract basis, the pharmacist shall perform duties which include but are not limited to the following:

(1) receiving the original, or direct copy, of the physician's drug treatment orders;

(2) reviewing the drug regimen for any changes, for potentially adverse reactions, allergies, interactions, contraindications, rationality and laboratory test modifications and advising the physician of any recommended changes, with reasons and with an alternate drug regimen;

(3) maintaining for each resident an individual record of all medications dispensed (prescription and non-prescription), including quantities and frequency of refills;

(4) participating, as appropriate, in the continuing interdisciplinary evaluation of individual residents for the purpose of initiation, monitoring, and follow-up with individualized habilitation programs.

G. Only appropriate and trained staff shall be allowed to administer drugs."[8]

The protection-checks for safeguarding medication prescriptions include: (1) a review of the patient's record, including extensive documentation; (2) review of whether the drug to be prescribed is standard in the program; and (3) the full understanding that the patient and/or the patient's parents/guardian are informed of both benefits and hazards of the drugs.

If the above conditions are met, the outcome is acknowledgement that the use of medication is helpful to the patient. The outcome of the protection is to ensure that there are corrections of any wrong dosage levels quickly and to prevent abuse, e.g. the use of medication as a restraint device. The right to refuse medication and the right to be free from abuse and restraints are addressed in Chapters 4, 8, and 9.

Case 1. Naughton v. *Bevilacqua* involves a plea for injunctive relief and damages based on the use of tranquilizers to which the patient, Naughton, had exhibited allergic reactions.[9] Naughton, a voluntarily committed patient at the Rhode Island Institute of Mental Health was diagnosed as moderately mentally retarded and autistic. As part of his treatment, doctors administered tranquilizers. The use of tranquilizers to control the behavior of patients such as Naughton is not unusual.

At the time Naughton was admitted to the Institute, his parents informed hospital officials of Naughton's adverse reaction to tranquilizers of the phenothiazine family. Since his admission to the institution, however, Naughton had been given phenothiazine without prior testing for allergic reactions. After one particularly severe reaction the hospital notified both his parents and their attorney.

Procedures to protect Naughton from further incidents, such as posting notices, were agreed to, but plaintiffs alleged that Timothy subsequently was given phenothiazines and again suffered severe adverse reactions. Naughton's parents blamed this latest incident on poor record-keeping practices at the Institute. They felt strongly that nothing short of an injunction forbidding the Institute staff from administering phenothiazines to Naughton would prevent such an incident from being repeated. The court sympathized with Naughton's parents' concern with preventing a similar incident from reoccurring but felt that an injunction aimed at the Institute would be useless as a corrective.

Notes. This is a case in which the parents of the patient clearly and consistently informed the institution that the patient would have a severe reaction to tranquilizers. Yet the process and procedure of drug prescription and the medication planning of the treatment center were so deficient as to allow this to happen despite the warning. The case illustrates the difficulties that can be encountered in managing the individual needs of patients, but it does not excuse the failure to do so. In this case, severe adverse reactions resulted. In other cases, death can be caused when a patient is given medication that is not part of a medication plan individually tailored to that patient. Cases such as the one above indicate deficiencies in the organization processes which should be monitored to protect this right and the health and safety of the patients.

MEDICAL SERVICES: SPECIFIC TYPES

Definition. Patients have the right to specific and auxiliary types of medical services as the need arises.

This right is an extension of the access right reviewed above. Its primary purpose is to stress the importance of the need to have available either on-site or by referral the kinds of supportive medical services that are available outside the treatment setting. For example, because there is no dentist in the unit is not sufficient reason to deprive patients of dental care. Such problems are seemingly elementary, but they do happen. The author is aware of one case in which the unit ran out of medical supplies needed to perform a certain medical service. They were hard to locate and in short supply. Because supplies were difficult and scarce, they simply stopped providing the service, a weak response to a troublesome problem.

The requirements for meeting this right in terms of a protection process are as follows:

- ongoing reviews of the medical needs of the patients
- referrals to in-house and out-of-house service providers as needed
- follow-up to ensure that the care was provided and in a quality way

Essentially, this right demands that mental health care providers recognize the needs of the "whole" patient. Just because their interest is primarily psychological/psychiatric, they are not free to disregard other needs of the patient.

The outcome of this right is the matching of patient needs for services with appropriate available providers. It is a matching that would occur normally outside the treatment setting, either by the patient or by friends and family.

Case 1. Patient, Barbara Doe, was in need of several types of dental work — a root canal and an extraction to be exact.* The organization's dentist had scheduled her for 8 weeks from the date on which she requested the service. However, during this time, the dentist resigned to take a better position elsewhere. A recruitment effort was started, but after two months few dentists had applied and none were found suitable.

Meanwhile, patient Doe's teeth became more troublesome. When dental help was requested, the patient was informed that someone would be hired shortly. The patient complained that since dental service was required immediately, the hospital had an obligation to provide it. The hospital refused to fulfill the request by bringing in temporary help or contracting out the work, citing expenses and the difficulties of finding willing providers.

The court found the hospital's rationale to be insufficient, adding that auxiliary services are billed as part of the patient's per diem costs. Thus, it might be viewed that she had already paid for the service which was not being provided by the setting.

---

*Fictitious case.

Notes. This case is a typical example of the lack of provision of auxiliary services which are stated as offered by the treatment setting. The rationale for not providing them at the time of the need did not hold up here and will not hold up in other situations. It is in some areas difficult to make arrangements with private providers. The costs tend to be overestimated by providers, since there is not such a tremendous demand for special services that a few instances of outside contract work would bankrupt the organization. The case also points to the need to maintain good relationships with contract providers for just such circumstances.

SUMMARY

The purpose of guaranteeing a right to medical care is to ensure that the patient's physical/medical needs are met by providing a minimum quality of medical treatment and specialty medical services as needed. The standards of medical care are maintained by monitoring what and where services are provided and by whom and when (i.e. soon after complaints or not). Medical care quality should match the care provided in the local community.

Specifically, patients are guaranteed the access to medical care as needed, a physical exam as part of the admission procedure, and the continued use of their private physician if so desired and if payment is arranged by the patient. Patients are to be guaranteed an appropriate rationale for the use of medication. Essentially, this means following a carefully prepared drug treatment plan that is reviewed and checked to note patient reactions. Medication is not to be used for administrative efficiency (e.g. sedating an unruly patient because of inappropriate staff levels) or as punishment.

Specialty or auxiliary medical services are to be provided as needed. This includes dental work, eye exams, and so forth. The treatment setting is responsible for recognizing and meeting all medical needs of the "whole" patient in an effort to provide the most beneficial treatment possible.

REFERENCES

1. Fiori, F.B., "Bureau of Health Facilities' Increasing Responsibilities in Assuring Medical Care for the needy and Services Without Discrimination," *Public Health Reports* 95(2) March–April 1980, p. 164.
2. Goldsmith, S.B., "Jailhouse Medicine – Travesty of Justice?" *Health Services Reports,* November 1972, vol. 87, p. 767–774.
3. Health Law Project, *Health Care and Conditions in Pennsylvania's State Prisons,* Univ. of Pa. Law School, Governor's Justice Commission, 1972.
4. Zalman, M., "Prisoners' Rights to Medical Care," *J. of Criminal, Criminology and Police Science,* 63, p. 185–199, 1972.

5. Joint Commission on Accreditation of Hospitals, *Consolidated Standards for Child, Adolescent and Adult Psychiatric, Alcoholism and Drug Abuse Programs,* Chicago: JCAH, 1979.
6. Kiely, W.F., "Psychiatric Syndromes in Critically Ill Patients," *JAMA,* 235(25), June 21, 1976, p. 2759.
7. Joint Commission on Accreditation of Hospitals, op. cit., (item no. 5).
8. *Wyatt* v. *Stickney,* 344 F. Supp. 373 (M.D. Ala. 1972).
9. *Naughton* v. *Bevilacqua,* 605 F. 2d. 586 (1st Cir. 1979).

6
Confidentiality and Disclosure

OVERVIEW

Patients have the right to keep confidential all aspects of their relationship with the mental health system, but they have the right to access to that information for themselves.

The general purposes of patient rights in this area is the protection of confidentiality and the monitoring of the disclosure of information with regard to its necessity, to the amount and type of data, and to the recipient of the information. This protection and disclosure screening ensures for patients some basic access to data about their treatment and their overall progress in the program, but limits access to other persons.

The purpose of confidentiality rights are threefold: (1) to safeguard privacy; (2) to minimize the negative effects of mental patient status; and (3) to reduce interpersonal obstacles to regaining acceptance status in the community. Confidentiality rights protect the patient's recognized position in his or her own community. Because a stigma is still attached to mental patient status, the release of information connecting any person with treatment or mental disability results in a lowering of status in the community.[1,2] Although not appropriate, it is fact. Thus, the rights to confidentiality are designed in part to interfere with and to avoid that status-lowering process.

The mechanism by which confidentiality rights are protected involves the development of organizational policies and procedures for the release and distribution of information about patients to outsiders and to patients themselves.[3] The type of patient-related information frequently sought ranges from very basic demographic data (age, sex, race, former employment) to detailed clinical information regarding the patient's behavior and progress in treatment. To assist the development of protective mechanisms, the confidentiality rights issues addressed in this chapter include the following topics:

- identification of patients as clients of the mental health system
- examination and tests of patients
- patient case records
- privileged communication
- interviews, photographs, and tests
- the patient's right to know

The point of this discussion is that the confidentiality protection processes used in the organization, and the complementary individual staff behaviors, must be established to ensure that the patient's confidentiality is not violated. The possibilities for violation include for example: identification of the patient to outside persons; release of examinations and results; distribution of case records; or verbal communications about patient status.

The rights are protected by a dual system involving both behavioral and mechanical methods. Behavioral approaches include development of staff knowledge of the limitations of their freedom to distribute information.[5,6,7,8,9] Those limitations involve strict control of the type of data, to whom it is given, and for what purpose. Mechanical methods of control include locked files, established codes for patient records, and a strict enforcement of the usage of written patient consent forms for the release information. The combination of behavioral and mechanical processes ensures that the patient's status as a member of the service system is protected. Distribution of confidential information is limited to only those persons absolutely requiring that knowledge to render service or financial reimbursement.

The outcome of this protection is twofold. First, it ensures that the patient's involvement with the treatment unit is as private or as open as the patient himself desires. Should he decide to communicate his status to others, it is his own decision, not one taken for him by others who will neither lose nor gain status and stigma.

Second, if few people know of an individual's struggle with mental disability, the patient is less resistant to return to the circle of family and community from which he has come. In that sense, the patient's right to privacy supports a therapeutic process which attempts in most cases to return the patient to his original social system.

IDENTIFICATION

Definition. Patients have a right to keep the identification of their patient status confidential.

The purpose of the identification right is to maintain individual privacy. Every American citizen has the right of privacy in his or her personal and property affairs. Mental patients are no different. A second purpose of this right is to minimize the negative consequences deriving from status as a mental patient, as noted above.

Identification is limited through a careful, controlled monitoring of the release of information. This monitoring process is based on five questions:

1. Who wants to identify the patient as a patient?
2. What identifying information do they want to know?
3. Why do they need to have this identifying information?
4. When do they need this information?
5. Who will receive the identifying information in addition to the individual requesting it?

There are a limited number of reasons for which the patient should be identified. Among them are the following:

- treatment
- referral
- financial reimbursement/payment
- research
- training
- program evaluation
- notification of family and/or next of kin

Regardless of which of the above stated purposes is given, each of the questions should be addressed. For example, if the answer to the question "Why?" is referral, the staff person should inquire as to who is requesting the information, what they need, when they need it, and who will receive it. Logic and common sense should follow the initial questioning. If a referral is to be made, the recipient of the information should be an appropriate referral resource, that is, either another physician, service care giver, or auxiliary service provider (e.g. speech or vocational rehabilitation therapist, etc.).

The outcome of controlled monitoring is that the identification of patients as patients is severely limited. The only reasons for identification are treatment or administrative necessity. Beyond those concerns, identification of patients as patients should be resisted. At the very least, requests for identifying information should be withheld until the staff member has developed satisfactory responses to the above five monitoring questions.

Case 1. In *Carr* v. *Watkins,* the patient, Carr, claims that in April, 1960, an officer in the security division of the Naval Ordnance Laboratory and officers of the Montgomery County Police Department transmitted information about him to his present employer.[10] The receipt of this information by the employer caused Carr to lose his job.

Six years before this incident, Carr was working at the Naval Ordnance Laboratory when he was charged with molesting children and with being drunk. The charges were heard by the appropriate officials within the laboratory and Carr was exonerated of any wrongdoing. He continued working there until he resigned.

However, the defendants told Carr's present employer that he had been fired from the laboratory due to these incidents. The issue is whether the defendants were acting within the scope of their employment when they passed this information to Carr's employer. If they were, then they are immune from prosecution. The original court thought that the defendants were immune and so ruled. On appeal, however, the Appellate Court sent the case back so that evidence could be presented to determine whether they were "acting within the scope of their employment."

Notes. In this case, the defendants passed on information identifying charges of which the client was cleared. Ostensibly, this information was passed on to prevent the patient's committing a further offense at the laboratory. While the defendants have some obligation to pass on information relating to the dangerousness of the client, in this case the identification apparently was unnecessary.

Case 2. In *Felber* v. *Foote* the plaintiff, Dr. John Felber, is a licensed psychiatrist who was seeking to avoid a statute compelling practitioners of the healing arts to report the names of, and other information about, drug dependent persons to the Connecticut State Commissioner of Health.[11] Dr. Felber claimed that the statute involves his and his patients' right to privacy. He also claimed that the statute violated his right to due process of law guaranteed by the 14th Amendment. The court rejected both contentions.

The court found that the privilege of confidentiality between the doctor and his patient is not rooted in the constitution; therefore, there is no guaranteed right of privacy protected in this area. Additionally, the 14th Amendment stipulates that no person can be deprived of life, liberty, or property without due process of law. Under the Connecticut statute which is being questioned, there is no threat to life, liberty, or property, so Dr. Felber's due process claim was not appropriate.

Notes. Here the law as defined by this court allowed identification of a patient as a drug dependent person. The questions listed earlier as a test of whether to release information have been answered. The identification here is provided to a state government agency in connection with its administrative and treatment services funding. Should that information be used in some way to commit the patient to an institution, the question of a constitutional claim to privacy and ultimately liberty could be raised. There would then be a real question of deprivation of freedom based on the release of the information relating to patient status.

EXAMINATIONS AND TESTS

Definition.   Patients have the right to be free from examinations and tests unless they are specifically and directly related to their treatment and/or are voluntarily agreed to by the patients.

The purpose of this right is to extend the rationale of privacy regarding the patient's personal information, i.e. through examinations and tests. The right provides the basis for patient rejection of any examination or tests that are not an integral part of a patient's treatment. It is specifically to avoid the use of patients as test subjects for both formal and informal investigations, some of which are research.

The purpose generates four questions which the staff should review with regard to the use of examinations/tests and the results:

1. What are the examinations and tests (are they substantively related to the program's therapeutic purpose)?
2. Why are the examinations and tests to be given (rationale)?
3. What will happen to the results (data analysis—individual versus group— and to what use)?
4. Who will receive the results (and what is the distribution system)?

The purpose of this questioning is to establish a process for determining the appropriateness of examinations and tests and the use and release of results. The guidelines include the following steps involving both staff *and* patients:

1. notice of the intent to give an examination or test
2. review of the purpose
3. insurance of the patient's understanding of the purpose and process of the test and of his right to refuse the test
4. patient's approval
5. supervised administration of the examination and test by appropriate individuals
6. privacy of results of the individual patient's tests
7. controlled distribution of the results, including aggregation of data.

Following this review process *prior* to giving examinations and tests helps to ensure confidentiality and privacy before the actions begin.

Patients have the right to review the purpose and process of examinations/ tests prior to their administration, and they have the right to question the use of the information gained from the tests. The outcomes of this monitoring process are three:

- freedom from unnecessary examinations and tests for patients
- the assignment of staff responsibility for establishing the rationale and the competence of the proposed examiners and their instruments
- the reduction of the "test subject status" of patients residing in institutions.

Too often patients become the subjects of one or more examinations and tests which are only peripherally related to their treatment. They become subjects of exploratory searches which are not sufficiently grounded in treatment theory and are not linked to an individualized treatment plan.

Case 1.   Berry v. *Moench* involved a patient's libel suit against a physician for publishing in a letter allegedly false and derogatory information acquired in connection with the treating of the patient.[12]

Dr. Moench, the defendant in the case, received a letter from a doctor requesting information concerning the patient Berry for the stated purpose of passing it on to a couple, parents of Mary Booth, who was dating Berry. Dr. Moench's reply contained statements on Berry's mental health (manic depressive and a psychopathic personality); on his family background (brother a manic, father committed suicide); on his character (gambled for money instead of attending classes, bad credit risk, trouble with authorities during the war, did not support a past wife and child); and finally recommending that the young girl involved with Berry "run as fast and as far as she possibly could in any direction away from him."

Dr. Moench had treated Berry 7 years previously, with four electric shock treatments. He had not seen Berry since that time. As a result of the correspondence, Mary Booth's parents violently opposed her marriage to Berry, later disowning their daughter because she went ahead and married Berry.

A legal defense to libel is the establishment of the truth of the statements, which in this case was possible. The court noted the uniqueness of the physician/patient relationship and the importance of confidentiality placed on this relationship by the law. Such a confidence should not be broken unless there exists an important interest to protect such as the life and safety or well-being of a third party. The court found that the lower court did not address this question and the case was remanded for a new trial.

The guidelines recommended by the court for the second review were used to determine if the statements published were:

a. in good faith and with reasonable care as to their truth;
b. fairly reported; and
c. conveyed only to such persons as needed the information.

Notes.   This case illustrates conflict generated by the release of information developed through a series of examinations and treatments conducted by a physician. The physician exercised his obligation to release information which he felt was important to the life, safety, and well-being of another party. However, as was obvious from the filing of the litigation, the patient whose confidential patient status was broken sued, alleging that that information was not to be passed on under any circumstances.

The case is again being reviewed by the court. But it would appear that the physician's position will be upheld since he apparently released the information:

   a. to satisfy an obligation to protect the safety and welfare of another person;
   b. in a way which reported truth and professional opinion;
   c. only to those persons who would be affected—the parents and the daughter.

The only area of concern from the facts presented here was the time lag since the physician had last seen the patient. If the facts are true and the patient is a "troubled person," the physician's opinion may be allowed to stand uncontested. However, the question could be raised concerning the patient's behavior in the seven years since he was last seen by the physician. The physician in effect discounted the possibility of change. A more recent interview could have been used to validate the opinion.

CASE RECORDS

Definition. Patients have the right to confidentiality of their case records and to all information contained therein.

The purpose of the confidentiality of case records is to ensure that all information transmitted, collected, and recorded throughout the process of treatment is kept in a file that is absolutely private. The "case record" is here defined to include the full range of reports, such as contact records, intake-admission record, preliminary assessment, level of functioning scales, individual direct service record, treatment plans, case management record, discharge evaluation record, discharge summary, and client satisfaction survey.[13]

This information is purposefully collected during the process of treatment *for* treatment and is not for distribution outside the service setting. Case records contain material derogatory to patients individually and to families, friends, or employers, which would not be constructively received if presented in any context other than the treatment setting. When extensive amounts of material from case records are presented as part of the treatment process, it is usually within the framework of family systems therapy, or group therapy in which confidentiality is stressed.

There are two ways in which the case records are kept confidential: through behavioral and through mechanical processes. First, as to the organization's behavior, it is important that the organization establish a policy in regard to the case records. That is, the organization must define which data can be released under what conditions. There should be development of clear rules (organizational policies) defining what can be done with information collected, irrespective of how it was gathered (e.g. through specific forms, tests, examinations, interviews, whatever). The policies aid staff in their day-to-day decision making by defining a management system for the collected information. Thus, the process for protecting confidentiality is demonstrated by employee responses to the organizational rules defining what information can be released, why, to whom, and under what circumstances.

The second protection method for case-record confidentiality is a series of mechanical constraints. Traditionally, these have been quite simple, locked files. However, with the increasing use of computerized information systems in many agencies, data is now safeguarded by computers which have limited access and codes which mask patient identity. Which type of mechanism is used will depend on the sophistication of the organization and the level of its information systems development. The important point to remember with regard to mechanical systems for collecting information is that in all probability a "shoe box" type of operation is likely to lead to some difficulty. As a minimum, case records should be in locked files with limited access.

Case records can be released for review by persons other than the patient's treatment team. Procedurally, there are several steps to be taken in order to help to ensure that the release is consistent with patients' rights. The patient must be informed and must understand the advantages and disadvantages of releasing the information. For example, a frequent purpose for release is for referral to another organization for special or follow-up care. The referral to whom and for what reason must be explained. If the purpose is outside clinical review, that same level of in-depth explanation must be given.

Employment recommendations are another release reason, but unfortunately they are the subject of some debate and moral conflict.[14] For employment reviews, both advantages and disadvantages of release must be stated to the patient including the possibility of losing the job if a review is or is not given. Currently, there is a dispute among some practitioners regarding the usefulness of releasing information in employment situations. The debate centers on the fact that when former patients admit to their "former patient status" they often do not get the job. The stigma and the uncertainty for prospective employers are such that they do not often "take a chance" on the patient's being recovered. Without employment, few patients have the opportunity to recover independence.

Alternatively, some practitioners discreetly recommend that patients not disclose their patient status. The patient is more likely to get the job but takes the risk of being fired if the "application misinformation" is found out. The law is moving toward a correction of this problem by eliminating the employer's permission to question the applicant about personal characteristics such as age, pregnancy, and former personal problems such as addictions and mental illness.

The patient must voluntarily agree to the release of the information. This means that consent must be given free of direct coercion generated by the treatment team and free of implied negative consequences should the patient not agree (e.g. lost privileges, opportunities, etc.). The voluntary consent must be informed; that is, patients must have full understanding of the advantages and disadvantages, as well as the fundamental questions which become guidelines for determining the fullness of the release decision:

1. What information is to be released (e.g. whole record, parts, which parts)?
2. Who needs the information (e.g. caregiver, administrator, researcher)?
3. Why do they need the information (e.g. treatment, management, research/ evaluation)?
4. When do they need the information (e.g. while patient is in treatment, following discharge monthly)?
5. How will they use the information (e.g. develop follow-up treatment plan, billing, evaluate treatment success)?

These questions and answers will be obvious in many cases, but they will be useful when record request purposes are not among the most common examples cited above.

In obtaining agreement to release, staff should remember that patients have a full right to question the release of the data—their resistance and/or reluctance should not be denigrated.

There is an allowance for an emergency release of information without the approval of the patient. Emergency release recognizes that there are times when release must be quick. For example, a patient may be undergoing emergency treatment in another setting, perhaps after being on a leave of absence. The emergency treatment team can better perform its task with certain parts of the patient's case record in hand, e.g. drug effectiveness notes. It is permissible to release the information under emergency circumstances when the benefit of the patient is the primary purpose. However, staff should be careful to account for three concerns:

1. They must fully document the situation which is suggesting the breach of confidentiality.
2. They must have sufficient rationale for that release and be ready and willing to defend it should the release be questioned after the fact.
3. They should themselves be persuaded that a breach of confidentiality is warranted and feel confident that a court can be convinced to the same degree (as actually could be the case if a confidentiality violation is cited).

The concluding point on emergency release of information is firm acknowledgment of its necessity in some situations. However, in those situations staff must document the rationale to the degree that allows them to be prepared should they have to defend it, a very real possibility.

The outcome of case-record confidentiality is that the privacy of the patient's process through treatment is protected. It helps to guarantee that any remarks made which are derived from the disability and which surface as a part of working through the treatment process are not distributed to a wide audience. The right protects against haphazard release, because case record information is often perceived negatively by family, employers, or others. Typical outcomes of inappropriate release are developed or reinforced stigma and additional reintegration conflict generated by denigrating remarks made by the patient about significant others in his social system. Because of the considerable range in the litigation to date, several cases will serve as examples of the types of conflicts which can arise with regard to this right.

Case 1.   In *Clark* v. *Geraci,* the patient was an accountant in civilian employment with the U.S. Air Force.[15]   He was discharged from the Air Force when they received a letter from his doctor stating that the cause of his frequent absences was due to alcoholism.   Since his discharge, he has been unable to find other employment.   He therefore initiated this suit for breach of confidentiality.

Normally, a doctor is a confidant of the knowledge and medical information that comes to him while treating his patient.   The doctor learned of the alcohol problem while treating the patient for asthmatic bronchitis and respiratory infections which were the resulting ill effects of the addiction.   Disclosure of the patient's alcohol problem would normally be inappropriate action for the doctor, but in this case the patient requested that the doctor furnish certain information (a part of his file) to the Air Force in order to explain his frequent absences.   However, the doctor's duty to disclose the underlying causes of the patient's illnesses and absences when requested to do so by the Air Force overruled his duty of confidentiality to his patient.   This higher duty developed when the doctor realized he furnished incomplete information at the request of the patient earlier.

Notes.   In this case, the patient asked the physician to disclose information to the Air Force which would assist the Air Force in determining the continuing employment of the patient.   The physician, based on the consent of the patient (implied full disclosure), proceeded to release the full information which he was in possession of, including the information that the patient was an alcoholic.   There is no breach of confidentiality since the patient had voluntarily agreed to the release of the information, and in fact, requested that it be done.   The request that partial information be submitted would have placed the doctor in the position of unethically providing only part of what he knew. Although it ultimately interfered with the patient's obtaining other employment, it was the patient's inappropriate behavior which produced the employment problem, not the physician's.

Case 2. In *State ex rel Carroll* v. *Junker,* a law professor and two students conducting a class research project under a Superior Court order examined 189 randomly selected mental illness files.[16] The prosecuting attorney challenged this order as a breach of confidentiality. With regard to case records or commitment hearings concerning mental illness, the State of Washington's laws afford the right of privacy. It was revealed during proceedings that all communications between the law professor and the judge stressed the need for absolute confidentiality of the materials to be reviewed. The students involved read through the files for three months until the prosecuting attorney moved for both temporary and permanent injunctions.

The question at issue is whether the court, on its own and without notice to the patients whose files were involved, properly ordered the records opened to the research team. The court stated that under the statute closing mental illness records to the public, a judge of the Superior Court in the exercise of sound discretion may permit such files to be opened. The criteria a judge must use weighs the harm or embarrassment to anyone involved in the case files which are opened, against the private and public benefit gained in the opening of the records.

In the present case, no notice whatever was given to anyone who had a direct and viable interest in preserving the privacy of the 189 mental illness files. Except for the representation of anonymity and confidentiality made by the two students and their professor, and the court's order, there were no safeguards of privacy and confidentiality. The court ruled that the previous order appeared to be unsupported by adequate reasons. There were not readily available tenable grounds of sufficient weight or merit to overcome the public and private interests of the legislatively ensured confidentiality and privacy.

Notes. In this case, the judge might have had sufficient rationale for securing the records and completing the review by the professor and the students. However, the judge neglected the process of presenting the rationale for inspection. He also neglected to discuss this with both patients and the treatment team responsible for safeguarding that confidentiality and to persuade patients and staff (without the coercion of the court) that there was a greater public interest to be served. The fact that they did not follow those steps lead the reviewing court to conclude that there was a breach of confidentiality without a significant gain for the public good. Since appropriate protection procedures were not followed, what might have been a legitimate and useful project was ended.

Case 3. *Gaertner* v. *State* involves the issue of whether a state hospital may lawfully bar the legal guardian of a minor patient, who is mentally ill, from access to the patient's hospital records.[17] The plaintiff, guardian of a mentally incompetent minor, requested access to the records of her ward that showed treatment given to the patient at a state home and training school. The request was accompanied by a waiver of the physician/patient privilege signed by the guardian.

On the advice of the State Attorney General, the request was denied. At the trial-court level, an injunction was granted forbidding the state from keeping the records from the guardian. The law permits no one but the patient to waive physician/patient confidentiality. However, in the case of a mental incompetent, the law recognizes that a legal guardian must act in the patient's place. The Appellate Court therefore held that the state hospital may not lawfully deny the guardian of an incompetent minor access to the records of his ward on the basis of the physician/patient confidentiality.

Notes. Here the staff rejected the idea that anyone other than the patient could gain access to the case records. However, they neglected to consider the fact that incompetent patients are by definition unable to make those decisions. When a guardian is seeking information on behalf of his ward, he is acting for the patient in matters of confidentiality determination. To hold for the staff would have denied the incompetent patient's guardian any way to review his ward's treatment; i.e., it would keep the guardian from fulfilling his responsibility.

Case 4. In *Clarkson Memorial Hospital* v. *Reserve Life Insurance Company,* the non-release of record information was found inappropriate.[18] Reserve Life Insurance Company was the insurer of some patients of Bishop Clarkson. In connection with a claim for reimbursement against Reserve, patients authorized representatives of Reserve to examine and copy as necessary their original hospital records. All authorizations were made in writing. The hospital refused to allow Reserve's representatives to see the records, so Reserve took the matter to court.

The court held that when Reserve received authorization from a patient having a proprietary interest in his or her own record and where legitimate need existed, then the hospital had no right to deny Reserve access to the records in question. The only basis for the hospital to deny access to the records was if the patient's doctor in the exercise of his professional judgment determined under oath that the records should not be released in the best interests of the patient's health.

Notes. In this case the rationale for the release of records was the appropriate purpose of settling an insurance claim. The steps to ensure protection of confidentiality were taken prior to seeking the release, i.e., authorized signed approvals by the patients, and so forth. The hospital was in error in attempting to withhold the records.

PRIVILEGED COMMUNICATION

Definition. Patients have the right to privileged communication between themselves and treatment professionals, unless such privilege is overruled by its considerable danger to identifiable individuals and/or to an identifiable general public.

The right of privileged communication is a key component of the therapeutic process. It is the basis on which much of the information is shared between patient and therapist. Without the right of privileged communication, the patient-therapist confidences established to enable that free flow and discussion would be cut off. It is not inconceivable to consider that without privileged communication, the therapeutic process would be significantly damaged or even rendered inoperable, particularly in processes such as psychoanalysis.[19]

The basic purposes of the right to privileged communication are three: (1) the right is established to safeguard the privacy of verbal and/or written transactions between patients and therapists and/or a therapeutic team; (2) it facilitates the free flow of information by guaranteeing to the patient that what is said and done in the confidence of the therapeutic discussion will not be distributed beyond that discussion, and (3) it is to prevent harm in the form of damaged interpersonal relations sometimes generated by derogatory information exchanged in the therapeutic process.

The verbal exchanges, as well as the notes taken regarding these exchanges, are kept confidential in the clinical files. They are not released for review to anyone outside the patient's immediate system, which may include a guardian if the patient is incompetent.

This covers fairly well the case of privilege between patient and therapist. The issue in group therapy has not yet been tested and is a matter of concern for both privileged communication and confidentiality.[20] The concern underscores the need to make clear to group members that the information is private. A contractual agreement may be useful.[21]

There are two occasions on which data may be released. The first occasion is that of an emergency. The privileged communication can be broken if it is done in the best interests of preserving the patient's health or safety as defined by an emergency situation. It must be remembered that this is an extraordinary procedure that may need to be defended in court. The question "Would this be defensible in court?" should guide the decision accompanied by "Will the staff judgment hold up under public scrutiny?"

The second occasion on which privileged communications may be released is with regard to danger to the public. One of the cases to follow is quite well known because litigation resulted from an instance in which a therapist did not release information which may have saved someone's life.[22-29] The key point is that the danger must be to an identifiable person known to the patient or to an identifiable person in the public. A general threat of "I want to kill someone" is not sufficient because the group to be protected is too large.

The outcome of this protection is that therapeutic process which is dependent on communication is both facilitated and maintained. Withholding of communication out of fear of what would happen to the information would effectively negate the exchange. Thus, the outcome of the right to privileged communications is preservation of a therapeutic process, an aspect of the right to privacy.

Case 1. In *Tarasoff* v. *Regents of University of California,* the patient, Poddar, informed his therapist, Dr. Moore that he was going to kill a young girl who was unnamed.[30] He described the girl as someone he had been seeing whom he would kill when she returned from Brazil. Since the description was detailed, it was easy to identify the target. The therapist informed a colleague and a supervisor that the patient was potentially dangerous and should be hospitalized at least for observation. Police detained the patient, although he resisted commitment.

After satisfying themselves that the patient was rational, they released him on his promise that he would stay away from the girl. On the young woman's return from her summer vacation, the patient did kill her as he threatened. The parents of the young woman initiated the litigation claiming that the therapist failed to warn them of the patient's repeated threats and the danger to their daughter. Their position was that communications are privileged except in the case where there is a significant and imminent danger to someone in the general public or to some other identifiable person.

Notes. The case surfaced two points which are summed up by the following: "...a hospital must exercise reasonable care to control the behavior of a patient who may endanger other persons. A doctor must also warn a patient if the patient's condition or medication renders certain conduct such as driving a car dangerous to others."[31] The resultant effect of this case is to qualify the privileged communication position. Communication is not privileged in all cases, in all situations, but is instead tempered by the characteristics of the case in relation to the dangerousness to others.

Prior to this case, the privilege was regarded as beyond qualification, untouched by limits of any type. For staff treating violent patients, the case must stimulate a review of the threats made. A series of questions should be the response: Are the threats individualized? Are they repeated? Is there a likelihood of action to carry them out? Can a warning be given without affecting the therapeutic process? If all or even several generate yes answers, the staff person should provide a warning to the target.

Case 2.   *In re: Lifschutz* is a habeas corpus proceeding initiated by Dr. Lifschutz, a psychiatrist, who was imprisoned after he was adjudged in contempt of court.[32]   He refused to obey an order of a County Superior Court instructing him to answer questions and produce records relating to communications with a former patient. Dr. Lifschutz contends that this court order unconstitutionally infringes on his right of privacy, his right to practice his profession, and the privacy of his patients.

Dr. Lifschutz's imprisonment results from a lawsuit instituted by a former patient against another person for injuries resulting from an alleged assault. During a deposition before the trial, the patient revealed that he had received psychiatric treatment from Dr. Lifschutz for a period of 6 months—some 10 years earlier. Dr. Lifschutz was subpoenaed by the victim and was ordered to bring all medical records relating to the treatment of his former patient. He appeared at the deposition, but refused to answer any questions relating to his treatment of patients and failed to produce the requested medical records.

Dr. Lifschutz was then ordered by the court to answer questions and to produce the medical records. At no time did the patient claim the physician/ patient privilege of confidentiality. Dr. Lifschutz again refused to cooperate. The court also noted that the patient had made the condition of his mental and emotional state an issue in his own proceeding.

The court concluded that the order requiring Dr. Lifschutz to answer appropriate questions concerning communications with the patient did not infringe on the psychotherapist's constitutional rights. Under the facts of this one case, the doctor could assert no statutory authority to refuse to comply with the request of disclosures. The Appellate Court found the trial court correct in its judgment that Dr. Lifschutz was in contempt of court for intentionally violating valid court orders.

Notes.   It is again clear from this case that the confidentiality of privileged communication can be overcome by significant judicial requirements. In this case, the information from the therapeutic process was important for sorting out a criminal court conflict. Privilege was shown to have limitations. In a case where the assessment of criminal wrong required testimony of material acquired in the treatment, the court found privilege to be non-binding. However, this is not now law in all states. For it to become law, the difficult problem of whether any privilege exists with patients involved in the criminal justice system would need to be resolved. Generally, the case illustrates that therapists treating patients with criminal involvement must consider privilege to be possibly non-binding in any given case at any time.

INTERVIEWS, PHOTOGRAPHS, AND TOURS

Definition.   Patients have the right to be free from interviews, photographs, and tours which are not a necessary and integral part of their treatment, or of the general treatment program.

The general purpose of this right is to protect privacy. It is to assist in differentiating the treatment facility from the extremes of visitation which create a "zoolike" atmosphere. Although the use of the term "zoo" as an adjective is a somewhat inflammatory, it was indeed a function of mental asylums in the past.[33]   Institutions functioned in part as amusement places for townspeople. While we have moved beyond that point, this right ensures that there is no regression. Specifically, the two purposes of this right are the following:

- to ensure privacy of the person's status as a patient, and
- to reduce the numbers of people who may potentially endanger that privacy.

With regard to these purposes the prohibitions and/or limitations on interviews, photographs, and tours are efforts to maintain the general confidentiality of the patient. Obviously, the more people who tour the facility the greater are the chances of someone breaking the confidentiality.

The process through which permission for interviews, photographs, and tours is established involves several aspects of review.

First, there is the process of individual screening. Any time that outsiders come on the wards or into the hospital other than for formal visiting, each individual staff member has a responsibility to inquire as to their purpose and whether or not permission was given for them to enter. In general hospitals, this is logistically difficult because of the volume of visitors. Mental institutions have fewer visitors with much greater levels of privacy from outsiders.

Second, this same process should be formalized as an ongoing ward policy. Regardless of the time of day, ward staff should be adhering to a general policy of questioning newcomers to the ward as to purpose and permission. Penalties for poor staff compliance should be developed with each staff person responsible for aiding compliance.

Third, there should be an administrative screening process through which requests for interviews, photographs, and/or tours would be reviewed by the treatment facility administrator. Cases with either specific reasons for visitation, such as family or attorney, or general reasons for visitation (e.g. friendly visits or a regular basis), would be documented and approved by the administrator and/or a group of persons functioning as a review team. A staff person could volunteer to chair the committee.

The review procedure, whether operated by an individual or team would include four steps:

1. A notice in writing of the intent to request interviews, photographs, and/or tours.
2. A hearing (open session to involved persons) to establish the purpose, the methods, the results, and the distribution of interviews and photographs and any other material gathered on visits. The rationale might include specific reasons useful to the treatment center as well (e.g. research or training).
3. The absence of alternatives to the taking of tours, photographs, and/or interviews of patients.
4. The development of a written agreement which specifies the above purposes, methods, and outcomes and which is signed by all involved.

One of the sample cases (Wiseman[34]) will demonstrate that this procedure does not absolutely ensure that no person(s) will inappropriately use the results. It does, however, assist in ensuring that the treatment facility has taken purposeful steps to minimize the likelihood of a negative outcome, for example, violation of patient privacy or even exploitation of the material for commercial or political purposes.

The outcome of this procedure is the reduction of the likelihood of the treatment center assuming a zoolike atmosphere, whereby outsiders are frequently parading through, asking questions, conducting interviews, and/or taking pictures. A second outcome is that it reduces the potential secondary violations of patients' confidentiality. For example, a student snapping a picture with the best intention of illustrating hospital conditions finds that the picture gets widely circulated through a classroom or a community discussion group. The limited usage with the patient privacy intact that was originally intended is lost.

Case 1. Commonwealth v. *Wiseman* concerns the making of a film in Massachusetts.[35] A filmmaker, Wiseman, requested permission from the superintendent of a mental hospital and from the State Commissioner of Mental Health to make an educational documentary film concerning the conditions at an institution. The request to make the film was reviewed by the superintendent and referred to the Attorney General in order for officials to grant permission. There were several conditions established for this permission: "(1) that the rights of inmates and patients. . .would be fully protected, (2) that there would be used only photographs of inmates and patients. . .legally competent to sign releases, (3) that a written release would be obtained from each patient whose photograph is used in the film; and, (4) that the film would not be released without first having been approved by the Commissioner and the superintendent." The intent of the hospital was to support the educational purpose of the filmmaking. To protect patient rights it established a series of conditions which were to ensure that patient confidentiality would not be violated.

The filming was approved. Filmmakers were given free access to all units of the hospital except for one whose center director strongly objected.

However, pictures were taken which "showed mentally incompetent patients. . .in the nude. . .and in the most personal and private situations." The Commissioner, the superintendent of the institution, and the Attorney General rejected the results. On reviewing the film, they felt that the type of pictures taken and the way in which the film was assembled resulted in a severe invasion of the privacy of the inmates shown in the film. They also noted that mentally incompetent patients were included (which was against the original agreement) and that in general the film was not suitable for presentation as an educational documentary.

Mr. Wiseman, the filmmaker, then made an agreement with a film distribution company to distribute the film to the general public. The film was shown in New York City in 1967.

Reactions to the film reviewed in court showed very different views of the situations presented. "Reactions to the film set out in the record varied from the adversely critical conclusions of the trial judge to those expressed by witnesses who [variously] regarded it as fine journalistic reporting, as educational, and as art."

The comments of witnesses included the following: "The Bridgewater atmosphere is one of aimless hopelessness. . .a psychiatrist turns an interview with an inmate into a sadistic baiting, or with malicious cheerfulness force feeds a dying old man, while we wonder whether the ash from the doctor's carelessly dangling cigarette is really going to fall into the glop being funneled into the convulsively shuddering throat. The society's treatment of the least of its citizens. . .is perhaps the best measure of its civilization. The repulsive reality. . .forces us to contemplate our capacity for callousness. No one seeing this film can but believe that reform of the conditions it reports is urgent business. . .We cannot forget that. . .the actors are there to stay, trapped in their own desperate inventions. When a work achieves that kind of power, it must be regarded as art. . . ."

The above comments suggest that the film should have been judged as a documentary, a piece of artwork, and a compelling statement for reform. However, as the court noted, there is the conflicting problem of confidentiality and privacy: "The film shows many inmates in situations which would be degrading to a person of normal mentality and sensitivity. Although to a casual observer, most of the inmates portrayed make little or no specific individual impression, others are shown in closeup pictures. These inmates are sufficiently clearly exhibited (in some instances naked) to enable acquaintances to identify them. Many display distressing mental symptoms. There is a collective indecent intrusion into the most private aspects of the lives of these unfortunate persons in the Commonwealth's custody."

Notes. The court halted commercial showings but allowed showings to students and professionals for educational purposes. The outcome of this conflict is certainly a question of balancing the individual rights of these patients to privacy against the desire to reform the conditions under which they are forced to live. There were several problems with the agreement developed to avoid this type of conflict.

First, the agreement was not in writing. This failure simultaneously allowed an opening for the conflict to arise and did not present a mechanism for resolution to be unambiguously determined. Second, the assurances which were given in terms of securing consents from patients, not invading their private lives, and restricting the degree of degradation in the scenes presented were violated. Third, the conditions, although matters of grave public concern and of demonstrated usefulness for generating public response, would not necessarily demand, as noted in the opinion, that the film be shown commercially in such places as New York City.

The original intent was for it to be educational and documentary in nature. Showings at universities and screenings for attorneys and other professionals in positions to make policy change would be appropriate. But the court review showed that it was not used initially and primarily for "training legislators, judges, lawyers, sociologists, social workers, doctors, psychiatrists, students in these related fields, and organizations dealing with social problems of custodial care and mental infirmity." The planned audience as originally intended was educational personnel but that planned intent (the basis on which permission was given) was violated.

THE PATIENTS RIGHT TO KNOW

Definition. Patients have a right to know what is written about them in their case records and other administrative files.

The purposes of this right are as follow:

1. To provide patients with the same access to their records that others within the system have.
2. To ensure that all viewpoints are represented in the files, particularly the patients'.
3. To enhance the therapeutic process by generating additional discussion with patients based on the comments they read.

The intention of the right is to diminish the mystery of the patient's records and to open them to review, including debate as appropriate. Most important, the sharing of that information can be educational and therapeutic.[36-40] It can also be useful in correcting mistakes in the patient's file, which follow each patient indefinitely.[41]

The process for protecting this right to disclosure is direct. Clinical files are to be available to patients for *supervised* patient review. At the patient's request, a staff member (preferably the patient's primary clinical staff) should schedule a time for the review. A brief explanation of what the patient is to find is in order and any organizational rules governing changes in the record. The presence of supervision helps to ensure: (1) that there will be discussion of the material in the files, and (2) that any material that is disturbing to the patient can be dealt with at that time. Thus, the process for protection is not elaborate or difficult, requiring only an open "treatment oriented" discussion with the patient. The volume of requests is not high, with one study finding few patient inquiries after the announcement of open files.[42]

The outcomes of this patient "right to know" are three. First, access to the records helps to increase and to ensure the accuracy of those records by virtue of the realization that inspection is continuous.[43] Should there be a large disparity between the writing of the staff and the view of the patient, then that conflict will be surfaced and negotiated, although it does not happen often.[44] Second, patients' insight into their difficulties may increase as a result of this information access.[45] And, third, patients have a method of redress to effect a correction of errors in fact or interpretation.

Case 1. In *Gotkin* v. *Miller,* Janet Gotkin was voluntarily hospitalized between 1962 and 1970 because of a series of suicide attempts.[46] As of 1973, she had received no treatment since September of 1970. She contracted to write a book about her experience with the service system. To assist her in developing the book, she wrote to three hospitals where she had received service and requested that they send her copies of her records. The hospitals refused.

Gotkin then filed suit against the directors of the hospitals alleging that the policies of the hospitals violated her rights as a former mental patient under the First, Fourth, Ninth, and Fourteenth Amendments of the Constitution. The court found that there was no constitutionally protected right to access to the records and that, in particular, the purpose for which Gotkin requested the records had no special overriding power.

Notes. In the absence of a therapeutic purpose for securing the records, there was no compelling rationale for the request presented by the former patient. Since there is no constitutional right (and apparently not even a constitutional "sense") that identifies a patient's records as property of the patient, an overriding therapeutic purpose must be developed in order to gain permission for review. Should the patient require that review for therapeutic purpose, an outside physician could be enlisted to receive the records and supervise their review by the patient. In that way, the physician would be present to assist in the resolution of conflicts and in interpretation should they cause distress to the patient.

Apparently not at issue here was whether there was an overriding public welfare need to assist in the development of the book. If Gotkin had made a plea similar to Wiseman's, stating that her book would have educational and training value, she may have been given access. Conversely, a direct attempt to commercialize for profit would not likely be viewed as a compelling rationale.

Again, we find the courts attempting to review the purposes and the outcomes in relation to the law. The opening of the records requires time and expense for the hospitals. Any material that is controversial will create further concerns for review. Therefore, the court in attempting to establish a balance between the right of the patient and the hospital's private records inspects the rationale, looking for a compelling reason to support the patient's request. Absent such a reason, it supports the hospital.

Case 2.   *Bush* v. *Kallen* concerned a New Jersey statute mandating that records of patients in a mental hospital are to be kept confidential and are not to be disclosed to anyone except under proper inquiry.[47] The inquiry can be from a relative, friend, or attorney if it appears the information is to be used directly or indirectly for the benefit of the patient.

The plaintiffs, except for one, were involuntarily committed and gave written authorization to their counsel to inspect and copy their medical records in connection with legal problems related to their commitment and the care they were receiving. The superintendent of the institution in which they were committed denied their request. He stated that the records were confidential and that he would not permit inspection and copying of the records by counsel unless: (1) the Essex County Council authorized the release, and (2) he personally determined that each patient was mentally competent to sign the necessary authorization.

The superintendent's position was found to violate the rights of the patients. The finding was based on the fact that since the information sought was to be used for the benefit of the patients, their attorneys were entitled to access to the confidential records.

Notes.   In this case, the patients requested that attorneys representing them in a mental health issue secure copies of their records. The superintendent rejected a legitimate and appropriate method for patient review of the records with the assistance of the attorney. The case does not fully define the rationale for the superintendent's rejection. A part of the "hidden" concern may have been for the potential problems which could be created by the attorneys' examining records of services rendered and the methods used. Although that may have been an outcome of the attorneys' review, it was not sufficient cause for denial of the right to inspect when the patients approved the reviews.

SUMMARY

A patient has the right to keep confidential all aspects of his records, and he has the right to access to them himself. The purposes are to safeguard patient privacy, to minimize the negative effects of mental patient status, and to reduce interpersonal obstacles to regaining acceptance in the community. The protections should be both behavioral and mechanical.

Behaviorally, staff should know the limits of access to records and should act accordingly. Mechanically, there should be constraints such as locked files, established codes for patient records, and strict enforcement of written forms of patient consent.

The outcome of these protections is that the patient controls who should know about his status and how much they should know.

Under the right to individual privacy, the patient has the right not to be identified as a patient. To monitor this right, staff should concern themselves with the following questions:

- *Who* wants patient information?
- *Why* do they want it?
- *What* specific information is needed?
- *When* is the information needed?
- *Who* besides the requestor will get the information?

Communication between the patient and treatment professionals is held to be privileged. This guarantee of privacy facilitates the free flow of communication in therapy and prevents damage to other interpersonal relationships. Releasing any of this communication can only be done in an emergency situation where it is needed to help the patient, or if there is a danger to an identifiable person.

The patient has a right to be free from interviews, photographs, and tours. The purpose is to protect privacy by reducing the number of people who may break that privacy structure. Informally, staff should screen any visitors who arrive at times other than visiting hours. There also should be a formalized ward policy for screening persons wanting access to the ward. In addition, there should be an administrative screening to review requests for interviews, photographs, and tours. A procedure to follow is this: (1) notice of intention to request interviews, photographs, and/or tours; (2) a hearing to establish the purpose, methods, results and distribution of results; (3) absence of alternatives to achieve the same purpose; and (4) the development of a written agreement.

Patients also have the right to be free from examinations and tests unless they are directly related to treatment and/or are agreed to voluntarily. The purpose of this right is to avoid using patients as test subjects. Again the questions of what tests, why, processing the results, and distribution of results must be considered. Steps to shield the patient include the following: advanced notice of testing; making sure tests are necessary and that patients know the purpose and process of the testing, and that they can refuse the testing; supervising the administration of tests; and controlling the distribution of the data.

Case records are collected for treatment purposes, not distribution. As such they are confidential. Staff should use the behavioral and mechanical protections listed in paragraph one to ensure this confidentiality. Legitimate reasons for releasing case records with patient consent include referral to another organization and employment recommendations (though usefulness is debated). An exception can be made in the case of an emergency so long as it is a primary benefit to the patient's well-being and is fully documented.

Patients have the same right of access to their own files as other members of the mental health system. This ensures that all viewpoints are adequately represented in the file and can help therapy by discussing recorded comments. It is important that patient reviews be supervised so that disturbing material can be discussed immediately. This right ensures and increases the accuracy of record keeping. It can help to improve patient insights, and importantly, it provides a method of redress for patients to correct errors in their files.

REFERENCES

1. Armstrong, B., "Stigma: Its Impact on the Mentally Ill." *Hosp. & Commun. Psychiatry,* 31(5), May 1980, p. 342.
2. Goffman, E., *Stigma,* Englewood Cliffs: Prentice Hall, 1963.
3. Seitz, J. & Ward, Dobbs W., "Granting patients access to records: the impact of the privacy act at a federal hospital." 29 *Hospital & Community Psychiatry,* (5) 288 (May 1978).
4. Drake, E.; Bardon, J.I., "Confidentiality and Interagency Communication: Effect of the Buckley Amendment," *Hosp. & Community Psychiatry,* 29(5), 1975, p. 312.
5. Swoboda, J.S., et al., "Knowledge of and Compliance with Privileged Communication and Child-Abuse-Reporting Laws," *Professional Psychology,* 9(3), Aug. 1978, 448–457.
6. Keith-Spiegel, P., "Violation of Ethical Principles due to Ignorance or Poor Professional Judgement versus Willful Disregard." *Professional Psychology,* 8, 1977, 288–296.
7. Shah, S.A., "Privileged Communications, Confidentiality, and Privacy: Privileged Communications," *Professional Psychology,* 1, 1969, 56–59.
8. Shah, S.A., "Privileged Communications, Confidentiality, and Privacy: Confidentiality." *Professional Psychology,* 1, 1970, 159–164 (a).
9. Shah, S.A., "Privileged Communications, Confidentiality and Privacy: Privacy." *Professional Psychology,* 1, 1970, 243–252 (b).

10. *Carr* v. *Watkins*, 227 Md. 578, 177 A. 2d 841 (1962).
11. *Felber* v. *Foote*, 321 F. Supp. 85 (Conn. 1970).
12. *Berry* v. *Moench*, 8 Utah 2d 191, 331 p. 2d 814 (1958).
13. Gifford, S. & Mayberry, D., "An integrated system for computerized patient records." 30 *Hospital & Community Psychiatry*, 532 (August 1979), 408, 508.
14. Weber, D., et al., "Ethical and legal considerations of confidentiality in the treatment of hospitalized health professionals," *Psychiat. Q.*, **503**:237 (Fall 1978).
15. *Clark* v. *Geraci*, 29 Misc. 2d. 791, 208 N.Y.S. 2d, 564 (1960).
16. *State ex rel. Carroll* v. *Junker*, 79 Wash. 2d. 12 482 p. 2d. 775 (1971).
17. *Gaertner* v. *State*, 385 Mich. 49, 187 N.W. 2d. 429 (1971).
18. *Clarkson Memorial Hosp.* v. *Reserve Life Ins. Co.* 350 F. 2d. 1006 (8th Cir. 1965).
19. Plant, R.A., "A Perspective on Confidentiality," *Am. J. Psychiatry*, **131**(9), 1974, p. 1021.
20. Slovenko, R., "Group Psychotherapy: Privileged Communication and Confidentiality," *J. Psychiatry and Law*, Fall 1977, p. 405.
21. Ibid.
22. "Tarasoff and the psychotherapist's duty to warn," **12** *San Diego L. Rev.* 932 (July 1975).
23. *"Tarasoff* v. *Regents of University of California:* The psychotherapist's peril," **37** *U. Pitt. L. Rev.* 155 (Fall 1975).
24. "Tort law: Psychotherapist-patient privilege, patient's dangerous condition, confidentiality, legal duty to warn potential victim," 9 *Akron L. Rev,* 191 (Summer 1975).
25. "Torts—confidential communications—psychiatry—psychotherapist has a duty to warn an endangered victim whose peril was disclosed by communications between the psychotherapist and patient," 44 *U. Cin. L. Rev.*, 368 (1975).
26. "Torts—the dangerous psychiatric patient—the doctor's duty to warn," 10 *Land & Water L. Rev.*, 593 (1975).
27. Roth, L.H. and Meisel, A., "Dangerousness, confidentiality, and the duty to warn," **134** *American Journal of Psychiatry*, 508, 510 (May 1977).
28. Note. "Untangling Tarasoff: *Tarasoff* versus *the Regents of the University of California*," 29 *Hastings Law Journal*, 179 (Sept. 1977).
29. J.G. and Maximov, B., "The patient or his victim: The therapist's dilemma," **62** *California Law Review* 1025 (1974).
30. *Tarasoff* v. *Regents of Univ. of Calif.*, 13 Cal. 3d. 177, 529 P2d 553, 118 Cal. Rptr. (1974).
31. Ibid., p. 558.
32. *In re Lifschutz* 2 Cal. 3d. 415, 467 P. 2d. 557, 85 Cal. Rptr. 829 (1970).
33. Rothman, D.J., *The Discovery of the Asylums*, Boston: Little, Brown & Co., 1971.
34. *Commonwealth* v. *Wiseman*, 356 Mass. 251, 249 N.E. 2d. 610 (1969).
35. Ibid.
36. Burch, E.A., Benggio, E., "Using Personalized Consumer Charts in a Partial Hospitalization Program," *Hosp. & Community Psychiatry*, **31**(2), Aug. 1980.
37. Shenkin B., Warner, D., "Giving the patient his medical record, a proposal to improve the system," *N. Engl. J. Med.* **289**:688–692, 1973.
38. "Medical record in patients' hands," (letter to ed), *N. Engl. J. Med* **290**:287–288, 1974.
39. Golodetz, A.; Ruess, J.; Milhous, R., "The right to know: giving the patient his medical record," *Arch. Phys. Med. Rehabil*, **57**:78–81, 1976.
40. Simonton, M.J., Neuffer, C.H., Stein, E.J., et al, "The open medical record: an educational tool," *J. Psychiatr. Nurs.* **15**:27–29, 1977.
41. Stein, E., et al., "Patient access to medical records on a psychiatric inpatient unit," **136** *American Journal of Psychiatry*, (3) 327 (March 1979).

42. Seitz, op. cit., (item no. 3).
43. Stein, et al., op. cit., (item no. 41).
44. Golodetz, op. cit., (item no. 39).
45. Bouchard, R.; Tufo, H.; Van Buren, H.; et. al., "Problem-oriented record," in *Applying the Problem Oriented System,* edited by Walker, H., Hurst, J., Woody, M., New York: Medcom Press, 1973.
46. *Gotkin* v. *Miller,* 514 F. 2d. 125 (2wd Cir. 1975).
47. *Bush* v. *Kallen,* 123 NJ. Supe. 1975, 302 A2d 142 (1973).

7
Communication and Visitation

This chapter, the right to communication and visitation, concerns the patient's ability to maintain contact with those outside the treatment setting.[1,2] Secondarily, it concerns maintaining the patient's ability to secure and coordinate resources on his own behalf. Once the patient begins contact with the treatment system and is admitted, all communications within that system could potentially work to maintain involvement in the system. Only through continuous and open contact with non-involved persons is the ability to correct possible mistakes maintained.[3] This ability is dependent upon two related mechanisms: communication and visitation.

In general, patients have the right to communicate with anyone of their choosing. They are in treatment, not in prison.[4,5] The primary mechanisms of communication, and the situations in which communication occurs, are person-to-person, telephone, and mail. Any restrictions on the use of these mechanisms for transferring information potentially reduces the patient's ability to inform "outsiders" of his situation. Adherence to this right is particularly important when the patient is admitted involuntarily. When the right is abridged, it must be for an administrative or clinical reason that then appears in the patient's record.[6]

Conversely, open access to the communication media also provides the patient with the opportunity to communicate with those not desirous of the communication. The most startling example is that offered by one administrator of an institution, as noted by two commentators:[7]

> "One hospital administrator reported that a 70-year-old patient wrote to her 10-year-old granddaughter at school stating: 'Your mother is a whore. She sent me away to get rid of me so she could entertain men at home. She will do the same to you unless you send her away.' The child was brutally shocked."[8]

There is little data documenting the incidence and prevalence of "harmful" patient communications. The above incident illustrates that there is certainly some amount that must be controlled. It must be emphasized that any situation which restricts liberty and freedom of speech must be scrutinized for absolute necessity; that is, there must be a compelling rationale absent of less restrictive alternatives.[9] Unfortunately, there is no way to accurately predict the inappropriate use of communications—patients must in effect abuse the system before constraints can be justified.

Rights concerns in this area will be addressed under the following headings: person-to-person communication, mail and telephone communication, attorney communication and visitation, and media communication.

PERSON TO PERSON COMMUNICATION

Definition.   Patients have the right to person-to-person communication.

In general, patients have the right to talk with persons who have come to visit them in a person-to-person fashion without having to rely on mail and telephone mechanisms. Even prisons allow prisoners to meet visitors from the outside, although with some precautions to ensure the necessary administrative security.

The right to person-to-person communication serves three purposes:

1. To ensure continued contact between the patient and significant others, e.g. members of the family, friends, relatives, etc.
2. To provide for the enhanced communication quality generated by personal interaction, (e.g. expressions, body language).
3. To ensure the safety and well-being of patients and others by allowing outsiders to see the condition of the patient for themselves.

The purpose of person-to-person communication is to ensure that the patient maintains the communication links that were established in the outside community. Although this contact can be maintained through telephone and mail mechanisms, there is little substitute for the enhanced quality of observing the person to whom one is talking.

This right is maintained by organization/staff permission and support of person-to-person communication. There is no extraordinary process required to establish this type of communication. It should exist quite naturally in all treatment units that have at least some degree of freedom for patients, i.e., non-maximum security units. The rights protection process is activated when there is a necessity to limit or abridge altogether the person-to-person linkage. If person-to-person communication is to be limited, there are four characteristics of the limiting process:

1. There must be a compelling reason and supporting rationale for the limiting of communication;

2. There must be notification of the patient that such limitation will be in place;
3. There must be exploration with the patient of all possible alternatives; and
4. The limitation of person-to-person communication should be defined by time with scheduled periodic reviews.

Treatment-system status quo should be to allow and encourage person-to-person communication. Communication is traditionally structured by specified visiting times and places similar to the systems used by community hospitals. An unusual (rights limiting) structure is created when there is a necessity to abridge that communication.

A need for treatment is not necessarily a safe and sufficient restriction rationale. While communication for some patients is a part of their clinical difficulties, the halting of the right to communicate does little for the resolution of that problem. When clinicians feel that communications problems are great, e.g. between patient and the family, then person-to-person communication problems should be brought into treatment, not cut from it, and thereby generating clinical and legal questions.

The outcome of the protection process is continuance of two-way communication for the great majority of patients. Limitation is defined as non-normal, for patients are person-to-person communicators in their normal, as well as their treatment environment.

The following case is an example of one communication difficulty which developed into litigation. The other cases in this chapter expand on the communications rights. They also include, by extension, the person-to-person situation.

Case 1.   Stowers v. *Ardmore Acres Hospital* is a legal action by the patient against her psychiatrist for false imprisonment and assault and battery.[10]

The patient, on a court order initiated by her husband, was taken from her home on January 4, 1964, to a private psychiatric hospital where she was prevented from communicating with people "outside" and was given medication over her objections. Both of these actions were ordered by her psychiatrist. The court concluded that her detention and seclusion went beyond that contemplated by the court order, thus rendering her psychiatrist liable for false imprisonment and assault.

Prior to January 4, the defendant's psychiatrist at the request of the patient's husband, visited her home and talked with her for a short period. Several days later, he again talked with her, this time over the telephone. On the basis of these two conversations, the psychiatrist concluded that she was suffering from paranoid schizophrenia and should be hospitalized.

The husband then obtained a court order which was required by statute. The statute, however, only authorizes treatment of a patient temporarily detained in state hospitals, not a private hospital. Furthermore, Michigan's medical malpractice guidelines state that the patient has an absolute right to refuse treatment unless the patient has been judged mentally incompetent.

In this case, the patient was *not* adjudged incompetent and was released on January 27, 1964, on the recommendation of two other doctors appointed by the probate court to examine her. Therefore, the psychiatrist had no right to temporarily detain the patient in a private hospital and to administer medication without the patient's consent.

Notes. It is unclear from the details of the case whether or not the woman was seriously mentally disabled. Disability is difficult to determine without extensive testing beyond brief telephone calls. What is clear from this situation is that a "second opinion" provided by two additional doctors on the order of the court did not find it necessary to maintain her detention in a private psychiatric hospital.

Not allowing her to communicate with people outside the hospital eliminated her ability to question her detention. Additionally, the psychiatrist conducted an examination over the telephone, which was a main part of his rationale for admitting the woman. Without person-to-person interaction, it is difficult to ascertain, except in the presence of extreme and obvious symptoms, the degree of disability. Person-to-person communication with outsiders would have allowed other family members, friends, relatives and/or an attorney to help determine whether detention of this patient was appropriate.

MAIL AND TELEPHONE COMMUNICATION

Definition. Patients have the right to communicate by mail and/or telephone.

This is a follow-up to the person-to-person communication question. The telephone and the mails are the next most common means of communicating with others. It is necessary, therefore, to protect this right for the same reasons the above case demonstrates.

In particular, the purpose of the right is intended to: (1) provide for communication of the patient's situation by the patient to those outside the treatment system, and (2) provide for outside contact as a part of the normal life process. Again, it is emphasized that mail and telephone communication processes are a part of normal life patterns outside the treatment system. The assumption is that as many of those normal life processes as can possibly be maintained should be maintained within the treatment system.

Additionally, mail and telephone communication is the basic linkage between the patient and those outside the system who are not accessible personally. To reduce or eliminate these means of communication, there must be sufficient rationale, including an absence of feasible alternatives to limitation. The protection of this right requires three aids:

1. The provision of writing utensils and paper.
2. The provision of postage (in limited amounts).
3. The provision of adequate numbers of telephones in places accessible to patients.

With these elements present, the right has a reasonable expectation of protection.

Limitation of mail and telephone communication requires the four step process noted in the person-to-person communication section:

1. Definition of a compelling rationale.
2. Notification to the patient of the proposed restriction.
3. Exploration with the patient of all alternatives to limitation, and
4. Time limits for the restriction with periodic review.

At times it is necessary to restrict the mail and telephone communications, particularly with extremely disoriented or violent patients. The test is that the process for implementing restrictions and limitations must be fair, reasonable, and defensible in a review by non-involved professionals.

The outcome of the right's protection is assurance that the communication process existing outside the treatment system is continued. Secondarily, this right promotes the correction of inappropriate situations (e.g. harmful or abusive conditions, inappropriate admissions) by its pressure to transmit information that is internal to the system to the outside.

Case 1. *Brown* v. *Schubert* involves two patients confined in a state hospital in Wisconsin.[11] On July 27, 1972, the superintendent of that institution ordered the plaintiffs transferred from minimum security facilities to maximum security facilities. This transfer was effected after the superintendent learned that they had mailed letters to a Madison Urban League Official and a Madison newspaper reporter. (The case does not mention specific contents of the letter, although it was presumably derogatory information about the operation of the institution.)

As a result of the transfer, the patients suffered the loss of various liberties and rights, including the freedom of movement enjoyed on minimum security wards. The superintendent dismissed the patient from his position as institution photographer and rescinded a recommendation to the department of health and social services that the patient be transferred. The superintendent also ordered the censorship of all the patient's mail.

The court ruled that the "corrective measures" were for punishment only and, as such, could not be implemented without procedural due process safeguards including a hearing into the matter. The court found that the patients were entitled to be restored to their former status and ward assignments, and it prohibited the censorship of the patient's mail.

Notes. Although the case does not identify the contents of the letter that was mailed, the letter evidently contained information which the superintendent perceived to be detrimental to the treatment system. His response on review was found to be punishment directed at the mailing rights of the patients at the state hospital. The superintendent's rationale for restriction of mailing rights was not sufficient to convince the court that it was an appropriate part of the treatment process. Therefore, the court ordered that the patients be returned to their original status and that their mailing rights be protected.

Case 2.   The second case, *Eckerhart* v. *Hensley* focuses on visitation, telephone, and mail issues and will be quoted extensively since it provides a detailed picture of the conflict of rights and security.[12]   The following is quoted directly from the case, a class action undertaken by involuntarily confined patients complaining about the treatment and conditions at a state hospital. There was close court scrutiny of visitation, telephone, and mail rights.

"Visiting hours in the Biggs Building are from 1 p.m. to 2:40 p.m. every afternoon. On weekends and holidays a morning visiting period from 9 a.m. to 10:45 a.m. is also permitted. Visits may last the entire visiting period unless the visiting room is crowded, in which case visits may be restricted to 30 minutes. No person under the age of 15 is permitted in the Biggs Building Visiting Room. Patients may be visited by their children under 15 by special arrangements. These visits take place in a separate room and are limited to 15 or 20 minutes. In the visiting room patients visit across a table, no personal contact such as touching or holding hands is permitted.

The visiting policy in the Rehabilitation Unit is more liberal. The visiting hours are 9 a.m. to 11 a.m., 1 p.m. to 4 p.m., and 7 p.m. to 8 p.m. daily. No ex-patients or employees may visit patients without the prior approval of the treatment staff. Children under 14 may not visit on the wards of the rehabilitation unit; families with children must visit in the canteen.

Patients in the Biggs building may receive incoming telephone calls from their attorneys only if such a call is arranged and approved in advance. Patients may receive no other incoming calls. A patient may place an outgoing call only if request is made and approval is received from the treatment staff. Approval is given only in case of an emergency (e.g. death or serious illness in the patient's family) or when it is determined to be beneficial to the patient. Patients may place collect calls to their attorneys only prior to a 90-day staffing, before a court appearance, or prior to 'other legal technicalities regarding their case.'

Rehabilitation Unit patients have access to pay telephones in the main administration building which may be used during patient's pass time. At other times, they may call their lawyers at any time and may place collect calls to their families once a week. Rehabilitation unit patients apparently may receive incoming calls provided callers identify themselves, except that no calls may be received from ex-patients or employees without approval from the treatment staff.

All outgoing mail for patients in both the Biggs Building and the Rehabilitation unit may be sealed by the patients and is not screened by forensic unit staff in any way. Postage for two free letters per week is provided to each patient. Incoming mail to patients in the Biggs Building and the two locked wards of the Rehabilitation Unit, is opened and checked for contraband before it is delivered to the patients. Correspondence is not read by hospital staff. The screening for contraband is done in an administrative office, outside the presence of the patient addressee, except for attorney or court related mail which is opened and screened for contraband in the presence of the addressee.

Plaintiffs challenge certain aspects of the visitation, telephone, and mail policies on the grounds that they are unduly restrictive, in many instances counter-therapeutic, and violative of the patient's constitutional rights. As discussed above, this type of institutional regulation is particularly within the province of the forensic unit administration, and it is not the constitutional role of the court to substitute its judgement for that of the state officials responsible for the forensic unit, absent a constitutional violation. Defendants argued that none exist . . . . Defendants legitimate interest in the efficient administration of the forensic unit also would justify limits and restrictions placed on visiting hours and telephone use to insure that facilities are used in an orderly manner and that neither visitation or telephone use by patients interferes with the normal operations of the forensic unit. However, the restrictions imposed on patients by the Biggs Building visitation and telephone policies are so extreme as to be not reasonably related to legitimate interests in either security or orderly hospital administration. The patient confined in the Biggs Building is effectively precluded from using the telephones; he may not receive calls from relatives, friends, his wife, or children. In the absence of an 'emergency' he may not make calls out of the building. The combination of short visiting hours (1 hour and 40 minutes) and the completely inadequate capacity of the visiting room (where visits are restricted to 1/2 hour if the room is crowded) discourage long and comfortable visitation.

These severe restrictions isolate patients from the outside world and constitute an excessive and arbitrary response to a legitimate interest in institutional security. Additionally, these policies are completely at odds with the therapeutic objective of the forensic unit. Visitation and telephone contacts are important to maintain ties in the community outside the mental hospital. To impose so complete a limitation on outside contact deprives patients of needed support from family, friends and other resources in the community. The result of isolation from the outside world can be counter-therapeutic and actually harmful. The court finds that the visitation and telephone policies of the Biggs Building are so restrictive as to constitute punishment and are therefore violative of patients' rights under the due process clause of the 14th Amendment. The court further finds the restrictions imposed by the visitation and telephone policies of the Rehabilitation Unit to be not so severe and that such policies fall within defendant's broad discretion to define institutional regulations."

Notes. This case provides considerable detail regarding topics the court will examine when involved in a review of communication restrictions. The policies of the unit must be defensible in terms of meeting the joint needs of administrative security and efficiency and the patient's right to communicate. Any restriction of those communication rights must follow the conditions required by the due process clause of the 14th Amendment, namely: adequate notice, a hearing, and exploration of less stringent alternatives. The concepts of fairness and balance are thus reiterated. The communication policies must allow for a balancing of the interests of the patient and the institution. If the restrictions are out of balance in favor of the institution, the courts can be brought into the situation through assertion of the violation of the constitutional rights to freedom of communication and due process.

ATTORNEY COMMUNICATION AND VISITATION

Definition. Patients have the right to communicate with their attorneys and to receive visits from their attorneys.

The assertion of the attorney communication and visitation rights follows the same reasoning as the person-to-person and mail and telephone communication discussions above. It is necessary to stress the importance of allowing and promoting attorney communication and visitation for patients. Legal representation is a fundamental right and is the basis for much of the additional help patients can receive given a problem of some severity such as confinement.[13-16]

The purposes of attorney communication are twofold: (1) to provide for the constitutional rights of legal representation and (2) to encourage and allow attorney/patient interchange as a desirable preventive law mechanism. The first purpose is based on the position that all citizens have constitutional rights to legal representation. The assistance applies to situations criminal in nature or to an involuntary admission to a mental health facility.

The second purpose addresses the idea that communication between an attorney and a patient may lead not only to litigation but to the uncovering of problems which can be corrected before litigation is required. Attorneys are accustomed to negotiating conflict without resort to the courts. The promotion of communication between patients and attorneys is one mechanism for increasing the number of negotiations and decreasing the amount of litigation arising from operational and pure rights conflicts.

The process for promoting this communication is the provision of mechanisms for the actual communication itself, that is, telephones, mail, and visitation times. To the extent that these are severely limited (e.g. in maximum security facilities), the attorney may be allowed exceptions to the visitation times and/or to additional mail.

The importance of balancing the visitation to ensure that necessary administrative requirements are met is acknowledged. This point is particularly relevant to security measures when mental health clients are violent or simultaneously involved with the justice system due to criminal offenses.

One outcome of protection of attorney communication and visitation rights is to ensure that minimal constitutional safeguards are protected and upheld within the treatment system. A second outcome is that some problems which may lead to litigation are avoided or resolved prior to litigation. As the body of mental disability law increases, this litigation prevention point should not be understated.[17]

Case 1. In *Wetmore* v. *Fields* the plaintiffs, inmates of the federal correctional institution at Oxford, Wisconsin, contended that federal prison officials had interfered with their constitutional rights of access to the courts.[18] Furthermore, they wanted the federal correctional institution to provide and maintain an adequate law library or an inmate legal assistance program. The court ruled that if a prison provides inmates with adequate legal assistance from persons trained in the law, then the prison can prohibit inmates from giving legal assistance to other inmates and does not have to maintain a law library. If on the other hand, the prison does not provide outside legal help, then the right to inmate legal assistance applies and the prison must maintain an adequate law library. It then cannot prohibit inmates from helping other inmates.

The problem in this case arose when the prison arbitrarily reassigned three inmates from the prison law library to the prison maintenance staff. Consequently, inmates who were depending on help from the three reassigned inmates were unable to get adequate advice on upcoming legal proceedings. The court felt that the prisoners' basic right of access to the courts was jeopardized, thus requiring the implementation of the above guidelines.

Notes. Although this case directly concerns the provision of prison law libraries as a substitute for outside legal expertise and as an aid to developing inside legal expertise, the case parallels our communication problem. Without access to attorneys and continued communication with them, inmates or patients are effectively denied one of their remedies for correcting problems, the courts. The court in this case felt that without the assistance of the inmates who had become "inside legal specialists" other inmates were denied legal representation. Any restriction of the attorney communication and visitation process in mental hospitals in effect creates the same problem. Without access to attorneys, the use of the legal system as a remedy for patient problems is effectively reduced.

MEDIA COMMUNICATION

Definition.   Patients have the right to communicate with the media (print, television, etc.).

The media communication right is separately identified and discussed because it appears to be qualitatively different from personal, mail, and telephone communications with friends, family, and significant others. Complications are acknowledged because the media can interfere with treatment and administrative processes in certain situations.[19]

The three primary purposes of patient communication with the media are: (1) to ensure the patient's ability to communicate his situation to those outside the system; (2) to aid and promote public review of the treatment system; and (3) to expose abuses and identify needs for change (i.e. development of the system).

In some cases friends, family, attorneys, or significant others are not able to effectively communicate the patient's situation, particularly when fears of retribution exist. This view recognizes that the media has the power to initiate change actions which may correct an individual patient situation or a whole class of patient problems (e.g. poor facilities, no treatment). As an illustration, there might occur cases where environmental conditions at a mental institution are seriously substandard, or where abuses resulting in physical harm are suffered by a single patient or a class of patients. The use of the media in these instances puts them in the role of "systems level" advocates.[20-24]

But it is also suggested that media involvement may interfere with the smooth functioning of both administrative and service programs, for example, security or systems stability. Media persons can be used to manipulate the authority system, to disrupt the routine, and to promote organizational change. For these and other reasons, media interaction is often avoided or rejected by staff. But in order to effectively demonstrate that administrative considerations should prevail over free and unlimited media contact, several steps must be taken. They are derived from previous rights and from the influence of due process.

First, there are several prerequisites necessary to the consideration of a patient's right to communicate with the media:

1. Any communication rights limitations must safeguard the access of other patients to the media.
2. The right to communicate with the media is limited by standards of libel and slander to which patients need to be accountable.
3. The right to communicate may be limited by administrative requirements of the institution such as security.
4. The rights are limited only while the patient is a part of the treatment system.

To restrict patient communication with the media, the identical process is used as in the other communication limitations:

1. the creation of a rationale for restriction;
2. the notification of the patient of the coming limitations;
3. the exploration of possible alternatives to limitation with the patient; and
4. a time limited restriction on media communication, with periodic review.

The outcome of the right is maintenance of a patient's general right to freedom of speech with whomever he chooses. As a fundamental civil right, it deserves special support. The outcome of limitations that are imposed with the above procedures ensures that patients still have access to the media. But the access is provided in the context of other considerations which must be made to ensure efficient and effective functioning of both the treatment and the administrative systems.

Case 1. *Pell* v. *Procunier* involves prison inmates, but the case is especially relevant to maximum security mental health care.[25] Reporters requested permission from the appropriate corrections division to interview three inmates. In addition, the editors of a certain periodical requested permission to visit an inmate to discuss the possibility of publishing some of his writings and to interview him concerning conditions of the prison. All of the journalists were denied permission to interview the inmates.

The inmates and the journalists initiated the litigation contending that the denial of permission was a violation of their free speech rights under the 1st and 14th Amendments. The journalists cited the limitations on news gathering as a significant constitutional problem.

The court did not see a problem with the time, place, and manner of the regulations. The court noted that "in light of alternative channels of communication that are open to the inmate appellees [the restriction] does not constitute a violation of their rights of free speech." Furthermore, the court noted that "alternative means of communication remain open to the inmates; they can correspond by mail with persons (including media representatives); they have rights of visitation with family, clergy, attorney and friends of prior acquaintance; and they have unrestricted opportunity to communicate with the press or public through their prison visitors."

Notes. In this case, the court used the presence of alternative mechanisms of communication to offset the civil rights problem, supporting the administrative necessities of operational efficiency and stability. The court considered the availability of the various mechanisms for communication that were addressed in this chapter, including person-to-person, mail, telephone, and media interviews. They found that the denial of media interviews still allowed person-to-person visitation, and mail and telephone communication to take place. That is, there was not complete restriction on contact. The denial of media interviews did not interfere totally with the patients' ability to communicate with the media. Denial involved a structuring of the way in which communication would take place to aid administrative processes. The need to structure was sufficiently documented and therefore withstood court scrutiny.

SUMMARY

A patient's right to communicate includes maintaining contacts outside the treatment setting and the ability to secure and coordinate resources on his own behalf. Essentially, patients have the right to communicate with anyone on a person-to-person level, or by telephone or mail.

Person-to-person communication (visits) should exist naturally in all treatment units. The purposes of visitation are: (1) to ensure continued contact with significant others; (2) to enhance communication quality; and (3) to allow others to see the patient's condition and hear his comments on treatment. Telephone and mail communication have the same basic rationale. These two types of communication should be ensured by the provision of writing materials, a limited amount of postage, and telephones accessible to patients.

To limit or deny communication, there must be, first and foremost, a compelling reason with supporting rationale and documentation of it. The patient then must be notified and alternatives explored. The denial of this right must be time-limited with a guarantee of periodic review. Safeguarding this right is essential, especially for involuntary patients, to ensure that reporting of any mistreatment is possible. There is a need to balance administrative security and efficiency with the patient's right to communicate, but the balance must be fair or in the patient's favor.

REFERENCES

1. Annas, G.J., Glantz, L.H., Katz, B.F., *The Rights of Doctors, Nurses and Allied Health Professionals,* Cambridge, Mass.: Ballinger Pub. Co., 1981, p. 361.
2. Annas, G.J., *The Rights of Hospital Patients,* New York: Avon Books, 1975.
3. Brakel, S.J., Rock, R.S., eds., *The Mentally Disabled and the Law,* Chicago: The University of Chicago Press, 1961, p. 155.
4. Szasz, T.S., *Law, Liberty and Psychiatry,* N.Y.: MacMillan, 1963.
5. Adams, S.F., "The Committed Mentally Ill and Their Right to Communicate," 7 *Wake Forest Law Rev,* 297, 1971.
6. Lindman, F.T., McIntyre, D.M., *The Mentally Disabled and the Law,* Chicago: Univ. of Chicago Press, 1961.
7. Schwitzgebel, R.L., Schwitzgebel, R.K., *Law and Psychological Practice,* N.Y.: John Wiley & Sons, 1980, p. 58.
8. Davidson, H., "Mental Hospitals and the Civil Liberties Dilemma," *Mental Hygiene* 374, 1967.
9. Ennis, B., Emery, R.D., *The Rights of Mental Patients,* New York: Avon Books, 1978, p. 159.
10. *Stowers* v. *Ardmore Acres Hospital* Mich.: App. 115, 172 N.W. 2d 497 1969.
11. *Brown* v. *Schubert,* 347 F. Supp. 1232 (E.D. Wisc. 1972).
12. *Eckerhart* v. *Hensley,* 475 F. Supp. 908 (W.D. No. 1979).
13. *Powell* v. *Alabama* (287 U.S. 45).
14. *Betts* v. *Brady,* 316 U.S. 455 (1942).
15. *Gideon* v. *Wainwright,* 372 U.S. 335; 9 L. Ed. 799; 83 S. Ct. 792 (1963).
16. *Argersinger* v. *Hamlin,* 407 U.S. 25 (1972).
17. Amer. Bar Association Commission on the Mentally Disabled, *Mental Disability Law Reporter.* Series published bimonthly by the Mental Disability Legal Resource Center, American Bar Assoc., Washington D.C.
18. *Wetmore* v. *Fields,* 458 F. Supp. 1131 (W.D. Wisc. 1978).
19. Smith, D.C., "Media Manipulation of the Mental Health System: An Administrative Reality." *Hosp. & Community Psychiat.,* 30(4) April 1979, p. 275.
20. Howard, J.M., Somers, R.H., "Resisting Institutional Evil From Within," in *Sanctions for Evil,* N. Sanford, ed., San Francisco: Jossey Bass, 1971.
21. Eklund, E., "Promoting Change Through Systems Advocacy," in *Advocacy Systems for Persons with Developmental Disabilities,* L. Baucom & G. Bensberg, eds., Lubbock, Texas: Research & Training Center in Mental Retardation, 1976.
22. Brown, M.R., "Context and Potential of Systems Advocacy," in *Advocacy Systems for Persons with Developmental Disabilities,* L. Baucom & G. Bensberg, eds., Lubbock, Texas: Research & Training Center in Mental Retardation, 1976.
23. Weingold, J.T., "Some Approaches to Systems Advocacy," in *Advocacy Systems for Persons with Developmental Disabilities,* L. Baucom & G. Bensberg, eds., Lubbock, Texas: Research & Training Center in Mental Retardation, 1976.
24. Boggs, E.G., "Collective Advocacy (Systems Advocacy) Versus Individual Advocacy: An Issue Paper," in *Advocacy Systems for Persons with Developmental Disabilities* L. Baucom & G. Bensberg, eds., Lubbock, Texas: Research & Training Center in Mental Retardation, 1976.
25. *Pell* v. *Procunier,* 417 U.S. 817 (1974).

8
Freedom of Movement

This chapter concerns both the degree of liberty accorded to patients as an ongoing part of treatment and the extent of the restriction of liberty at any time during the patient's stay in the treatment system. The freedom of movement-liberty conflict exists within individual units in the hospital and in day-to-day life on the ward. Deprivation of freedom to move about is significant in relation to theoretical concepts of treatment, to constitutional positions in law, and to daily operations. This chapter addresses the following topics: least restrictive alternatives; individual restrictions; organizational restrictions; restraints, seclusion; transfers; access to transportation; and leaves of absence.

In general, the purposes of the patient's right to freedom of movement are:

1. to maximize patient freedom to the greatest extent possible, i.e. to approximately match the freedom which exists outside the treatment setting; and
2. to maximize patient freedom so as to contribute to "independence" learning and to help in maintaining a state of normality (normalization).[1,2]

Outside the treatment setting, patients must manage their freedom and their responsibilities. The complete restriction of freedom establishes an unreal situation which does not coincide with life outside the protection of the treatment system.

The critical questions for rights integration are as follow: how to maximize freedom, how to restrict it, and how to protect the patient's right to free movement while in treatment when that movement must necessarily be constrained at certain times. Emerging are some guidelines for the restriction process which are slowly gaining acceptance:

- Provide the least restrictive service in total.
- Keep individual and organizational restrictions to the absolute minimum necessary for patient, staff, and public safety, using alternatives whenever possible.

- Use restraint and seclusion only as mechanisms for handling emergency and problematic patient situations, viewing them as treatment techniques.
- Use transfer only as necessary for patient treatment, not as an administrative convenience.
- Restrict and/or cancel leaves of absence only when fully justified by the patient's lack of progress or difficulties encountered when on leaves.

The process by which liberty restrictions are effected is based on the ever present notice, hearing, exploration of alternatives, documentation, and periodic review. That is, restraints, transfers, cancelled leaves are only used after notice, hearings, and other procedural protections are completed. The degree of formality can be light, but the procedural elements must be present.

The outcome of the freedom of movement right is to maximize patients' freedom of movement given occasional limitations required by treatment. Both the conditions of patients and the constraints of administration require that some freedom must be limited. Ensuring that these patients' rights are safeguarded minimizes the controlling and often detrimental effects of individual and organizational restrictions. Restraints, seclusion, and the limiting of leaves of absence are not to be used as punishments or retribution but only as part of a treatment plan, and even then only as part of a treatment technique found superior to others. Further exploration of these issues will identify some of the specific conflicts which can surface.

LEAST RESTRICTIVE ALTERNATIVES

Definition. Patients have the right to be treated in the least restrictive environment.

Increasingly, it is recognized that patients have a right to be treated in a setting which is the least restrictive of their liberty.[3-5] This limitation on restriction involves two levels: (1) the general setting of the treatment service, and (2) the individual actions which are taken toward the patient which restrict his freedom of movement within the setting.

The purposes of this right are:

- to ensure that alternatives to total confinement are fully explored, and
- to ensure that maximum freedom of movement is provided to the patient in all cases.

These purposes relate to the point of admission to the service system and to the types and nature of service provided once in the setting. They are based on the idea that infringement of freedom and liberty is negative by traditional societal standards and on the allied clinical point that infringement of personal freedom

is clinically harmful. The patient's right to be treated in the least restrictive setting involves a civil right of liberty that society has long held to be of considerable value. The treatment team should regard freedom as clinically useful in
helping the patient learn to cope with the level of freedom found outside the
confines of the treatment system.

However, this principle is not absolutely established, with several commentators describing the two-level problem quite well:

> "The principles [of least restrictive alternatives], will require greater justifi-
> cation of decisions to commit clients to psychiatric hospitals as well as of any
> restrictions of freedom within the hospital (such as placing the client on a
> locked rather than an open ward). The matter of safeguarding the client's
> right to treatment in the least restrictive alternative raises serious diagnostic
> questions. . . .While this issue may seem straightforward, it necessitates an
> application of clinical procedures beyond traditional methods of diagnosis
> and assessment; in particular it calls for a much more direct behavioral assess-
> ment process and requires that the assessment outcome be describable in a
> precise manner for legal testimony during the commitment hearing."[6]

In short, clinicians will need to closely consider alternative settings and sharpen
their diagnostic abilities to meet the possible test of hearing scrutiny. Screening
methods are now developing.[7]

The process by which this right is protected is a continuous and ongoing exploration of alternatives, whenever patient freedoms are considered for restriction. That position necessitates a review, for example, of community residential
program alternatives when commitment to a mental hospital is proposed—i.e.,
the total setting problem.[8] It also means that each clinical step taken with the
patient, which involves a restriction of the patient's freedom, must consider alternative ways of achieving that clinical goal. The alternatives must be developed,
presented to the patient, and fully documented so that a review of their rejection
can be conducted at some time in the future. The extensiveness of the presentation can be limited as long as the elements that comprise the rationale for
restriction are there.

Staff have an option of extending the detail of their review as far as they are
able to. One commentator summarized environmental factors in a survey of the
scientific literature on placement of patients in programs as follows:[9,10]

Type of residential facility.
Location: urban versus rural, "low profile" versus
   high visibility, and so on.
Staffing: types and distribution of personnel.
Specific programs and treatment modalities provided.

Selection of patients: mix according to level of functioning, diagnosis, demographic and socioeconomic characteristics, previous hospitalizations, and so on.

Presence of normal catalysts: mix of patient and nonpatient residents.

Rehabilitation efforts: degree and kind emphasized.

Expectations of patients: anticipations of capabilities and behavior.

Degree of autonomy accorded patients.

Extra residential programs for patient.

Limitations on length of stay.

History of facility: record of success in providing care.

Stated and unstated program goals: degree of precision or ambiguity in program goals and subgoals.

As noted by that writer and others, the right of least restriction is a matter of the best judgment for each patient, which may mean institutionalization.[11-14]

The above list of criteria is not exhaustive. Staff should be encouraged to extend the list with the assistance of patients. After this extension, the items can then become a "least restrictive checklist" that would be used at initial treatment planning sessions and at any time that transfers are to be made which affect the patient's degree of freedom.

One view of the specifics of the least restrictive alternative conditions was stated lucidly in *Wyatt* v. *Stickney* as follows:

"To this end the institution shall make every attempt to move residents from (1) more to less structured living, (2) larger to smaller facilities, (3) larger to smaller living units, (4) group to individual residence, (5) segregated from the community to integrated into the community living, (6) dependent to independent living."

The result is more independent freedom for patients.

The outcome of this right is that any proposed restrictions on patient freedom, beginning with the commitment process, are thoroughly reviewed and all less confining alternatives explored. Few persons would find defensible the argument that at no time in a severely disabled patient's career does the patient need to be restricted. To advocate absolute freedom at all times with the absence of organizational and individual restriction would be to deny the general path of mental disability. Carefully controlled and time-limited restriction of freedoms and liberties is really the intended purpose.

Case 1.   *Ploof* v. *Brooks* involves the transfer of a mentally ill juvenile delinquent from the open ward of a state hospital to a secure ward containing severely disturbed mental patients.[15] The plaintiff remained in the ward for two days, at which time a bed became available in a second security ward. The patient had a history of being hostile and abusive toward both patients and hospital staff. He repeatedly refused to participate in educational therapy programs.

After a short release in 1970, the patient returned to the hospital where he continued to be uncooperative in any attempt by the staff at rehabilitation. Both the patient's social worker and a physician believed the transfer to a secluded ward would be beneficial. Of the two choices available, Ward 2A, where young patients without serious mental problems are held, was the preferred. Ward 2A, however, had no available beds. The patient was subsequently transferred to another ward for two days where he was exposed to patients with severe mental and emotional problems.

During the course of this court procedure questioning the legality of the transfer, Ploof testified that his experience on the ward brought on recurrent nightmares while at the hospital and since his release. No evidence exists in the hospital records to support such complaints. The court found that the decision to make the transfer was essential to the patient's welfare and that of the orderly administration of the hospital facility.

The selection of Osgood 3 over Ward 2A was dictated by the lack of adequate staff and available beds in Ward 2A. It was not motivated by malice or for the purpose of punishment. The court stressed that in reviewing an administrative decision made by hospital staff, the judicial function is not to judge the correctness of the decision but to assure that it was based on relevant information.

Notes.   The patient filed a suit contending that he was not in the least restrictive environment. On review, the court found that both the social worker and the physician believed that the reduction of freedom would be beneficial to the patient. During the judicial hearings, the court attempted to discover whether the transfer was for punishment or was based on a treatment rationale. It was the court's opinion that the treatment rationale was the determining factor for the transfer. However, it is important to note that the staff were asked to provide their rationale for the transfer, including full documentation of both the decision-making process and any negative outcome, e.g., whether the patient complained of nightmares as a result of the transfer.

The case also illustrates that a matching of individual and organizational needs may be sanctioned. The unruly behavior of the patient was coupled with the absence of a bed in the most appropriate unit. An alternative unit was chosen that was appropriate, and it met administrative constraints.

INDIVIDUAL RESTRICTIONS

Definition.   Patients have the right to be free from individual restrictions that are not related to their treatment plan.

This right is directed at the singling out of individual patients for restrictions on their freedom of movement. The general purpose of the right is to ensure that patients are not unduly restricted in response to a need for administrative convenience and/or as punishment or retribution for acting out. For example, the denial of grounds privileges to a patient is an appropriate response if that patient is found to be losing control (e.g. assaultive). But it is not appropriate if the denial results from a shortage of staff or a staff interest in reducing the perceived chaos of the unit.

The process by which this freedom from individual restriction right is maintained involves the following steps:

1. identifying the problem;
2. presenting the rationale for individual restriction;
3. developing evidence that alternatives are not available;
4. explaining and exploring the problem with the patient; and
5. periodic review of the restriction once it is in effect.

The outcome of this right is to ensure that restrictions are for the benefit of the patient, that is, to ensure his or her safety, or the safety of others. Restrictions are also used as a part of the patient's treatment plan. Punishment, retribution, or administrative convenience are not justifiable uses of restriction. Adherence to the right helps to ensure that the latter outcomes do not occur.

Case 1. In *Williams* v. *Robinson,* the patient questioned not the legality of his hospitalization at St. Elizabeth's Hospital, but the decision to transfer him from St. Elizabeth's to the maximum security unit located at John Howard Pavilion.[16] According to available records, Williams was an amiable patient and was looking forward to an early release. On August 7, 1969, he was reported absent from his industrial therapy assignment and was placed on unauthorized leave. When he was located several hours later, he was restricted to the ward. A week later, he was transferred to the maximum security unit following the administration's determination that on August 7th, Williams had robbed an employee of $22.00 by threatening her with an ice pick.

Williams protested the move and requested an opportunity to show that he was in class at the time of the robbery. After a perfunctory response by the hospital, Williams remained in confinement at John Howard. No hearing was ever held by the hospital.

Williams then initiated legal proceedings, arguing first that the procedures used to resolve the robbery question were not adequate to ensure the accuracy of the hospital's determination. Second, the hospital failed to consider possible alternatives less restrictive of his liberty and of greater therapeutic value. And third, he was not receiving adequate treatment for his illness.

In the opinion, the court recognized that judicial review of the merits of internal hospital decisions is strictly limited. At the same time, the court stressed that the judicial duty in reviewing administrative acts is to guarantee that the ultimate administrative decision is based on sufficient evidence. The deciding body must show the information on which it relied in reaching a decision and explain the course of reasoning by which the result was reached.

Consequently, the court stressed that carefully kept hospital records are extremely important to judicial review of any hospital's administrative decision. The court also noted the Hospitalization of the Mentally Ill Act of 1964 which cites the patient's right to have access to his own records. The court urged that procedures be implemented to permit dissatisfied patients the opportunity to question hospital adminstrative acts. They should be able to present their grievances to the hospital's administration for review, and all such grievances and responses should be included in the patient's records. The court concluded that until such mechanisms were initiated, judicial review could not be restricted to the use of such inadequate records as those presented in the case at hand.

Notes. The case identifies hospital bypassing of key steps in placing a patient in individual restriction, namely the holding of a hearing, the development of the rationale, and the exploration of alternatives. The records were too inadequate to determine whether the patient was wronged or whether the hospital acted correctly in this case. The fact that records were inadequate was, in the view of the court, a problem in itself. It *denied the hospital* the ability to demonstrate that it was taking the individual restriction action appropriately. Simultaneously, the absence of adequate record keeping *denied the patient* the ability to demonstrate that adequate rationale was not presented, nor were alternatives explored.

As a result of the litigation, the case is still not fairly resolved. Neither the patient nor the hospital is free from the suspicion that they acted incorrectly. The action of the hospital demonstrates that restrictions can be applied in the absence of supporting "data." Without the supporting information, there is no basis for subsequent review—and importantly—no protection for either hospital or patient.

ORGANIZATIONAL RESTRICTIONS

Definition. Patients have the right to be free from general organizational restrictions.

This right is an extension of the previous discussion on individual restrictions. The same guidelines apply, although there is now consideration of all of the patients as a group either in wards, in units, or in the hospital as a whole. This is the freedom from restriction right at the organizational level.

The purpose of the right is to maximize freedom during the patient's stay in the treatment setting. It is to ensure that patients as a group are denied freedom of movement only in the service of clinical progress. The purpose of organizational restrictions can not be to punish or provide retribution for acts conducted by a group of patients or the acts of one of the members.

Organizational restrictions range from locked dayrooms, to whole locked wards and can include the restriction against movement on the grounds, or in the community, or against travel to recreational or educational sites.[17] Staff are sometimes tempted to confine patients when administrative problems arise such as short staffing, or acting out by one patient. Emergencies allow for problem-solving restrictions—but prolonged use is not sanctioned.

The essentials of the process for protecting the freedom of movement with regard to organizational restrictions are:

1. the clear identification of the problem;
2. the rationale for the use of organizational restrictions;
3. the documentation of that rationale, including the discussion with the patients in question;
4. the full exploration of alternatives to restriction; and
5. periodic review of those restrictions.

If these five steps are taken, organizational restrictions can be used as clinical demands require.

The outcome of this review is to ensure that organizational restrictions are for the benefit of the clinical service and/or to ensure the safety of an individual or a group of patients.

Case 1. In *U.S. Ex Rel Souder* v. *Watson* a Pennsylvania state prisoner, Souder, filed a petition for a writ of habeas corpus challenging the constitutionality of a state statute providing for commitment of prisoners to a mental facility.[18] Sentenced to life imprisonment in 1962 for murder in the first degree, Souder requested a transfer to Farview State Hospital in 1967.

After four years at Farview, he returned to the State Correctional Institution at Pittsburgh. About a year later in April, 1972, the prison's deputy superintendent commenced proceedings to commit Souder to a mental facility for the second time. A hearing on the deputy superintendent's initial position was held on April 27, 1972. Souder received no personal notice of the hearing nor was he present at the hearing. Notice was served to his mother who did not attend, to the officials of the Western Penitentiary, and to the County Public Defender.

After the hearing began, but before any testimony was presented, the Public Defender came into the courtroom and entered his appearance on Souder's behalf. However, Souder was not represented by counsel in any of the proceedings prior to the hearing.

All of the experts who evaluated the prisoner were court appointed and were employed as consultants by the State Correctional Institution in Pittsburgh. No independent expert was appointed to assist Souder at the commitment hearing. In addition, Souder was not informed of the purpose of the examinations or that he had a right to remain silent during the questioning. The public defender presented no testimony on Souder's behalf. Following a hearing lasting 27 minutes, the court committed Kenneth Souder to Farview State Hospital.

After a number of court proceedings, Souder succeeded in obtaining his release from Farview and was transferred back to the State Correctional Institution in Pittsburgh where he initiated the present habeas corpus action.

Souder requests that the state statute be declared unconstitutional and that all references to his second commitment be erased from his files. The court found that because the existing procedures used to commit prisoners to mental facilities differ from those used to commit civilians, the statute was unconstitutional.

Notes. In this case, one patient filed suit (representing a class of patients) objecting to his transfer to mental facilities without the benefit of appropriate hearings and the due process normally provided in the criminal justice system. The patients were not given the opportunity to explore the question of their need for this transfer and, importantly, consider whether the new unit would be more restrictive than the one they were currently in.

Although it is not certain from this case, the question arises as to whether all patients who are transferred to more restrictive units should receive personal notice of the hearing. In general, the case illustrates that the five steps of the protection process were ignored. It appears that there was a one-sided presentation of the problem, rationale was weak, the patient was not allowed to be involved in the discussion, there was no exploration of alternatives, and there was no mention of periodic review of his status.

It is conceivable that one or two of the steps would be missed without adequate preparation. But the wholesale disregard for the protection process justifiably generated litigation. As a result, the organizational participants expended considerably more time, energy, and resources than would have been required for the protection process.

RESTRAINTS

Definition. Patients have the right to be free from physical or chemical restraints, except when those restraints are a part of their treatment plan and/or when necessary for the safety of the patients themselves or others.

Restraints in long use were physical ones, such as straitjackets and leathers. In the past twenty years, the term has come to include the use of drugs in dosages which restrain and/or diminish the behavior of patients. Mechanical restraints were the first to be questioned with the result that alternatives are now offered.[19]

The general purpose of the right to be free from restraints is to limit the use of physical and chemical restraints. Restricted uses are for treatment, emergencies, and situations which threaten the safety of the patient or others (protection from impending harm, i.e., prevention). Programs exist for helping staff identify both the situations and responses.[20-24] Accepting occasional use acknowledges that at some times restraints are necessary to check a patient who is unable to control himself and who is not responsible for his own safety and/or the safety of those around him. It can be regarded as a clinical technique with indications, dosages, contraindications, and side effects.[25] Accepted needs for the restraint are clinical intervention and administrative securing of safety, but not administrative management or convenience.

The process of ensuring appropriate use of restraints involves consideration of the following six topics, in effect aspects of a restraint use approval:[25a]

1. identification of a problem for which the clinical response is restraint;
2. rationale for the use of restraint as the best response;
3. time limits for the restraint;
4. periodic review of the restraint as a needed response and the development of a justification for continuation of that response if desired;
5. review by the clinical director at the beginning and end of each time limit;
6. concern that the restraint does not interfere with personal care including meals, bathing, and the use of the toilet.

These considerations are minimal requirements for the use of restraint in a clinical situation. Emergencies will not allow time for thoughtful review of all points. But once restraints are in use, any continued application to the same patient should provide ample opportunity for thorough exploration of alternatives.

The outcome of limiting the use of restraints under the above parameters is a focused, specialized, and appropriate use of this clinical technique.[26] Importantly, one outcome of the protection is a continued monitoring by the staff of both the justification and the time periods of restraint use. It is often not a single application of a restraint that is damaging but the repeated return of the patient to restraints or continuation of restraints without freedom.

Case 1. Morgan v. *State* involves a claim for damages based on Morgan's confinement in a state hospital.[27] She was charged with having committed a felonious assault on a man by stabbing him, mistakenly believing him to be a judge who had dismissed a damage suit for $8 million against several state officials and judges.

The next evening an order committing Morgan to Kings County Hospital for a mental examination and observation not to exceed 60 days was signed by a magistrate. Approximately one month later on the basis of physicians' certificates, the court ordered the hearing to be held after notifying both Morgan and her attorney. The hearing resulted in Morgan's commitment to a state hospital for 60 days. At the end of that period, the director of the hospital filed the proper certificate stating that the patient was in need of further care and treatment. The commitment order became final. Later Morgan was transferred to an institution for the criminally insane.

Testimony on the hospital records indicated that Morgan was restrained in a camisole (i.e. strapped to her bed) for a period of 13 days. On another occasion, a protective sheet was the mechanism for restraint. Similar occurrences were noted in the hospital records concerning Morgan at various times. In addition to being restrained physically, Morgan complained of being beaten by an attendant while confined to a room for approximately six days. She described her confinement vividly: "in solitary, she could not lie in her cell all day; she could not make up her cot to lie in, or have her eyeglasses or reading matter; she could not wash and her toilet needs remained in the cell with her; she laid on the stone floor during the day and was only allowed on the cot at night."

During each incident of restraint, Morgan claimed she was denied bathroom privileges. The state produced no witnesses who contradicted these incidents. Instead, both hospital records and witnesses corroborated the occurrences. The court concluded that although Morgan received adequate medical attention while in the hospital, she had been subjected to unnecessary cruel and unusual punishment. Accordingly, $15,000 in damages for pain and suffering was awarded to Morgan.

Notes. This case presents an example of the use of restraints which may have been clinically appropriate at the outset of their use, but which were obviously continued well beyond any clinical justification. Compounding the extended use of the restraints was the denial of basic personal care needs, e.g. bathroom and sleeping arrangements. For documentation, the hospital records and witnesses corroborated the patient's story.

What questions are raised by the facts of the case? Why did staff not intervene? Were there no alternatives to the restraints? Are there many cases in which a patient must be strapped to a bed for 13 days—or any cases? Since the actions were not considered appropriate professional behavior (obviously), the court awarded damages to the patient.

SECLUSION

Definition. Patients have the right to be free from seclusion except when seclusion is part of the treatment plan or when necessary for the safety of the patient or other persons.

As with the other freedom of movement rights, the seclusion right concerns the restriction of its use to clinical needs or for the safety of other persons. Directly stated, the purposes of the seclusion right are to limit the use of seclusion to treatment necessity, (containment, isolation, decrease in sensory input), to emergency situations, and to situations which threaten the safety of the patient or others (protection from impending harm and prevention).[28-32] There is some question whether seclusion as a technique is needed at all and whether it represents failure.[33] It arouses fear and confusion in the patient.[34] But a strong case can be made for selected use as a part of a treatment plan, particularly for patients who cannot be helped in any other way.[35,36]

In *Wyatt* v. *Stickney,* the opinion stated that "seclusion, defined as the placement of a resident alone in a locked room, shall not be employed. Legitimate 'time out' procedures may be utilized under close and direct professional supervision as a technique in behavior shaping programs."[37] The conversion of the term "seclusion" to "time out" is intended to be more than a semantic difference. It is to promote the idea that isolation of one patient from other patients and from the culture of the unit is designed to shape behavior. It is used as a part of the clinical program, and must be accompanied by close clinical assessment and monitoring of the patient by staff, with orders renewed every 24 hours.[38] One group even monitors continually with closed circuit camera.[39,40]

The process for the use of seclusion if it is to be employed, follows the same procedures as noted above:

1. identification of a problem for which the clinical response is seclusion;
2. rationale for the use of seclusion as the *best* response in comparison to other alternatives;
3. time limits for the seclusion;
4. periodic review of seclusion as a needed response and development of a justification for continuation of that response if needed;
5. review by the clinical director at the beginning and end of each time limit;
6. concern that seclusion does not interfere with personal care including meals, bathing, and the use of the toilet.

The above points assume continual documentation of each of those aspects. The review of alternatives is significant because there are almost always options. One clinician listed the seclusion alternatives as administrative (e.g., transfer), interpersonal (e.g., increased staff contact), and somatic (e.g., psychotropic medication).[41]

The outcome of this right is that the use of seclusion is restricted to very limited circumstances. And in those circumstances there should be both careful documentation of the need, the process of implementation, and continued monitoring of the time limitation, as demonstrated in one case.[42] The position here is that seclusion can be used for emergency purposes without written orders, but qualified clinical staff must review it and a psychiatrist must eventually approve its use.[43]

The outcome of this right is to identify the use of seclusion as an extraordinary clinical procedure. It is not likely to be used for every patient, or for many patients at all. When it is used, it is used for a specific reason, for a limited period of time, with the attention of the clinical director, and with constant monitoring of the length of time of application.

Case 1. The case example is the *Morgan* v. *State* illustration just presented.[44] The patient was confined to a room for six days. During this time she was not given reading matter; her personal hygiene needs were disregarded and her health was threatened.

Notes. The case does not review whether there was an existing clinical necessity for the seclusion of the patient. To continue the seclusion, there would have had to be a *continuing* clinical necessity as well. In addition, even if justifiable need existed, the way seclusion was carried out was so poor as to threaten the patient's health.

TRANSFERS

Definition. Patients have the right to be free from transfers.

There are two purposes for this right. First, it is to recognize the disruption to patients of changing their physical environment. Their living situation is their temporary home, particularly for long term patients. The right recognizes that changes are in effect a disruption of home.[45-48] Second, the right sensitizes staff to the possibility that a transfer of a patient to another setting may change the level of restriction. If additional restrictions result, the change to a greater level of restriction must be justified.

The process of transfer requires four steps:

1. identification of the clinical or administrative need for transfer, including the rationale for transfer as an appropriate response,
2. notice to the patient that a transfer is to be initiated;
3. holding of a formal or informal hearing to explain the coming change with the patient, including possible alternatives if the patient objects;
4. development of time periods and points of periodic review.

The process follows the same path as previous movement processes. Staff are responsible for ensuring that the patient has notice, has the right to present his or her side of the transfer questions, is present through an exploration of alternatives, and fully understands what is to happen to him or her. Last, this process must be documented and must be reversible.

The outcomes of this protection are two. First, clinical stability is reinforced by maintenance of the treatment setting in which patients are being treated. Second, there is reduced use of transfer as punishment and as an administrative efficiency or convenience.

Case 1. *Romero* v. *Schauer* involves Colorado State Hospital patients who were transferred to the state penitentiary after an administrative determination that they were too dangerous for continued confinement in the hospital.[49] The action was brought by two of the patients transferred to the state penitentiary, one of whom was afterwards killed by an inmate. The patients challenged the constitutionality of the administrative procedure used, claiming it violated their 5th, 6th, 8th and 14th Amendment rights.

The court focused on the patients' claim that such a transfer was a violation of due process law. The court presented guidelines to be followed in making such a move. The guidelines are as follows:

1. A patient alleged to be so dangerous that he cannot safely be confined in the state hospital must be provided with written notice of the facts upon which the accusation is based.
2. The hearing must be held by an impartial body prior to transfer or within a reasonable time after transfer, if made for safety or security reasons.
3. The patient must have the opportunity to call witnesses and present evidence on his own behalf.
4. There must be a written statement by the hearing body, containing the evidence they relied upon and the reasons for their decision.
5. The patient must have the choice of assistance by legal counsel during the hearing process.

In addition, the court stated that members of the plaintiff class who are transferred to the state penitentiary must receive psychiatric treatment *substantially* equivalent to that provided patients at Colorado State Hospital so as to guarantee them equal protection under the law.

Notes. In this case, the transfer of the patient without appropriate due process may have resulted in a loss of life. If that was avoidable by a hearing and use of other alternatives for solving the problem, a patient died because of an inappropriate transfer procedure—the worst possible outcome. The court states that certain minimal steps must be taken in order to transfer patients in a way that is consistent with their rights. Those steps include notice, hearing, patient viewpoint, documentation, and the right to be represented. They are similar to the steps recommended throughout this chapter that demonstrate appropriateness in a variety of situations, including other transfer cases.

At the hearing, the court should expect to find a clinical or a safety justification for that transfer. The finding rests on the idea that the right to liberty is a fundamental civil right for all citizens. Placing patients in more restrictive settings decreases the patient's degree of liberty. Therefore, a transfer is not a simple shift in treatment setting. In cases where restrictions increase, it is a serious incursion on freedom.

Patients who do not have a means for reviewing and/or contesting the transfer decision are left without a means to protect one of their most basic civil rights. Certainly the court has a role in that type of rights review and could potentially be brought in on any case.

TRANSPORTATION ACCESS

Definition. Patients have the right to access to transportation to and from the service facility, on admission, on discharge, and for the purposes of treatment.

The general purposes of this right are these: to ensure that patients can get to the facility, to ensure that they can get out of the facility, and to ensure that they have access to transportation which promotes their treatment progress. While transportation is not a problem for all patients or even perhaps for many, it is a problem for those in state mental hospitals. They are frequently without the personal financial resources that pay for automobiles, taxis, and other means of travel. Their families are often not able to help.

The process by which the right is protected involves notifying the facility of the need for transportation, identification of the absence of any alternatives to hospital or service-system-provided transportation (no buses, trains, taxis), and a matching of transportation needs with the constraints of administration. Staff must assist in identifying the need and exploring alternatives while allowing for administrative efficiencies. Patients must be provided with transportation needed for activities in their treatment plan.

The outcome of this right's protections is that patients have the freedom to move in and out of the facility. It is a literal insurance of physical assistance when needed. Protection of the right also guarantees that patients will not be excluded from certain essential treatment activities by reason of transportation difficulties (e.g., educational or recreational trips).

Case 1. John Doe, a patient at the Oak State Hospital, was a member of a group of patients scheduled to visit a museum in a city located 45 miles from the hospital.* The trip was to cost each patient $10.50, which included transportation, a luncheon, and admission to the museum. All of the patients were able to pay the costs from personal funds except for John. Since John did

---
*Fictitious case.

not have the money, he was not able to go. He requested that the hospital pay for his transportation stating that he would borrow lunch and admission money. Staff were unable to obtain permission to cover transportation costs for John. The hospital administration stated that to pay for one patient would necessitate the hospital's paying transportation for all patients. The whole group except for John went to the museum.

John Doe sued the hospital claiming that his rights to transportation were violated and that he was denied treatment that others in the hospital received; i.e., he was discriminated against with regard to the treatment program.

Notes. The hospital had a "special treatment" costs account but it was low in funds. The available resources would not allow for extensive funding of special treatments or the payment of costs for many people. The hospital was in one view correct in denying the payment for this particular trip.

However, the result of the denial was an exclusion of this patient from a key treatment component and the singling out of the patient for discriminatory handling. The hospital would be directed to find a means to accommodate cases where a single patient would be denied useful service. In this case, they should have paid and concerned themselves with paying for all only if the problem arose. This would appear to be a common sense solution which was not followed at the time due to hypothesized fears of the negative results of special handling.

LEAVE OF ABSENCE

Definition. Patients have the right to a leave of absence if that is clinically required.

The purpose of the right is to ensure that patients have an opportunity to secure a trial leave from the hospital and/or a break from the treatment regimen. Unless patients are involuntarily committed, the patient should be able to utilize the leave of absence as a part of his treatment protocol with some degree of ease. Even involuntary patients are sometimes allowed leaves as their program warrants.

This right is protected by a series of steps similar to other movement rights:

1. identification of a situation for which the clinical response is a leave of absence
2. rationale for the use of the leave as the best response
3. time limits for the leave
4. periodic review of the leave as a useful method and the development of justification for continuation or discontinuation of the leave
5. review by the clinical supervisor at the beginning and end of each time limit
6. full documentation in the treatment plan and records as to the purpose and results of the leave

If leaves are to be denied after specific patient request, they must follow the process with these elements: notice to patient, hearing, patient participation, exploration of alternatives, and documentation. Otherwise arbitrary revocation can be unconstitutional, following criminal law protections for due process.[51,52]

The outcome of this right is that leaves are used as a part of the treatment process. It reduces the use of leave denial as a punishment for inappropriate patient behavior.

Case 1.   Meisel v. *Kremens* involves an action brought by Meisel, a patient in a Pennsylvania mental health facility.[53] This suit challenges the constitutionality of the state statute which summarily revokes leaves of absence granted to patients and which does not provide those patients a hearing at which the factual and medical basis of the revocation may be questioned.

On March 12, 1973, after a hearing, the court committed Meisel to Haverford State Hospital for evaluation. Further hearings were held on March 19, 1973, where it was disclosed that Meisel had behaved assaultively toward his parents and where Meisel's term of commitment was extended. Approximately 7 months later on October 12, 1973, the hospital director authorized Meisel's discharge on a long term leave status. According to Section 419 of the Mental Health and Mental Retardation Act of 1966, the director of any facility may terminate the leave of absence and direct the law enforcement officer to apprehend and return the patient to the mental health facility.

After his discharge, Meisel and his family attended outpatient individual and family therapy. During this time Meisel lived at home. On the evening of May 30, 1974, Meisel's father called the police after an incident occurred at the patient's home. The facts of the incident are disputed. Under the authorization of the hospital's director, the police took Meisel to Haverford State Hospital.

Following his reincarceration, Meisel's long term leave was terminated. The director based his decision to terminate the leave of absence on information received from Meisel's father. The information was not reviewed at any formal hearing. After discussing the consequences of curtailing the liberty of an individual for an indeterminate period without any form of hearing, the court found this statute unconstitutional. It excluded from this opinion emergency commitments of the mentally ill.

Notes.   The case illustrates the linkage of the leave of absence to the question of denial of liberty. In this case, the patient was allowed liberty on the basis of his leave of absence. Other cases have indicated the degree of importance placed by the court on patient freedom. Meisel was denied freedom by revoking his leave of absence. The court indicates that, because revocation is a means of limiting patient liberty, it is subject to the same procedural guidelines as other more often used methods, e.g., commitment. However, an emergency situation will be sufficient cause to revoke without procedural safeguards. But any continuation of confinement will require all of the protective steps, including a hearing, patient and attorney representation, exploration of alternatives, and documentation.

SUMMARY

The right to freedom of movement focuses on providing the least restrictive alternatives to patients. It allows them to be free from organizational and individual restrictions, restraints, seclusion, and transfers as punishment or to facilitate administrative efficiency. The right supports transportation as a necessity and due process to protect leaves of absence. The overall purpose of this right is to maximize freedoms, especially when they contribute to learning independence. The guidelines used to protect freedom of movement rights generally follow the rule of providing the least restrictive environment within the constraints of patient and societal safety. It also states definitively that restriction of movement cannot be used as a form of punishment, only as part of a treatment plan or in extreme emergency situations.

The patient has the right to be treated in the least restrictive environment in which he can function. The desire is to maintain as much integration with society as possible. Any restrictions on patient movement require a treatment rationale.

The imposition of restrictions must follow these procedures: (1) identification of the problem; (2) rationale for the restriction; (3) documentation that alternatives are not available; (4) explanation to patient; and (5) periodic review for the purpose of removing restrictions. In the case of seclusion or restraints, the clinical supervisor must also review the situation at the beginning and end of the period of use. Restraints and seclusion must not interfere with the patient's personal care (e.g., meals and bathroom needs).

With regard to transportation, the patient must be able to get to and from the hospital setting and must be provided transportation to activities that are a part of treatment. The purpose here is to provide mobility assistance as needed and to see that patients are not excluded from certain essential treatment activities.

Leaves of absence are to be provided as they become clinically desirable. Again, rationales for change, notification, and review are necessary. Cancelling a leave requires the same procedures as any other imposition of restriction.

The overall concern with freedom of movement issues is that the patient should be housed in the least restrictive environment available. Such a concern insures that restrictions are considered extraordinary clinical procedures. The right guarantees that the patient may not be punished by loss of his right to freedom of movement.

REFERENCES

1. Nirje, B., "The normalization principle and its human management implications," in *Changing Patterns in Residential Services for the Mentally Retarded,* R. Kugel & W. Wolfensberger, eds., Washington: President's Committee on Mental Retardation, 1969.
2. Wolfensberger, W., *The Principle of Normalization in Human Services,* Toronto: National Institute on Mental Retardation, 1972.
3. Rapson, R., "The Right of the Mentally Ill to Receive Treatment in the Community," *Col. J. of Law & Social Problems,* 16(2), 1980, p. 193.
4. Ennis, B. & Siegel, L., *The Rights of Mental Patients,* New York: Avon Books, 1973.
5. D.L. Chambers, "Community-Based Treatment and the Constitution: The Principle of the Least Restrictive Alternative," in *Alternatives to Mental Hospital Treatment,* L.I. Stein and M.A. Test, eds., New York: Plenum, 1978, pp. 23-39.
6. Hasazi, J.E., Surles, R.C., Hannah, G.T., "Client Rights in Psychiatric Facilities," in *Preservation of Client Rights,* G.T. Hannah, W.P. Christian, and H.B. Clark, eds., New York: Free Press, 1981, p. 372.
7. Allen, R.H. et al., "A Multi-Tiered Screening System for the Least Restrictive Setting," *Am. J. Psychiatry,* 137(8), August 1980, p. 968.
8. Rapson, R., op. cit., (item no. 3).
9. Bachrach, L.L., "Is the Least Restrictive Environment Always the Best? Sociological and Semantic Implications," *Hospital and Community Psychiatry,* 31(2), Feb. 1980, p. 97.
10. Carpenter, M.D., "Residential Placement for the Chronic Psychiatric Patient: A Review and Evaluation of the Literature," *Schizophrenia Bulletin,* vol. 4, No. 3, 1978, pp. 384-398.
11. Bachrach, L.L., "Planning Mental Health Services for Chronic Patients," *Hospital & Community Psychiatry,* vol. 30, June 1979, pp. 387-393.
12. Rachlin, S., Grossman, S., and Frankel, J., "Patients without Communities: Whose Responsibility?" *Hospital & Community Psychiatry,* vol. 30, January 1979, pp. 37-39.
13. Rabiner, C.J., and Lurie, A., "The Case for Psychiatric Hospitalization," *American Journal of Psychiatry,* vol. 131, July 1974, pp. 761-764.
14. Peele, R., Luisada, P.V., Lucas, M.J., et al., "Asylums Revisited," *American Journal of Psychiatry,* vol. 134, October 1977, pp. 1077-1081.
15. *Ploof v. Brooks,* 342 F. Supp. 999 (D. UT. 1972).
16. *Williams v. Robinson,* 432 F. 2nd 637 (D.C. Cir. 1970).
17. *Shapiro v. Thompson,* 394 U.S. 618 (1969).
18. *U.S. Ex rel Souder v. Watson,* 413 F. Supp. 711 (M.D. Pa. 1976).
19. Guirguis, E.F., "Management of Disturbed Patients: An Alternative to the Use of Mechanical Restraints," *J. Clin. Psychiatry,* 39, 1978, p. 295.
20. Gold Award — "A Program for the Prevention and Management of Disturbed Behavior," *Hosp. Commun. Psychiatry,* 27(10), Oct. 1976, p. 724.
21. Guirguis, E.F., "Management of Disturbed Patients: An Alternative to the Use of Mechanical Restraints," *J. Clinical Psychiatry,* vol. 39, April 1978, pp. 295-300.
22. Gertz, B., "Training for Prevention of Assaultive Behavior in a Psychiatric Setting," *Hosp. & Communit. Psychiatry,* 31(9) Sept. 1980, p. 628.
23. Edelman, S.E., "Managing the Violent Patient in a Community Mental Health Center," *Hosp. & Commun. Psychiatry,* 29(7), July 1978, p. 460.
24. Snellgrove, C.E., Flaherty, E.L., "An Attitude Therapy Program Helps Reduce the Use of Physical Restraints," *Hospital and Community Psychiatry,* 26(3) March 1975, p. 137.
25. Rosen, H., DiGiacomo, J.N., "The Role of Physical Restraint in the Treatment of Psychiatric Illness," *J. Clinical Psychiatry,* 39, 1978, p. 228.

25a. Joint Commission on Accreditation of Hospitals, *Consolidated Standards for Child Adolescent and Adult Psychiatric Alcoholism and Drug Abuse Programs,* Chicago: JCAH, 1979.

26. Rosen, H., DiGiacomo, J.N., op. cit., (item no. 25).

27. *Morgan* v. *State,* 319 N.Y.S. 2nd 151 (1970).

28. Gutheil, T.G., "Observations on the theoretical bases for seclusion of the psychiatric inpatient," *Am. J. Psychiatry,* **135**:325–328, 1978.

28a. Mattson, M.R., Sacks, M.H., "Seclusion: uses and complications," *Am. J. Psychiatry,* **135,** 1210–1213, 1978.

29. Kilgalen, R.K., "The Effective Use of Seclusion," *Journal of Psychiatric Nursing and Mental Health Services,* vol. **15,** January 1977, pp. 22–25.

29a. Gutheil, T.G., "Restraint versus treatment: Seclusion as discussed in the Boston State Hospital case," *American Journal of Psychiatry,* **137**(6), June 1980.

30. Binder, R.L., "The use of seclusion on an inpatient crisis intervention unit," *Hospital & Community Psychiatry,* **30,** 1979, pp. 266–269.

30a. Wells, D.A., "The Use of Seclusion on a University Hospital Psychiatric Floor," *Archives of General Psychiatry,* vol. **26,** Mar. 1972, pp. 410–413.

31. Fitzgerald, R.C., Long, I., "Seclusion in the treatment and management of severely disturbed manic and depressed patients," *Perspect Psychiatric Care,* **11,** 59–64, 1973.

32. Goldberg, A., Rubin, B., "A method of pacification of the psychotic excited state: The use of the hospital as a transitional object," *Compr. Psychiat.,* **11,** 450–456, 1970.

33. Suga, B., "Seclusion," *J. of Psychiatric Nursing,* July-Aug., 1967, **5**(4), p. 328.

34. Wadeson, H., and Carpenter, W.T., "Impact of the Seclusion Room Experience," *Journal of Nervous and Mental Disease,* vol. **163,** November 1976, pp. 318–328.

35. Gutheil, T.G., op. cit., (item no. 28).

36. Wells, D.A., op. cit., (item no. 30a).

37. *Wyatt* v. *Stickney,* 325 F. Supp. 781 (M.D. Ala. 1971).

38. Gutheil, T.G., op. cit., item no. 28.

39. Fitzgerald, R.C., Long, I., op. cit., (item no. 31).

40. Derman, R.M., "Use of a Closed Circuit Camera to Monitor a Seclusion Room," *Hospital & Commun. Psychiatry,* **31**(7), July 1980, p. 496.

41. Gutheil, T.G., op. cit., (item no. 28).

42. *Rogers* v. *Okin,* 478 F. Supp. 1342 (D. Mass. 1979).

43. Joint Commission on Accreditation of Hospitals, op. cit., (item no. 25a).

44. *Morgan* v. *State,* 319 N.Y.S. 2nd 151 (1970).

45. Cotton, P.G., Bene-Kociemba, A., Roses, S., "Transfers from a General Hospital Psychiatric Service to a State Hospital," *Am. J. Psychiat.* **137**(2), Feb. 1980, p. 230.

46. Har-Esh, E., "Transfer of the Chronically Ill," *Amer. J. Psychiatry,* **135**(4), April 1978, p. 499.

47. Lieberman, M., Tobin, S.S., Slover, D., "The effects of relocation on long term geriatric patients," Final report, project 17-1328, Chicago: Illinois Department of Health, 1971.

48. Marlowe, R.A., "Effects of environment on elderly state hospital relocatees," Presented at the annual meeting of the Pacific Sociological Association, Scottsdale, Ariz., May 1973.

49. *Romero* v. *Schauer,* 386 F. Supp. 851 (D. Colo. 1974).

50. *Eubanks* v. *Clarke,* 434 F. Supp. 1022 (E.D. Pa. 1977).

51. Notes, "Mental Patients Furloughs Cannot be Arbitrarily Revoked in Pennsylvania, Judge Rules," *Hospital and Community Psychiatry,* **27**(1), Jan. 1976, p. 62.

52. *Meisel* v. *Kremens,* 405 F. Supp. 1253 (E.D. Pa. 1975).

53. Ibid.

9
Abuse

Patients have the right to be free from physical and psychological abuse. Does abuse occur? Is there an organizational tendency toward abuse? Yes, it is indigenous to mental health settings.[1, 2, 3, 4] The abuse question within treatment settings parallels that of abuse anywhere else. For example, in any given situation certain persons can abuse others whether they are patients, clients, employees, friends, family, or associates. Families abuse certain members, while neighbors ostracize those who do not fit a certain image, although there is not usually the severity of harm or the continuity of the problem that there is in a mental health treatment center.

The point of the "freedom from abuse right" in treatment settings is sharpened by the rather broad definition that abuse is deemed "abuse" if it is harmful and not in the service of the patient's treatment plan. This opens the possibility that in some cases certain treatment actions may be perceived by the patient, friends, or family as harmful (i.e., as abusive). Whenever harm is done to a patient, staff must have a complete rationale describing the "accident" or the method in terms of its contribution to the patient's individual treatment plan. There are two ways to harm patients—by accident or by abuse. Planned harm is not tolerated even as part of a "treatment rationale."

Michael Perlin has summarized the parameters of abuse as noted by the litigation under "freedom from harm":

"Among the rights owed to patients within the general rubric of a 'right to freedom from harm' (based on a composite Eighth Amendment/Fourteenth Amendment argument) are 'a tolerable living environment,'[6] protection from physical harm,[7] correction of conditions which violate 'basic standards of human decency,'[8] opportunity to exercise and have recreation,[9] and the 'necessary elements of basic hygiene.'[10] In addition, mental patients are owed a duty by those charged with their custody 'to preserve. . .their life, health and safety; beyond any duty owed to the general public,'[11] as well as a therapeutic, not punitive, confinement."[12]

There are essentially two types of abuse. Physical abuse is the hitting or striking of a patient, or in some way physically abusing the patient's person. Psychological abuse is the verbal and environmental pressures on patients which produce some harm to the patient's emotional status or psychological well-being.

Currently, there is an open debate regarding how much abuse exists within treatment settings such as state mental hospitals. Unfortunately, the conflicting but appropriate answer is that there is far more abuse than people believe but significantly less than others believe. One advocacy group found abuse to be the most frequent rights violation complaint.[13] Another found it to be the third highest category.[14]

Contrary to some advocates' notions, not many staff tour the treatment units searching for patients to put in closets, beat and torture with tales of threatened or actual harm if they do not behave. It is generally accepted that the day-to-day behavior on most wards does not include extensive and continuing amounts of physical and psychological abuse. Some units are apparent exceptions.[15] However, there are enough incidents to warrant serious concern for federal departments to stimulate program proposals from the states.[16, 17] For example, the types of abuse which do occur in some frequency include the following:

- the provision of drugs and alcohol in return for favors from patients
- the withholding of privileges in return for favors
- slapping and kicking when patients are felt no longer manageable
- physical handling of patients (e.g. restraining them) when other means are possible
- maintenance of indecent physical facilities
- verbal harassment (threats, etc.)
- general threats of harm if patients will not behave "appropriately"

The instances in which they occur range from direct, open and repeated to the occasional subtle "shaping of discipline."

There are three types of sources for abuse:

1. staff persons
2. the environment
3. the treatment program.

With regard to the first, there are a range of causes. A staff person may run out of patience, may not understand how to handle a given patient, or may, because of personal problems, begin slapping or kicking patients as a result of his own anger or frustration. In the second type, the whole institutional ward or treatment environment becomes abusive of patients.[18, 19] For example, there may not be enough treatment staff, enough toilets, enough private space, etc. In the third type, a treatment which normally appears to have some rationale is used in such a way that it becomes abusive.[20-24] For example, in a case reviewed later in this chapter, there was repeated administration of electroshock treatment when it was both physically harmful and emotionally terrifying to a patient.

Why does the abuse, particularly the staff-initiated abuse, happen? There are at least three major reasons why the majority of abuse occurs. First, certain staff are not suited for the work. They have neither the patience nor the understanding to deal with people who are at that time in their life not in control. Second, the stresses of the task may overcome any given staff person's level of tolerance. Although the staff may be suited to the work, some patients in certain phases of their disability may overcome anyone's tolerance. At that time, the staff person handles the problem in a way that he would not normally, i.e., in an abusive manner. Third, some staff persons *do* have a lack of knowledge of alternative means of handling patients. Patients are slapped or kicked because there are literally no other alternatives which quickly come to mind for handling a crisis situation.

The one direct way to combat the staff-based cause of abuse is to ensure that the staff selected are suited to the work. Ideally, the work should be a chosen career with individual knowledge and a definite understanding of its requirements. Not all prospective candidates can be adequately screened before entry, so some continuing review process must be developed.

Second, it is important to ensure that staff have knowledge of alternative means of handling violent or extremely frustrating patients, e.g., those who perseverate on certain topics, or who continually make a "pest" of themselves in the perception of the staff. Frustration develops because there is no way to manage the patient.

Last, there is a need to continually monitor and control the treatment situations so that staff who normally can manage are not left to do so without support when a critical situation arises. All staff will eventually reach a breaking point in their tolerance.

The critical issue in identifying abuse situations is that all actions must be justifiable in terms of the individual patient's treatment plan and the managing of that patient in any emergency situation. If staff can relate the emerging incident to both the treatment plan and the handling of the situation while realizing they will be responsible for actions taken, some abuse can be prevented. A sincere effort to manage a crisis in a way helpful to patients is usually apparent by the actions taken; the results are continued application and ready availability of alternatives. As demonstrated in the cases presented here for review, the extremes of abuse are quite easy to identify in a retrospective review.

PHYSICAL ABUSE

Definition.   Patients have the right to be free from physical abuse generated by the treatment setting, by the staff, and/or by the treatments.

The purpose of this abuse prevention right is to ensure that the treatment system (broadly defined) does not physically harm a patient. The physical abuse, as noted, can derive from individual staff persons, from certain treatment methods, and/or from the whole treatment setting. The reduction of abuse levels which already exist to their total elimination through prevention is brought about by interrupting these causes.

The right is protected and abuse is reduced and prevented through three processes. First, a monitoring process should be established to continually review the level of staff stress, the level of staff training with regard to problematic crisis situations, and the "difficulty" level of individual patients. Staffing ratios which are too low increase staff stress which, in turn, affects the type and extent of abuse experienced by patients. Without significant levels of continuing staff training, particularly with regard to alternative ways of handling difficult patients, patients will be the recipients of retribution abuse. Even well-trained, experienced staff have trouble handling certain patients in extremely agitated states.

Second, it is necessary to monitor the environment in which patients live to ensure that abuses are not present in the daily physical context of their treatment setting. The environmental issues are covered in a separate chapter. It is important to maintain significant and continuing monitoring of the environment. An environmental right violation can transcend what may be perceived as an important, but not devastating, right violation. For example, some hospital wards are not air conditioned. Several days of heat is unbearable. Thus, the placement of elderly patients in wards with temperatures above 90° for several weeks in the summer constitutes an abuse by the treatment setting.

Third, it is important to monitor the treatment process to ensure that all treatments, particularly radical treatments, are not carried to extremes. For example, a time-out chair may be effective. Using it repeatedly for days or weeks is abuse founded in retribution, ignorance of alternatives, or a continuing rationale for that single treatment, which is suspect.

The outcome of the abuse right is simply to prevent physical harm to patients which was not intended to be an outcome of their treatment. Presumably, patients were informed at admission and at the onset of treatment about the outcomes of their participation in treatment. It is certain that physical abuse was not one of the intended outcomes. The freedom from abuse right prevents this outcome from evolving as a part of a flawed treatment process, an aversive environment, or staff persons who respond inappropriately due to stress or lack of training.

Case 1. Patient Robert Jones has been on the ward for 12 years from the age of 15.* He has learned the system of varying confinement levels and has

---

*Fictitious case.

been discharged a number of times over the 12 years, always returning as a result of some acting out in the community. Documented in the patient's clinical record was a continuing behavior problem relating to repetition of requests for various activities, e.g., a daily pass, cigarettes, food, magazines, newspapers, friends, family, etc. When outside the hospital, the patient was repeatedly cited for "bothering" supermarket managers, landlords, etc., for a range of requests which were incessantly presented.

In the situation which developed, the patient made repeated requests to go outside even though he had been notified of confinement to the ward. At first when denied the requests, the patient merely restated them. However, the patient suddenly shifted the request to cigarettes, repeating again numerous times. By "repeated" the clinical log shows that there were 15 to 20 requests from him within a short period of time. With some of the requests, there was a simultaneous repetition without waiting for the negative response. This action continued for one whole day beginning at approximately 10:00 a.m.

After 7 difficult hours, a psychiatric aide on the second shift at 10:00 p.m. slapped the patient twice after the sixth cigarette request in one five-minute period. The patient filed a complaint of physical abuse. The staff person was reprimanded for his physical slapping.

Notes.   There were several problems with the staff person's response. He was a veteran with 12 years on the unit. The abuse occurred because: (1) he was emotionally exhausted, with diminished patience and tolerance; and (2) he admitted that he had a momentary lack of an alternative method of handling the task (of quieting the patient).

The problem here was not one of the staff person's being interested in the task, or understanding it. Nor was it a problem of initial lack of training. The aide was continually cited over a number of years for outstanding performance. However, in this case, the combined situation, i.e., a difficult patient and a momentary (perhaps continuing) lack of alternative ways of handling the task, led to physical abuse. Certainly the patient in this case recovered from the abuse and no permanent damage was done. However, as demonstrated by several other cases, that is not always the outcome.

Additionally, it is not the severity of the harm done which is the sole criteria for the judgment of abuse. Permission to slap opens the possibility that other physical interventions would also be tolerated. Severity of harm would then increase until organizational limits were set through some disciplinary action.

PSYCHOLOGICAL ABUSE

Definition.   Patients have the right to be free from psychological abuse generated by the setting, by staff, and by certain treatment methods.

The general purpose of this right is to ensure that the setting, the staff, and the treatment methods do not harm patients. This right recognizes the existence of the psychological aspect of patient life. Importantly, it considers the now accepted idea that settings and behaviors can inflict psychological pain without a physical mechanism. When a patient is slapped, kicked, or otherwise abused, it is readily apparent that the patient is physically harmed. There are, however, certain situations and methods which staff and other patients can willingly or unwillingly use to inflict pain or harm on a patient. Playing on the patient's fears and anxieties about certain treatments, such as electroshock, is a major way in which patients are harmed.

As noted in the section under physical abuse, there are three processes used to avoid or reduce the level of psychological abuse. First, monitoring is used to examine the level of staff stress, the level of staff training, and the difficulty level of individual patients. Each of these situations can be a cause of psychological abuse as easily as they can the physical. For example, if staff are extraordinarily stressed by one patient with especially aversive or bizarre behaviors, they can as easily threaten to withhold the patient's discharge or to contact friends or family members about his behavior as they can slap or kick him.

The second mechanism for lowering abuse levels is a review of the environment of the treatment setting to ensure that abuses are not present in the daily context of treatment. For example, an extensive seclusion period in a small room without furniture and with only padded walls establishes an environment that is psychologically abusive of the patient. It withdraws all stimulation from that patient, creating an unreal environment unmatched to the outside. While the seclusion may have had an appropriate purpose for a brief period of time, the extension of seclusion can result in psychological abuse.

The third mechanism for lowering psychological abuse is a constant and ongoing review of the treatment process. This review is used to ensure that all treatments, particularly radical treatments with very difficult patients, are not carried to the extreme. For example, the use of a timeout chair may be very effective. However, using it repeatedly for days or weeks is abuse founded in ignorance of alternatives or of the appropriate rationale for that treatment method. The continuance of the mechanism well beyond its limited usefulness results in an exposure to its definition as abuse.

The outcome of these processes for monitoring the behaviors of the treatment system and individual staff is the prevention of psychological harm to patients which is not a part of the intended treatment.

Case 1. This case involves an overweight woman who had been a patient in the state hospital for some time (14 years).* During hospitalization, she had

---

*Fictitious case.

been on numerous diets but none were followed. Despite a weight of 270 pounds, the woman continually ate pizzas and drank cokes yet remained very sensitive about her weight. She was again attempting to diet as a part of an intensive treatment plan and was beginning to be successful.

One day she purchased a large pizza and a quart of coke from the patient-run food store. A nurse, who herself had unsuccessfully attempted to diet, began to talk loudly about the patient's lack of control of her eating. The patient remarked that it was her own business and not the nurse's (who was not part of the patient's treatment team). The nurse remarked that "all patients were her business."

The patient suggested the nurse "buzz off." The nurse then began to repeat her assertion in loud, offensive, and profane language: "you - - - pig, you keep filling your - - - mouth with food. When the - - - do you think you'll lose weight." She continued berating the patient for some 10 minutes. The shouting so upset the patient that she dropped the soda, breaking the bottle. She became too upset to eat and in an act of defiance, threw her pizza at the nurse. The nurse called for attendant support to help in physically restraining the patient and asked to have her put into seclusion for acting out, which was done. The patient filed a complaint citing psychological abuse.

Notes. What was the problem in this case? The questions are: Is the nurse suited to the work, particularly when patients present problems closely related to hers? Was this an isolated case of the nurse's relations to patients or a typical one? This was clearly a case of psychological harassment stemming from an individual staff person's behavior, not the treatment setting or a part of the treatment plan.

A single incident such as this is a cause for disciplinary treatment such as a reprimand or suspension. The incident should also be reviewed by ward staff with a general reiteration of the dynamics of the situation and the resulting abuse of the patient. The loss of a pizza and coke are not overly devastating and may have been helpful to the patient in this case. But a court would view the resulting seclusion of the patient as a serious violation of the patient's right to liberty. In effect, inappropriate staff action resulted in a denial of a fundamental constitutional right—freedom. The court would also review the "treatment effects" of the staff behavior and would obviously find them wanting—perhaps exposing the staff (personally) or the organization to malpractice damages.

COMBINED PSYCHOLOGICAL AND PHYSICAL ABUSE

Definition. Patients have the right to be free from psychological and physical abuse that are simultaneously delivered.

This definition of the right is a combined repetition of the previous discussion. While the idea of a combined abuse method is obvious, the linking of physical and psychological methods is particularly onerous. In some instances, the combination of staff and treatment service aspects results in the abuse of patients, and stems from a lack of awareness of the patient's physical and psychological responses to certain treatments.

In the extreme, the problem is malpractice and subject to severe disciplinary action. However, the lesser degrees are harmful, and staff must be made sensitive to them. The following case is an extreme, but it does illustrate abuse stemming from malpractice and the combination of physical and psychological elements in one unfortunate incident.

Case 1.   Pettis v. *State* involves an action for damages for personal injury by Pettis, a state mental hospital patient, for multiple fractures sustained as a result of the administration of a series of shock treatments.[25] Pettis was committed to the Central Louisiana State Hospital by the court from an application signed by his sister. He previously received treatment as an outpatient in a mental health center at Rustin and as an inpatient at Confederate Memorial Hospital in Shreveport.

The staff diagnosed Pettis as schizophrenic, chronic, undifferentiated type and assigned him to the intensive care unit. After drug treatment failed, his physicians decided to administer shock treatments. Pettis received four shock treatments on May 21, May 24, May 26 and May 28. Records show that Pettis complained of back and shoulder pain after the second shock treatment, that he was confused concerning his environment after the third treatment, and that following the fourth treatment, he exhibited slow movement and confusion.

Pettis continued to complain of pain in his back, arms and legs. Records indicate that movement of his arms and legs was nonexistent. X-rays taken after the fourth shock treatment were not reviewed by a physician until May 31. The X-rays clearly indicated, and the physician noted, fractures of the bodies of three thoracic vertebrae. Examination of Pettis on June 1 by a physician followed. No further X-rays were taken. On June 4, a general practitioner was called to examine Pettis because his stomach was swollen and distended. Pettis was transferred to the medical-surgical unit of the hospital. Further X-rays revealed fractures of the left and right shoulder and of the hips. All evidenced signs of healing. The X-ray report noted that it appeared the injuries had occurred at approximately the same time. Pettis was transferred to a second hospital where surgery was performed on both hips. He claims that he has never fully recovered from the fractures and that he is totally disabled as a result of this incident.

Pettis received no tranquilizer or paralyzing drug prior to the shock treatment. Administration of such a drug normally prevents fractures from occurring during shock treatment. Defendants testified that rather than examine each patient prior to treatment, they rely on a "24-hour report" compiled by the nurses who note any complaints by patients. The physicians responsible for the shock treatments testified that no notations were registered on the 24-hour report. No contradictory evidence was presented at trial.

The court found that since Pettis did not have any fractures prior to May 21, but that he did have several following May 28, the breaks resulted from the shock treatments. The court concluded that despite the negligence of the nurse in failing to inform the doctor of plaintiff's complaint, the doctor had the duty of determining whether the plaintiff was experiencing pain as a result of the shock treatments prior to administering further treatments. This was basically a malpractice suit where the doctors and hospital were found to be negligent. The second reporting reversed the court's decision to hold the state immune. In conclusion, the doctor, the hospital and the state were held liable for Pettis' injuries.

Notes. In the terms of the law, this is basically a malpractice suit which stems from the physician's lack of review of the patient's situation. It can also be identified as an abuse case in which physical and psychological pain are rendered to the patient because of inappropriate treatment methods. One view is that abuse is an alternative way of viewing malpractice in situations similar to this.

In many cases of abuse, staff are in effect rendering nontherapeutic "treatments" or are behaving in ways which are not therapeutic for the patient (either physically or psychologically). As a result, the patients suffer physical and psychological harm because the staff members are not able to identify appropriate, professional, medically accepted treatment practices. It can be safely assumed that the treatment staff knew of alternatives to the administration of electroshock when physical injuries had been rendered but did not use them. It is, therefore, pure negligence with exposure to considerable liability. In other cases, abuse is the result of ignorance of alternatives.

SUMMARY

What is the underlying point of the foregoing discussion on physical and psychological abuse? The point is that patients are vulnerable to both physical and psychological harm. They are often less able to defend themselves against the physical and psychological attacks of others. While abuse is never appropriate, it does not happen when people have the ability to defend themselves, including the power to make change or force restitution. Patients frequently do not have these powers by virtue of their disability. Treatment staff are, therefore, under a greater obligation to ensure that abuse does not occur. It is recognized as a continuing professional and public health problem.[26, 27]

In summary, abuse is due to the following:

1. a mismatch between a given staff person and a mental health service task;
2. an accumulation of stresses or acute situational stress which overcome staff patience and rational responses to the task?
3. a lack of knowledge of alternative means of managing the task in a high-stress situation;
4. a continuation of a service procedure which is causing discomfort to a patient without rigorous or thorough review of rationale and with the absence of alternatives;
5. the ongoing existence of an environmental setting which is not therapeutically helpful to patients.

The mechanism for abuse reduction/elimination is a continual monitoring of each of these causal areas. More than any other right, the patient has the right to be free from abuse, the ultimate negative in rendering treatment services.

REFERENCES

1. Belknap, I., *Human Problems of the State Mental Hospital,* New York: McGraw-Hill, 1956, pp. 191–195.
2. Barton, R., *Institutional Neurosis,* Bristol, England: John Wright & Sons, 1966.
3. Freedman, J., "Encouraging Staff to Report Cases of Abuse," *Hospital & Commun. Psychiatry,* **30**(9) Sept. 1979, p. 636.
4. Armstrong, B., "A Question of Abuse: Where Staff and Patients' Rights Collide," *Hosp. & Community Psychiatry,* **30**(5) May 1979, p. 348.
5. Schwitzgebel, R.L. and Schwitzgebel R.K., *Law and Psychological Practice,* New York: John Wiley & Sons, 1980, p. 48.
6. *Willowbrook I,* 357 F. Supp. 752, 764 (E.D. N.Y. 1973); *Welsch v. Likins,* 373 F. Supp. 487, 502–503 (D. Minn. 1974).
7. *Hamilton v. Love,* 328 F. Supp. 1182 (E.D. Ark. 1971); *Rhen v. Malcolm,* 371 F. Supp. 594, 628 (S.D. N.Y. 1974), aff'd. 507 F. 2d 333 (2 Cir. 1974).
8. *Brenneman v. Madigan,* 343 F. Supp. 128, 133 (N.D. Cal. 1972).
9. *Hamilton v. Schiro,* 338 F. Supp. 1016, 1017 (E.D. La. 1970).
10. *Willowbrook I,* 357 F. Supp. 752, 765 (E.D. N.Y. 1973).
11. *Roberts v. State,* 307 N.E. 2d 501, 505 (Ind. Ct. App. 1974).
12. *Kesselbrenner v. Anonymous,* 33 N.Y. 2d 161, 350 N.Y.S. 2d 889, 892 (Ct. App. 1973).
13. Coye, J.L., Clifford, D., "A One Year Report on Rights Violations Under Michigan's New Protection System," *Hosp. & Community Psychiatry,* **29**(8), Aug. 1978, p. 528.
14. Ziegenfuss, J.T., "First Year Assessment of the Rights Advisor Program at Harrisburg State Hospital," Office of Client Rights, Department of Public Welfare, Harrisburg, Penna. 1982, 52 pp.
15. Notes & News, "Michigan Mental Health Department Trying to Eliminate Abuse in Mental Retardation Facilities," *Hospital & Community Psychiatry,* **29**(9) Sept. 1978, p. 621.
16. Office of Human Development Services Request for Proposals, Department of Health and Human Services, Washington, D.C. 1981.

17. Charette, J., Ziegenfuss, J.T., Byron, L., "A Patient Representative Program Model for Abuse Reduction," Concept Paper, Office of Client Rights, Dept. of Public Welfare, Harrisburg, Pa., January 1982, 13 pp.

18. Belnap, op. cit., (item no. 1).

19. Barton, op. cit., (item no. 2).

20. Spece, R.G., "Conditioning and Other Technologies Used to 'Treat'? 'Rehabilitate'? 'Demolish'? Prisoners and Mental Patients." *South Carolina L. Rev.*, 1972, **45**, 616–684.

21. Thomas, S.P., "Uses and Abuses of Electric Convulsive Shock Therapy," *J. Psychiat. Nursing and Mental Health Services,* Nov. 1978, p. 17.

22. Regestein, Q., Nurawski, B., Engle, R., "A Case of prolonged reversible dementia associated with abuse of electro convulsive therapy," *J. Nerv. Ment. Dis.,* **161**(3):200–203, 1975.

23. Pilette, P.C., "The Tyranny of Seclusion: A Brief Essay," *J. Psychiatric Nursing and Mental Health Services,* October 1978, p. 19.

24. Soloff, P.H., "Physical Restraint and the Non-psychotic Patient: Clinical and Legal Perspectives," *J. Clinical Psychiatry,* 1979(Jul), **40**(7), 302–305.

25. *Pettis* v. *State Dept. of Hospitals,* 336 So 2nd 521.

26. Sluyter, G.V., Cleland, C.C., "Resident Abuse: A Continuing Dilemma," *American Corrective Therapy J.,* 1979 (July-Aug.), **33**(4), 99–102.

27. Justice, B., Duncan, D.F., "Child Abuse in terms of a Public Health Model," *Mental Health & Society,* 1977 4(1-2) p. 110–114.

10
Money and Property

This chapter considers patients' rights to manage and control their own money and property. A very real concern for patients is what happens to money and valuables accumulated over many years. Patients enter the treatment system with both cash and valuables that are too frequently lost or stolen. Loss is an obvious negative side effect of securing treatment—their property must be protected.

Patients have all the money and property rights of other citizens. All citizen rights are maintained by patients both prior to their involvement with the treatment unit and while in that unit, unless they are specifically limited for clinical or administrative reasons, or through actions of the court. When restricted, the limitations must have a rationale, time limits, and adequate notice for the patient to understand what is happening and to prepare for and/or dispute the limitation.

Specifically, the treatment system must safeguard money and property by establishing procedures which guarantee that patients have the right to:

- access to their money and property
- safekeeping of their money and property
- purchasing and receiving money and property
- receipts for money and property
- safe storage of their money and property
- freedom from limitations on the use of their money and property, and
- public guardians if they are incapable of protecting their own money and property.

The treatment system must ensure these rights by first establishing protective organizational processes with regular monitoring to check on performance.

If these protection processes require special equipment, procedures, or personnel, then the treatment setting must provide them. A simple, but important point is that the high cost of paperwork and guardian personnel is not sufficient rationale for disregarding money and property rights.

Some states provide formal guardianship services for patients, while others more or less automatically gain some level of authority over patient property.[1] This institutional authority acts as a check and balance to prevent patient dissipation of assets, and it helps to ensure that the institution is compensated for services rendered.[2]

Those states that gain property control without a formal adjudication of patient incompetency must face the risk of litigation based on their conflict of interest—protecting patient monies and maximizing institutional returns for services rendered. Pennsylvania had that problem; but as a result of litigation, the state first organized a patient investment program, then a formal guardianship program.[4] Other states have also changed expropriation policies.[5] In addition, federal regulations now support money and property protection.[6]

The amounts of patient money in smaller treatment units is minimal, and business management for patients is limited. But in larger systems, the level of money can be quite significant. For example, the system in Pennsylvania manages approximately 25 million dollars under its guardianship system. When viewed as a total, that is an appropriate sum for safekeeping!

Organizational procedures are not intended to lose the individual patient in a complex process of steps and critical elements. A dominant theme in patient money and property management should be patient consultation and participation in every decision. The position is derived from Smiddy's agreement with Tribe.[7]

"The presence of these [procedural due process] safeguards will also provide the individual who is affected by the proceedings with an opportunity to participate in the process by which decisions concerning his future are made. This opportunity embodies the elementary idea that to be a *person,* rather than a thing is at least to be *consulted* about what is done with one!"[8]

This chapter also considers dissipation of assets, beneficiaries, and liability assessment as the final areas of patient money and property considerations. To reduce the redundancy of the purposes of this set of rights, the list cited above (access, safekeeping, purchasing, etc.) are combined and addressed jointly.

BEFORE ADMISSION TO TREATMENT CENTER

Definition. Prior to hospitalization, or entrance to any part of the treatment system, patients retain all generally accepted rights to money and property.

The prevailing standards of protection of citizen money and property pertain to patients as well as to all other citizens. The purpose of this right is to ensure that prospective patients are not prematurely restricted with respect to their money and property in preparation for their involvement with the treatment system. Neither family, friends, nor treatment personnel may acquire or manipulate a person's money and property under the rationale of mental disability, unless the state provides for such authority by the treatment setting, or there is a finding of incompetency.

Prospective patients retain access to money and property, have continuing rights to purchase and receive what they want, should receive safe storage with receipts, and, until clinical judgment is formed regarding the harmfulness of the patient's property, patient use of property should be free from limitations.

The outcome of this set of money and property rights is that control remains patient-centered, with limitations only occurring after formal involvement with the hospital or treatment center. Then, as will be demonstrated, the limitations are subjected to the constraints of due process and follow-up review.

Case 1. In one case, litigation was filed by a 45-year-old woman who owned considerable property.* Because of certain traumatic incidents, she suffered what two psychiatrists termed a nervous breakdown. Mrs. Jones applied to a private mental hospital for admission. At the admission conference, Mrs. Jones was interviewed regarding her present difficulties and her history. She was also asked several questions which seemed to be probing into the extent of her estate.

At the conclusion of the interview, she was informed that there was space in the center and that she could be accepted immediately. She needed to sign several release forms regarding confidential information and a form which entitled the center to bill all costs to the patient. In addition, a form was included which provided Power of Attorney to the center in the event that in the judgment of their clinical staff Mrs. Jones was incompetent to handle her own affairs. Fortunately, Mrs. Jones was accompanied by an attorney who recommended that she not sign the form since once within the treatment center she would be unable to control what happened to her. The treatment center then replied that they had no space available.

Notes. In this case, a private treatment center requested control of money and property from the patient. She was already under considerable stress from determining how to control her personal affairs, particularly her money and perhaps management of her property while she was in treatment. There is no absolute evidence that Mrs. Jones' property was in potential jeopardy beyond the bills she would accrue while receiving service. There was, however, sufficient concern for the power she was giving away to question whether her money and property rights were sufficiently protected by due process. While the center has every right to expect realistic assurances (including formal signatures) that they will receive payment for services rendered, the control of the property and the benefits to the organization could potentially go well beyond reimbursement for

---

*Fictitious case.

services. When the organization gains control, it is necessary to rely on their "fairness" in balancing the interests of the organization with the interests of the patient. Unfortunately, the balance is inherently hard to maintain and too often favors the organization, with little recourse for the patient without power.

MONEY AND PROPERTY RIGHTS
INSIDE THE SERVICE SYSTEM

Definition. Patients, once inside the treatment system, have the following rights regarding money and property:

- the right to safekeeping of their money and property
- the right of access to their money and property
- the right to purchase and receive money and property
- the right to receipts for their money and property
- the right to storage of their money and property
- the right to be free from limitations on the use of their money and property
- the right to be free from theft, loss, and destruction of their money and property.

The purpose of this right is to reinforce the understanding that once in the care of the treatment center or hospital, it is the responsibility of these organizations to maintain the safety of money and property. It is impossible to protect against all potential violations, but some degree of "reasonableness" must prevail in the organization's procedures.

This notion of "reasonableness" particularly concerns involuntary patients who have to depend on the institution almost solely for money and property protection. Two commentators, Samuel Brackle and Ronald Rock, have noted the following difficulties:

"Under many of the present involuntary hospitalization statutes no provision is made for a proper inquiry at the time of hospitalization to ascertain whether the patient has any business or property interests. The timely discovery of these interests may be very important to the preservation of the patient's property rights. To guard against the possibility that these interests may be overlooked, particularly in non-judicial proceedings, statutes should require that at the time of the hospitalization a prompt and thorough investigation be made to determine if there are any such business or property interests."[9]

Thus, the task of protecting the patients' money and property rights begins at the point of first contact with the treatment center. Involuntarily committed patients are particularly troublesome in that they are usually not "planned" admissions with the result that no plan for their money and property exists. There is, however, no security in the assumption that voluntary patients plan for their money and property management needs. Often they do not.

This comment leads us to ask how money and property rights are to be protected. There are several processes to accompany the investigation noted above:

- a thorough assessment of the patient's money and property management needs
- equipment and rooms for money and property storage which must be guarded and/or monitored
- receipts which should be provided when money and property are stored
- access to money and property which should be constrained only by administrative limitations (e.g. work times)
- a guaranteed responsibility for replacement of "disappearing" items whether money or property
- due process control of the patient's money and property which should rest with the organization.

In short, the organization must provide the equipment such as safes, and property storage rooms to ensure protection. Second, it must establish a monitor or guardian of patient valuables to ensure safekeeping and to provide patients with access.

The outcome of this group of rights is the establishment of a position that entering treatment for mental disability does not jeopardize a patient's money and property. Certainly, few persons would *voluntarily* agree to treatment if they were to be informed that when entering treatment they were likely to lose money or other valuables to theft or neglect.

The cases which follow outline sample problems patients have encountered in securing safekeeping for money and property while in treatment.

Case 1.   Nick McAuliffe v. *Carlson.*   The issues involved in this case concern fees and procedures which the State of Connecticut imposes on a select percentage of mentally ill persons.[10]   Plaintiff McAuliffe was sentenced to serve one year in the Hartford Community Correctional Center after conviction of breaking and entering. He served 218 days of his sentence in a state mental health facility. After his release, McAuliffe was billed by the state for his stay in the mental health facility a total of $1,098.07.

Later, the court committed McAuliffe to Norwich Hospital, a state hospital for the mentally ill. While at Norwich he deposited $150 in a patient's account, intending to save the money for future use. When he attempted to withdraw the sum, the officials informed McAuliffe that the money could not be returned. The Commissioner of Finance and Control had been appointed his

Conservator by a Connecticut statute. The $150 had been used to help pay for the Plaintiff's hospital treatment. No hearing was held to determine that McAuliffe was incompetent to handle his own affairs prior to appointing a Conservator. Normally, hearings are held.

The court decided, first, that a Connecticut statute which charged some prisoners for time spent in mental health facilities instead of jail because of the nature of their ailment, was unconstitutional. Second, the court ruled unconstitutional the Connecticut statute which permitted a Conservator to be appointed for a patient (who has assets worth less than $5,000) without the procedural safeguards of a hearing.

Notes. In this case, the treatment center attempted to *assume* incompetence on the part of the patient and to retain money which was deposited for safekeeping by the patient on his entrance to the center. The staff, in all probability, had cause for "assuming" incompetence. But without a hearing, a court will not find staff views to be above the level of untried opinions. Here we are not concerned with other patients, staff members, or outsiders appropriating the patient's money; the treatment system itself was about to do so. The system was not supported by the court because notice, hearing, and the right to legal representation were absent.

Case 2. In *Dale* v. *Hahn,* litigation focused on the commitment of Dale to Harlem Valley State Hospital under the mental hygiene law.[11] While Dale was a patient, the Director of the hospital petitioned the court to appoint a committee to manage Dale's personal and business affairs. A certificate was presented stating that both Dale and the hospital director received notice of the hearing to be held to appoint the committee. A committee was approved.

Dale alleges that the committee received $9,283.00 for her account. This sum was reduced to $5,972.00 shortly before her release due to expenses recognized by the court. After release, Dale received court certification of her fitness to handle her own affairs.

When Dale initiated the litigation (calling the New York State statute unconstitutional for lack of due process and invasion of her privacy right), she had still not received the balance of her estate. The court noted that since the patient was notified of her hearing, due process requirements were met. The court also stated that a connection between mental illness and incompetence in handling business affairs was not an unreasonable assumption. Dale had no standing (i.e. no present harm) to bring this suit since the balance of her estate would be returned after a court hearing.

Notes. In this case, the hospital correctly used the requirements of notice and hearing and were thus able to bill the patient for services provided her during her stay at the hospital. The court also supported the idea that a connection between mental illness and incompetence to handle business affairs was not an unreasonable assumption. However, this assumption must be scrutinized in each individual case since variations in disabled patients' competencies are great.

GUARDIANSHIP

Definition. Patients have the right to appointment of a guardian if they are unable to manage their own money and property.

The purpose of this right is to ensure that those patients unable to manage their own affairs, and particularly those adjudicated incompetent, have someone to manage their money and property interests. This is not an automatic occurrence but a step process in which there first must be demonstrated cause for the appointment of the guardian. In most cases, they are not provided unless certain criteria are met such as minimal levels of assets (e.g., $1500 or $2000). The elements of guardianship and incompetency individually, as well as their interrelationship, have been discussed in some detail, and periodically readdressed.[13-15]

The process of guardianship appointment is fairly complex in the systems operating in many of the states. However, five elements are somewhat common and necessary, including the following:

- a formal documentation of the need for guardianship
- identification of an appropriate guardian
- notice of a hearing that guardianship will be reviewed
- court adjudication with attorney representation for the patient during these proceedings
- establishment of procedures for periodic review and reversal.

The process requires that staff members define and provide evidence for the need for guardianship. They also must identify someone who can fill that function, either a treatment-system person who regularly provides the service or someone outside the system. Following preliminary steps, the guardianship process must include approval of the courts, with the patient having rights to notice, a hearing, and attorney support. This is in total the procedural due process requirement of testing for whether liberty and property are at stake and for defining which safeguards are required in each case.[16-17]

There is currently a move to develop a continuum of guardianship responsibility from total to what is termed "limited guardianship."[18] The new limited programs begin to recognize the variation in patient characteristics. The ultimate goal is that: "The more individualized approach of limited guardianship could be used to offer the protections a guardian can provide while maximizing the self-reliance of the mentally retarded [and mentally disabled] individual."[19]

Also, there is currently some debate as to who has the responsibility for training patients to manage their own money and property. Some people view this as the responsibility of the mental health staff as a part of their counseling-educating role. Others feel that the guardians should provide the service. But there is little debate that money management training is needed. As a result, training program models are being developed.[20]

The outcome of this guardianship service, and the special process by which it is provided to the patient, is insurance that those incapable of protecting their own money and property have help in doing so, but only when that help is required. The following cases involving money, property, and guardianship questions will illustrate both the needs and some of the difficulties that can arise in this area.

Case 1.   Rubinstein v. *Dr. Pepper Company* involves a contract disagreement between a bottling franchise and the Dr. Pepper Company.[21]   The defense contended that the plaintiff had signed an agreement giving up his license as a bottling franchise of the Dr. Pepper Company and releasing the Dr. Pepper Company of all future liabilities. In return, the plaintiff received a considerable amount of money.

The plaintiff claimed that he was mentally incapacitated at the time he signed the agreement to sell his franchise. The court held that a contract signed by a person claiming to be mentally deficient, but not under guardianship, absent fraud or knowledge of incapacity by the other party, is not void. It can become void only when the allegedly deficient party takes the proper steps to cancel the contract. He must give back all benefits received under the contract. Since the plaintiff-patient did not give back the money received for the franchise, his claim that the contract is null and void for incapacity was not upheld by the court.

Notes.   In this case, the patient sought to have a contract rescinded by using the position that he was incompetent and in need of guardianship. Presumably, the guardian would have recognized the disparity in the contract and recommended that the patient not go through with the franchise agreement. However, there were other circumstances.

To void a contract, the condition must be returned to its status before the contract. The money was not returned, so the court found that the patient was perhaps not serious about his incompetent status and/or that he was using it to reverse a bad business decision. Additionally, there was no evidence that the other side took advantage of his incompetence during the contract process.

The case also illustrates the importance of establishing guardianship needs at the time that a person first becomes a patient. Had that been done in this case, the guardian might have rejected the sale or, at the least, delayed the contract until the patient was better able to consider the long term impact. The lack of a guardianship assessment led to litigation.

Case 2.   Vecchione v. *Wohlgemuth* is a civil rights action brought by Mrs. Vecchione to contest the constitutionality of sections of the Pennsylvania Mental Health and Retardation Act of 1966.[22] One section provided that persons receiving diagnosis, treatment, care, and rehabilitation in state mental hospitals are responsible for all costs thereof. Another section stated that anybody admitted who had been adjudicated incompetent is liable to have all of his possessions and property seized by the revenue agent at the hospital without a prior court hearing. The cost of care is then deducted from the seized property.

The revenue agent must present prior notice and a judicial hearing before satisfying any claims from property of those admitted patients adjudged incompetent. The latter section further stipulated that any incompetent patient with assets of $2500 or more is entitled to have a guardian appointed to protect his interests, while a patient with less than $2500 in assets is not entitled to a guardian.

The plaintiff contended that the classification system violated the equal protection clause and also denied those declared incompetent due process of law by allowing the seizure of private property without notice or hearing. The court agreed.

Notes.   In this case, the state treatment system wanted the ability to seize patient money and property to ensure that they were reimbursed for services rendered. The outcome of the case upheld the concept that due process of law is required whenever private property is to be seized. Due process requires such elements as notice of a hearing, a right to be heard, and representation by an attorney. The effect of due process is to ensure that the patient has the opportunity to dispute the state's seizure of his property.

The case demonstrates that the court will support the patient's right to control his or her money and property to as great an extent as possible. "Even" incompetent patients have a right to due process in order to ensure that the *balancing* of both patient and treatment setting interests occurs.

DISSIPATION OF ASSETS

Definition.   Patients have the right to be protected from dissipation of their assets.

This is a rights problem which particularly involves judgments and values. What is the level of assets, if any, to be dissipated before a concern is raised? The purpose of the right is to ensure that a patient's actions to distribute his money and property are not driven primarily by his disability.

How is this right protected? Seemingly inappropriate actions to dissipate are confronted with an initial effort to "persuade" the patient of the inadvisability. If the patient should persist in distributing money or property, staff must take formal action to protect the patient's assets from actions derived from the patient's illness. Although some patients are initially and persistently angry about the intervention, many are grateful that they were not allowed to disburse a lifetime of accumulations in a period of illness.

If persuasion is ineffective and formal action required, there are several prerequisite steps:

- the patient must be identified as financially incompetent with evidence to document the position
- a guardian must be identified
- the court must be petitioned for adjudication of incompetency
- incompetency status must be reviewed periodically (i.e. at different time periods according to each state's statutes).

The formal action can restrict the patient's spending to limits set by a guardian.

The outcome of this interest in assets is that reasonable precautions are taken to ensure that patient assets are not lost primarily due to the patient's mental status during his illness.

Case 1.   In re: Turrell. This case involved application for the appointment of a guardian for a patient, Turrell.[23]   Mr. Turrell was an 85-year-old gentleman who in his younger days had been quite successful and had possessed an exceptionally keen and retentive mind. Before a guardian can be appointed, the prospective patient must be determined to be: (1) incompetent, and (2) unable to deal at arms length with people because of the incompetency. In this case, there was conflicting testimony.

On one side, it was presented that Mr. Turrell had spent over $9,000 in non-household expenses during the previous two years, including a total of $2,000 to a woman for no apparent reason. On the other side, there was testimony that Mr. Turrell had purchased a diamond ring for less than the normal selling price, that he had purchased a grave marker for only $400, and that he had made funeral arrangements for less than $1,000. The conflicting testimony thus showed him spending money "excessively" *and* being a good businessman.

Physically, the court observed that Mr. Turrell's smile was at times not normal, his eyes did not focus properly at all times, his gait and reflexes were not normal and he dropped his cane instead of laying it aside. These observations, in conjunction with the testimony, led the court to conclude that he was incompetent and could not deal at arms length (subject to undue influence) with sufficient ability to protect his money and property interests.

Notes. A part of this case involves a conflict of values. That is, does the patient have the right to distribute a certain amount of money when that money is his own? Was there sufficient evidence to demonstrate his competency to make that kind of decision? In short, was there enough accumulated evidence to demonstrate either his competency or his incompetency?

The court held that, given his personal characteristics at the time, he did not appear to the court to be able to manage his finances, including decisions to hold or to distribute his money and property. They determined that he was incompetent and appointed a guardian for him. Importantly, the patient had the protection of due process. Had he been able to convince the court of his capability, he would have been able to continue to manage his financial affairs. The proceeding served to surface a patient's problem (in controlling distribution of money) which if unchecked, could eventually have resulted in destitution.

BENEFICIARIES

Definition. Patients have the right to name their own beneficiary, or in the situation of adjudicated incompetency, have the guardian name one for them.

In general, the purpose of the beneficiary right is to ensure that patients have the right of other citizens, i.e. to pass on their money and property to persons of their own choosing. A question arises when patients are suspected of being or actually are incapable of making their own choice without being unduly influenced.

As in the other topics in this chapter, discussion with the patient may help to clarify the choice and to enable the patient to make the decision on his own. If the patient is incompetent, the decision is to be made by a court-appointed guardian. Should a change in beneficiary be the intention of the patient, a question will develop as to whether the change is stimulated by the patient's illness, particularly if a beneficiary was named prior to the onset of the illness. An adjudicated incompetent patient requires both guardian and court approval to effect the change.

The outcome of this right and the protective process is to ensure that the patient's right to name and to change beneficiaries remains. The right is aimed particularly at protecting the patient from those who want to influence the choice of beneficiaries to their own advantage.

Case 1.   Sluder v. *National Americans* is a case in which Sluder sued National Americans (a fraternal beneficiary organization) to recover installments due her as a beneficiary under a certificate issued to her sister.[24] The certificate provided that upon the death of the policyholder, the beneficiary should receive an annuity of $200 for 10 years, payable quarterly beginning on the first month after the death of the insured.

Prior to her death, Sluder's sister signed a new contract with the fraternal order. The second agreement specified that the fraternal order would pay

$20 per month to Sluder's sister, that the payment period would not exceed 24 months, and that in return Sluder's sister would turn over the certificate to the fraternal order. Further, if Sluder's sister would die prior to the expiration of 24 months, all liability of the defendant would cease. After receiving one payment, Sluder's sister died.

Sluder's argument is that her sister was mentally incompetent to agree to a second contract. The jury found that as a result of morphine injections, the deceased had hallucinations on the day the second contract was completed and, therefore, her mental condition rendered her incapable of understanding the agreement she signed. The court agreed.

Notes. Although it is not actually clear from the case, it appears that the fraternal order was to increase its gain by the shift in the contract terms of the beneficiary agreement. In its review, the court determined that the patient was not actually competent to make that sort of decision at the time in which the contract was signed. The result was that the patient's right to name a beneficiary *while fully competent* was upheld. The second contract which was developed while the patient was incompetent was denied.

The case indicates the importance of the patient's status at the time of the contract's signing. Although it may be possible at the proceeding to influence the patient in one or another direction, both the procedure and the outcome are subject to review. If full due process rights are not followed, there is a procedural problem. And if the patient is not competent on the day of the signing, that status will negate the outcome.

LIABILITY ASSESSMENT

Definition. Patients have the right to a fair assessment of their liability.

This right concerns the liability for services rendered to patients in a treatment center. The purpose of the right is to ensure that patient liabilities reflect a fair allocation of the cost of services to the patients and to their cost bearers, if any. The concern often emerges around the payment of care for involuntary admission and treatment. Who should pay? This is a difficult question, particularly in cases where the patient resisted treatment for the illness.

Since most treatment centers do not have a staff member designated to review billings, monitoring of this right is up to the patient plus family, friends, and attorney. There are very seldom formal processes to consider the accuracy or fairness of the billing system. Unless there is some special knowledge on the part of friends or family, it is usually quite difficult for them to identify a problem in liability assessment. However, the patient's caseworker, social worker, or other primary helper in the unit has some responsibility to act as the patient's advocate. Concern for the financial aspect of the patient is present in those systems where staff are asked to help the whole patient, which includes their financial needs.

The outcome of this right is the protection of patients' right to a fair assessment of costs when they are incapable of determining the fairness and accuracy of the assessment on their own.

Case 1.   In *Department of Mental Hygiene* v. *Kirchner,* the California Department of Mental Hygiene sued the administrator of the estate of a committed incompetent's daughter to recover costs for the care and maintenance of the mother in a state institution for the mentally ill.[25]   The mother was declared mentally ill by a court order and committed in January, 1953.   In suing her daughter for care and maintenance, the department relied on a statute which provides that the "husband, wife, father, mother, or children, of a mentally ill person or inebriate shall be liable for his care in a state institution of which he is an inmate."

The lower court ruled in favor of the Department, so the daughter of the estate appealed.   The appellate court reversed the ruling saying that when a state commits an individual to an institution, it is for the protection of society as a whole.   Therefore, the cost of maintaining that individual should be born by society.   To do otherwise would violate the equal protection clause.

Notes.   Here it is clear from the outcome of the case that patients placed in the treatment system primarily for the benefit of society (i.e. against their will), do not need to bear the cost of that treatment service.   That cost must be born by society, for it is society that is the initiator of the treatment service.

Do all guardians understand this point of view?   Since many incompetent patients are involuntarily hospitalized, it would seem that there would be a great number of guardians who would be able to reject payment.   Whether they are is an open question, but one which is certainly related to protection of an involuntarily committed patient's money and property.

SUMMARY

Patients have the right to manage their own money and property as any other citizen unless this is limited through court action.   The only reason for limiting this right is to protect the patient's assets.   Specifically, this right guarantees the patient:

- access to his money and property
- safekeeping of money and property
- ability to purchase and receive goods
- receipts for his money and property

- safe storage
- freedom from limits, theft, loss, or destruction of money and property
- public guardians for incompetency.

The hospital must provide the equipment, procedures and/or personnel necessary to ensure the above.

When a patient enters an institution, the institution does gain some control over the patient's assets by virtue of its responsibility to prevent dissipation and to ensure compensation within the constraints of due process. Patients usually have no plan for their money and property management needs. The process of providing a plan should include: (1) assessment of the need for management; (2) guarded equipment and rooms for storage; (3) provision of receipts for money and property; (4) access restricted only by administrative limits; and (5) responsibility for replacement.

Patients have the right to appointment of a guardian for their money and property if they are unable to manage it themselves. The procedure for appointing a guardian involves: (1) documenting the need; (2) identifying an appropriate guardian; (3) notification of the hearing at which guardianship will be reviewed; (4) court adjudicated financial incompetence with an attorney representing the patient; and (5) an established procedure for periodic review. A patient also has the right to be protected from the dissipation of his assets by his own actions. Again, financial incompetence must be adjudicated and a guardian appointed. Protection of the patient's estate includes the right to name his own beneficiaries or, if incompetent, to have his guardian name them. For incompetent patients, a change of beneficiary requires both a guardian and court action. This procedure is aimed at protecting the patient from those who want to influence his choice to their own advantage.

The patient has the right to a fair assessment of liability for services rendered. It is up to the patient, his family, and/or attorney to monitor this right. As it is extremely difficult to determine the correctness of service assessments, the case worker or other primary helper has some responsibility to act as the patient's advocate. Involuntary committment costs must be borne by society, not the family, if it was "society" that initiated the committment.

REFERENCES

1. Pennsylvania Office of Clients Rights. Guardianship Program. Department of Public Welfare, Harrisburg, Pa.
2. Lindman, F.T., McIntyre, D.M., *The Mentally Disabled and the Law,* Chicago: Univ. Chicago Press, 1961.
3. Kennedy, J.P., "Taking a New Approach to Investing Patient Money," *Hosp. & Commun. Psychiatry,* 25(3), March 1974, p. 137.
4. *Vecchione* v. *Wohlgemuth* 377 F. Supp. 1361 (E.D. Pa. 1974), 426 F. Supp. 1297 (E.D. Pa. 1977).

5. News & Notes. "Maryland, Virginia Alter Policies of Expropriating Patients' Social Security Checks," *Hosp. & Commun. Psychiatry,* **25**(2), Feb. 1973, p. 119.

6. Kapp, M.B., "Protecting the Personal Funds of the Mentally Retarded: New Federal Regulations," *Hosp. & Commun. Psychiatry* **32**(8), Aug. 1981, p. 567.

7. Notes (Smiddy, L.O.), "Guardianship for the Adult: A Need for Due Process Protections in Vermont," *Vermont L. Rev.* 4(1), Spring 1979, p. 95.

8. Tribe, L., *American Constitutional Law,* New York: McGraw-Hill, 517, A. 20 (1978).

9. Brakel, S.J., Rock, R.S., *The Mentally Disabled and the Law,* Chicago: Univ. of Chicago Press, 1971.

10. *McAuliffe v. Carlson,* 377 F. Supp. 896 (D. Conn. 1974).

11. *Dale v. Hahn,* 311 F. Supp. 1293 (S.D. N.Y. 1970).

12. Allen, R.C., Ferster, E.Z., Weihofen, H., *Mental Impairment and Legal Incompetency,* Englewood Cliffs, N.J.: Prentice Hall, Inc., 1968.

13. Mitchell, A., "Involuntary guardianship for incompetents: A strategy for legal services advocates," **12** *Clearinghouse Review* 451 (1978).

14. Langen, W., "Public guardianship protecting the interests of the ward," **2** *Law and Human Behavior* 267 (1978).

15. Alexander, G., "Premature probate: a different perspective on guardianship for the elderly," **31** *Stanford Law Review* 1003 (July 1979), (910).

15a. Note, "The Disguised Oppression of Involuntary Guardianship: Have the Elderly Freedom to Spend?" *Yale. L.J.* 676, (1964).

16. "Guardianship for the adult: a need for due process protections in Vermont," **4** *Vermont Law Review* 95 (Spring 1979).

17. *Morrissey v. Brewer,* 408 U.S. 471, 481 (1972).

18. Sanders, M.A., Wissel, K., "Limited Guardianship for the Mentally Retarded," **8** *U. Mexico L. Rev.,* 231 (1978).

19. Ibid.

20. Mueller, A., Pasternak, B., Handler, E., "Educating Deinstitutionalized Patients About Fiscal Realities," *Hosp. & Commun. Psychiatry,* **31**(7), July 1980, p. 472.

21. *Rubenstein v. Dr. Pepper Co.,* 228 F. 2d. 528 (8th Cir. 1955).

22. *Vecchione v. Wohlgemuth,* op. cit., (item no. 4).

23. *In re Turrell,* 174 Ohio St. 552, 190 N.E. 2d. 687 (1963).

24. *Sluder v. National Americans,* 101 Kan. 320, 166 Pac. 482 (1917).

25. *Dept. Mental Hygiene v. Kirchner,* 60 Cal. 2d. 716, 388 p. 2d. 720, 36 Cal. Rptr. 488 (1964).

11
Civil Rights

CIVIL RIGHTS

Civil rights are for everyone, and—contrary to some opinions and law—patients are no different. That is, these rights relate to patients as well as to all other persons—fellow American citizens. They are the rights of the social system in which both American "patients and non-patients" live. Then why are these rights included in this discussion? Are they not assumed? This chapter reviews specific civil rights which have come to be troublesome for mentally disabled persons.

These rights have become troublesome because the assumption that patients maintain them has historically not been the case.[1, 2] For example, mental health health systems specifically limit rights of access, education, compensation, voting, and contracts. Limitations are effected in some institutions by organizational policy, in others by informal organizational norms. The issues are exceedingly complex, particularly for involuntary patients. There are continuing problems in such areas as due process in commitment.[3] However, the stipulation that patients definitely have civil rights provides a basis for insuring that they do.

Civil rights for patients follows, or more accurately, should follow the list of civil rights provided to clients of the criminal justice system, an area considered to be a foundation of constitutional law. But patients and prisoners are treated quite differently:

"The analogy [between patients and prisoners] seems to deteriorate only when we realize that prisoners are incarcerated after exhaustion of complex and extensive procedures designed to insure due process of law. Even after commitment, a prisoner is entitled to recognition of certain basic constitutional rights. An inmate of a mental institution is generally accorded none of these protections. Although he has usually committed no offense, a mental patient is systematically deprived of those rights so jealously applied to the field of criminal law and deemed basic to the proper functioning of the Constitution."[3]

At the outset, then, there is a significant question concerning the degree to which patients are provided civil rights.

As noted throughout this book, the task is not to identify the problem of inadequate civil rights—that is done. Solutions are needed and are emerging. There have been substantive attempts to revise mental health procedures to reflect current thinking regarding rights for patients. For example, changes have occurred in the areas of due process and involuntary commitments.[4-7] This work is gaining increasing acceptance so that the regulations of service systems now more frequently include civil rights concerns.

The rights addressed here as civil, have several purposes which define their intent as a whole:

1. they are to maintain the patient's equality with other citizens;
2. they are to decrease the belief that patients are a different kind of citizen;
3. they are to ensure the maintenance of basic civil rights which no citizen should lose, except by judicial review; and
4. they assist patients in maintaining the "normality" of existence while in mental health treatment.

The process by which civil rights are protected is a matter of the organization's position with regard to the whole area of rights. In the diversity of the state services systems, the extent of rights accorded patients shifts by situation and by virtue of the patient's characteristics (e.g., competent-incompetent; voluntary-involuntary admission). Some states stress enforcement through advocacy systems. Others feel rights are best protected by the development of appropriate staff attitudes and knowledge of the state and federal law.[8-13] State responses widely differ. No generalization will cover adequately their varying approaches. However, there is common acceptance for emphasizing to staff that the civil rights of patients are to be protected as they would protect their own civil rights.

The outcomes of this protection are several. First, linking patients' civil rights with staff civil rights ensures that patients are accorded appropriate "citizen's rights." Patients do not automatically lose rights if there is no basis for losing them other than their patient status. Second, patients are helped to maintain their sense of sameness with the rest of the community. Third, a subgroup of American society is ensured that its rights are protected—equally—a fundamental constitutional goal of living in America. Patients are not a separate class of citizens—retention of civil rights demonstrates that they are not.

The list of rights for review could be quite long, as constitutionally based civil rights are extensive. However, there are a number which are regularly questioned and are considered to be most in need of conflict resolution:

- competency
- discrimination
- driver's license
- education
- labor and compensation
- voting

- marriage and divorce
- privacy
- religion
- sexuality
- custody
- contracts

Here, as throughout the book, there has been a studied attempt to avoid involvement in the legal analysis of each of these issues. Others have amply outlined the derivation from constitutional law and have made the point that legally some of these issues are far from a clear determination.[14, 15] Staff are advised to develop a checklist for their state's position on each. The protective processes outlined are intended to be a generic response altered by state views and individual clinical situations.

COMPETENCY DETERMINATIONS

Definition. Patients have the right to a fair and impartial determination of competency with representation of an attorney.

Competency determinations have two purposes for the patient. First, they are used to assess financial competency, i.e., a person's ability to handle his own financial affairs, independently. Second, the determination is used to assess a patient's functional competency, i.e., his ability to care for himself, including his ability to express and receive language, to move about, to learn, and to be economically self-sufficient. Two commentators, Brakel and Rock, have outlined the intentions of the determination process:

"Although it has been alleged that an adjudication of incompetency is entirely for the benefit of the individual and the protection of his estate, whereas hospitalization is intended for the protection of the public, this distinction does not withstand analysis. Many will dispute even the second part of this proposition, but more relevant for purposes of this chapter—the assertion that an adjudication of incompetency is solely for the benefit of the incompetent—is also questionable. It seems clear that incompetency and guardianship are intended not only to protect the assets of the ward for his own sake but also to prevent him from becoming a financial burden on the public. This is the admitted primary purpose of guardianship in cases of spendthrifts. In other cases of incompetency, it also appears that the state is acting to protect its treasury as well as to protect the assets of the individual. Furthermore, the public has a direct interest in other phases of incompetency. Incompetency not only deprives the individual of power to dispose of his property but also curtails other rights which may be of direct concern to the public, such as that of driving an automobile."[16]

The declaration of incompetency typically involves a hearing before a judge or master of the court (court representative). Both the patient and the treatment-setting staff are represented by attorneys who present the case for or against the incompetency position. The process is quasi-judicial. That is, it does not typically follow all the rules of the court process but is designed to allow for judicial judgment and what is known as discretionary justice.[17]

There is some question as to the reliability and validity of the competency determination process. The need for additional work is recognized. One examination revealed that there are "at least" serious questions concerning the elements of the test and the relationship of the patient's responses to the questions of actual competency.[18, 19] Most recently the question of competence has been linked with the question of the right to refuse treatment.[20, 21]

If a patient is incompetent, does he have the right to refuse treatment? And if incompetent, is he incapable of giving an informed consent to treatment or even to hospitalization? The question of the right to treatment and the right to refuse is still undecided.[22] What is clear is that both will require reliable assessment of patient competency either before admission or at the point of significant treatment decisions.[23, 24, 25]

It is not possible here to review the variety of competency assessment procedures.[26] However, note that if admission (through informed consent) and treatment refusal rights are to rest on competency assessments, the reliability and validity of the procedures in use at each unit must be thoroughly scrutinized. This scrutiny by staff can be viewed as a preventive action effected prior to a conflict over the quality of the assessment procedure.

Since an outcome must be decided with less than perfect clinical instruments and procedures, there is a need for a focus on the procedural protections of due process. The competency hearing requires the identical elements of the admissions hearing to ensure both fairness and accuracy, including:

- adequate notice of a pending hearing
- an actual hearing with patient participation
- representation/assistance by an attorney as needed
- an exploration of possible alternatives which have been considered
- an explanation of the assessment of the patient's competency including the criteria and examination results.
- explanation of the purpose and process of the proposed ruling
- an explanation of the patient's rights to a review of status at a time in the future.

These protective elements help to ensure a thoroughness of clinical review and the presence of formal due process procedural safeguards.[27] They also aid patient education and understanding of a most significant aspect of mental disability.

There are time periods after which the determination must be made again. Although this varies by state, patients can be declared either financially incompetent, functionally incompetent, or both. The outcome of the hearing and judicial review is a protection of patients' rights to handle their own affairs (both financial and personal) inside and outside of the treatment setting. Because of the potential consequence of the loss of personal affairs management, patients must be given a fair assessment with every opportunity to present their side.

Case 1.   In *Wieter* v. *Settle* the petitioner was charged with a misdemeanor violation when he allegedly gave false information about a bomb on an airplane.[28] As a result, he was confined to a medical center on the grounds of mental incompetency.

The original diagnosis of the petitioner/patient was "schizophrenic reaction, paranoid type in partial and tenuous remission manifested by hyperreligiosity, decreased self-control; life history of social instability; excessive dependency on institutional living; excessive suspiciousness and grandiose and persecutory ideas." A later examination revealed that "the prognosis of competency is good," that if the petitioner's "present improvement continues, he should be able to return to court at the time of his next N.P. Staff review in six months."

At that date, however, the patient had been confined, under arrest status, for a longer period than if he had been found guilty of the misdemeanor charge, for which he was originally taken into custody. As a result, the patient brought a habeas corpus proceeding.

At the habeas corpus proceeding, the court decided three issues, one of which was related to general competency concerns. A person is competent if it appears that the person under arrest status has the mental capacity: (1) to appreciate his presence in relation to time, place, and things; (2) to cooperate with counsel; and (3) to understand that a jury will pass on his guilt or innocence. Any psychiatric conclusion to the contrary was considered not legally binding, but at most opinion testimony.

Notes: The case demonstrates some of the court accepted criteria for competency: that the patient must have an understanding of the situation he is in with relation to time, place, and things; and that he must be able to assist in his own defense individually and through counsel. The court closely establishes the right of the judicial proceeding to determine competency—a ruling that is aided by, but does not fully depend on, psychiatric opinion. This point reinforces the view that an official ruling of incompetency is a judicial one—*not* a psychiatric one.

DISCRIMINATION

Definition.   Patients have the right to be free from discrimination resulting from their mental disability status.

The major purpose of this right is to ensure that mental patient status does not hinder patient access to jobs, housing, memberships, etc. The purposes of antidiscrimination rights are well known from the publicity regarding problems of blacks, women, and other minorities. The problems are much the same for patients.

Protection of the right does not require a special process. The protection rests on staff understanding of the potential for discrimination and on how the general public perceives information about mental disability. Unfortunately, attitudes have been, and continue to be, negative with some breakthroughs but no widespread acceptance.[29-33] When citizens, employers, and others perceive mental disability status in a negative light and act on it to deny patients their rights, then staff supplying the information are unwitting but helpful causes of discrimination.

Discrimination rarely occurs without information of mental disability status as a starting point. Therefore, the major issue is release of information identifying the patient's status as a patient. (The constraints and protections of the release of confidential information are reviewed in Chapter 6.)

Four sets of activities can help patients to avoid violation of equal treatment:

1. Assist patients in the development of strategies for avoiding discrimination in, for example, housing and employment.
2. Assist patients in identifying when they have become a victim of discrimination.
3. Assist patients in developing conflict resolution methods for their discrimination problems.
4. Provide patients with referral assistance (e.g. attorney representation) for solving discrimination problems if the above fail.

The activities can be as simple or as extensive as the situation demands. For example, staff might provide counseling with regard to the employee perceptions of the mentally disabled before and after interviews. If repeated rejections are received, staff might inquire as to reasons from the employer(s). Staff could arrange a patient-employer meeting to develop a compromise solution or a set of alternatives (other job possibilities). Last, if discrimination is apparent, staff can help patients gain redress for their grievances as other citizens are able to do.

The outcome of the rights protection here is insurance that patients are not denied employment and other opportunities based on the fact that they received services for mental disability.

Case 1. In a case summarized by the *Mental Disability Law Reporter* (*Hurley* v. *Allied Chemical Corporation*), "Joseph Hurley was denied a job as a coal miner because he had taken medication for depression. He brought suit under the West Virginia statute which prohibits denying a civil right to a person who has received services for mental illness, mental retardation, or addiction.

The Supreme Court of Appeals of West Virginia has ruled that that statute has an implied private cause of action. The court rejected the argument of Allied Chemical that private employment is not a civil right. The court went on in its discussion of the statute to add, 'this does not justify the conclusion that the employer must undertake any affirmative action or program in order to hire the individual.' "[34]

Notes: In this case, the corporation attempted to deny employment to a former patient because of his mental disability. The court held that the man did have a right to sue because he was unfairly discriminated against. A West Virginia statute specifically denies discrimination based on receipt of services for mental illness, mental retardation, or addiction.

DRIVER'S LICENSE

Definition. Patients have the right to a driver's license and to drive.

The purpose of this right is to protect a right held by other citizens and to express a concern for the patient's ability to be mobile. It is obviously difficult to travel without a means of transportation, particularly in rural or outlying suburban areas. A first thought for patients in residential care is loss of mobility. The loss of a driver's license both enhances the patient's perception of being locked in as well as his inability to travel in reality. There are other issues as noted below:

"The license to drive, whether it be a right or a privilege, is a valuable and necessary possession, the loss of which may lead to significantly diminished earnings, unemployment, or other hardship with a consequent increase in the individual's feeling of being different."[35]

But there is also a concern for society—with regard to public safety. Brakel and Rock summarize the problem succinctly:

"A person's inability to operate a motor vehicle properly can endanger public safety and is thus a matter of concern to the state. In most states mentally ill and mentally deficient persons cannot be issued drivers' licenses, and in many jurisdictions the restriction applies also to alcoholics, drug addicts, epileptics, and incompetents. Most of the statutes make the prohibition dependent upon an adjudication of the mental condition. However, it is often difficult to determine by reading the statutes whether the adjudication required is for hospitalization in a mental institution or for incompetency. Some states suspend the license as soon as a person enters a mental hospital, whether as a voluntary or a compulsory patient; some do not take action unless the patient has been involuntarily committed, and others are not concerned unless there has also been an adjudication of incompetency."[36]

For states that do restrict driving, the license loss often occurs through the incompetency process. If a patient is declared functionally incompetent, the clear implication is that he is also unable to drive an automobile. Denial of a driver's license is essential for protecting both the patient and others from that incompetence.

Short of loss of license as a part of an adjudicated incompetency process, the patient should be allowed to retain his license since there is only an undocumented "opinion" of his inability to drive. While the opinion may be firm, without a court review of the situation, the patient would be denied a civil right without due process—notice, hearing, representation. As a protective measure, staff should consider that driving is allowed unless there is denial based on a formal incompetency procedure subject to a review of its reliability and validity.

The outcome of the protection helps to ensure that patients do have the right to drive and to a driver's license unless their degree of functional competence is formally reviewed in relation to their driving ability.

Case 1. A lower court opinion, *Rodriquez* v. *Miera,* was summarized by the *Mental Disability Law Reporter:*[37]

"Plaintiff is an epileptic whose seizures are controlled by medication. She has never suffered a seizure while driving, and has never had an accident or been cited for a moving violation in the 14 years she has been driving. Plaintiff suffered a seizure in December 1977, and the Defendant Secretary of New Mexico's Department of Transportation initiated proceedings to suspend Plaintiff's driver's license. These procedures consisted of completion of a form by Plaintiff's physician, and review of the completed form by a review board composed of an orthopedic surgeon and an optometrist. Pursuant to the review board's recommendation, Defendant suspended Plaintiff's driver's license, as authorized by State law. Plaintiff challenged the suspension in a federal class action lawsuit, alleging deprivation of her license without due process.

The consent order requires Defendant to provide Plaintiff an opportunity for a hearing before an impartial decision maker prior to any deprivation of her driver's license. Plaintiff must receive reasonable notice of the hearing, must be informed of her right to counsel, must be allowed to present evidence and to confront witnesses, and must have disclosed to her the evidence and law relied upon by Defendant. The hearing must determine whether Plaintiff is suffering from 'any mental disorder or disease which would render her unable to operate a motor vehicle with safety upon the highways and has not at the time of hearing been restored to health. . .'

Similar hearings must be held prior to future deprivations of any person's driver's license on the basis of having had an epileptic seizure, except where the seizure occurred while driving. The consent order establishes procedures whereby the class members who have lost their driver's licenses because of epileptic seizures may request hearings as described above.

Finally, the consent order specifies that Defendant's actions were contrary to the Fourteenth Amendment's Due Process Clause."

Notes. This case indicates quite clearly the need for due process in any revocation of a patient's right—the subject here being a driver's license. As a license review process, this state's procedure was found to be inadequate. While the case is addressed to persons with epilepsy, the principle would apply to other types of mental and physical disability. The critical point is that denial of a driver's license is a serious deprivation both in terms of constitutional rights and the patient's practical ability to move about.

EDUCATION

Definition. Patients have the right to continue their education while in the treatment setting.

The purpose of this right is to ensure that patients are not denied education by virtue of their being in treatment and/or suffering from a mental disability. Education is a fundamental component of American society so well established that it is, in some ways, surprising to find problems in this area with regard to mentally disabled patients.[38] (See Chapter 4, p. 63 ff.)

Educational rights are particularly relevant to patients who are under 18 years of age and/or are in some phase of their primary school (here defined as schooling to achieve a high school diploma or equivalent). These rights ensure access to both academic and socialization experiences on an equal basis.[40]

The right to education is specifically targeted at those mentally disabled who were excluded from regular school systems on the basis of their disability. It also protects residents of large institutions for the mentally retarded where resources and programming levels are so low that the temptation to exclude educational activity is great.

The accepted standard for the protection is that any citizen has a right to education regardless of his or her disability. Organizations must either provide for the patient's education in the service unit or establish procedures for securing education from other providers. These procedures require formal written contracts and insurance that the education program is equivalent in content and duration to what the student would receive in a regular classroom.

The right is protected by the following considerations:

- ensuring that compensatory education is provided
- ensuring that appropriate classification and testing of the patients are provided
- ensuring the development of an educational plan
- periodic review of educational progress in relation to the educational plan
- provision of all due process rights if education is to be halted or denied.

The educational requirements mirror those for treatment in general. This right, as the others, includes the demands of due process when significant changes are made and particularly when they are contested by patient, parent, or guardian.

The outcome of this right's protection is very simply a guarantee of education for the mentally disabled.

Case 1. Mills v. *Bd. of Education of District of Columbia* was brought on behalf of seven school-aged children who had been labeled as behavioral problems, mentally retarded, emotionally disturbed, or hyperactive.[40] The suit was against the District of Columbia Board of Education for denying them an education. The court held that the Board violated the law and denied the children due process by refusing to give them specialized education.

Since this was a class action suit, all like children who are eligible for a free public education and who have been or may be excluded from the public school system have a right to specialized education at the public's expense. Several illustrations of the characteristics of the children involved in this decision are as follows:

1. Steven is eight years old, black, and resides with his mother. She is unable to afford private instruction for him and as a result he has been excluded from elementary school since his first grade year. Steven was slightly braindamaged and hyperactive and was excluded because he wandered around the classroom.

2. Janice is thirteen years old, black, and resides with her father, who is unable to afford private instruction. Janice has been denied access to public schools since reaching compulsory school attendance age because she is braindamaged and retarded, with right hemiplegia, resulting from a childhood illness.

3. Peter is twelve years old, black, and a committed dependent ward of the District of Columbia, residing at Junior Village. He was excluded from

school when he was in fourth grade because he was allegedly a "behavior problem."

All of the above were found to have a right to education at public expense. Children of this group were the cause of the litigation used to solve the problem for all such children.

Note. The fundamental concern here is that children are not excluded from the public school system because of their disability or "behavior problem." The issue transfers to those residents of public institutions for the mentally ill and the mentally retarded. If they are not provided with educational programs, they are in effect denied their public right to education. The summary point is that residents of any treatment setting must be provided with educational programming, either directly or through referral to other providers.

LABOR AND COMPENSATION

Definition. Patients have the right to work as soon as they are able, and to fair compensation for that work.

The purposes of the right are as follows: to ensure fair compensation for work, to ensure an opportunity for economic self-sufficiency, to prevent exploitation of patients, and to ensure the treatment-relatedness of any work. Although there is now common institutional regulatory support, this right derives from a history of patient work which was low-level in nature and unfairly compensated.[41, 42]

Some years ago (and perhaps in some states now), residents were compensated well below minimum wage on institution-operated farms which provided all necessary support for the institution. Patients were a part of what was labeled a "peonage system."[43, 44] To combat such exploitation, recent court rulings have stressed these requirements: that work required of patients be related to their treatment, that the work be supervised, and that work be fairly compensated with the exception that lower than minimum wages can be approved for state institutions.[45] While the regulations generated problems, institutions moved quickly to attempt to manage them.[46]

The right is protected by adherence to several guidelines for patient labor which are increasingly appearing in patient-worker regulations:[47]

1. work is not mandatory but voluntary
2. work must be agreed to without coercion according to the rules of informed consent
3. work must be part of a treatment plan with specific goals
4. work must be fairly compensated, i.e. there is an appropriate match between the nature of the work and the wages

5. work must be conducted according to all local, state and federal laws, e.g. hours, overtime, occupational hazards, etc.

The increased flexibility generated by new standards attempts to overcome some negative results from the minimum wage outcome, namely less work for patients.[48] But the overriding premise still is that a patient should "be paid what he earns."[49, 50]

The outcome of this right is decreased exploitation and a greater degree of attention to the matching of patients' needs with work characteristics. Patients are entitled to receive fair compensation for work that will help them achieve economic self-sufficiency.

Case 1. In *Downs* v. *Dept. of Public Welfare,* litigation was initiated for the purpose of ending the alleged "forced labor" of mental hospital patients in Pennsylvania.[51] The court granted an injunction halting the work in four hospitals mentioned in the complaint.

The pattern of the work programs and the forced labor at one hospital was representative of the work at other Pennsylvania mental institutions. Much of the work was alleged to be solely for the institution's benefit, non-therapeutic, and often degrading. The coercive pressure to do the work was derived from the boredom of institutional life, from the patient's perceived pressure from the authorities to work, and from outright denial of privileges for failure to work.

Some of the forced labor included repairing outdoor benches, sewing rag rugs, repair work in an electrical shop, furniture repair and refinishing, janitorial work, selling food in the snack bar, dishwashing, and car washing. Furthermore, patients were not compensated for the work done for the benefit of the institution. Although, by policy, patients were to receive 75% of any money paid for work done for the personal benefit of the staff, the patients rarely received anything.

The court ruled that the 13th Amendment restriction against involuntary servitude was applicable in the mental health institution context.

Note. This case identifies the range of problems surfaced in the area of patient labor and compensation. Patients were often used as "slaves" of the institution, perhaps not intentionally, but with that as a result. The court found the work to be degrading and in effect, not the type that would lead to economic self-sufficiency.

When wages were paid, they were not considered by the court to be "fair compensation." As a result, any treatment system must carefully scrutinize the amount of pressure on patients to work, the nature of the work and how it matches patient therapeutic needs, and the level of compensation relative to each type of work.

MARRIAGE AND DIVORCE

Definition. Patients have the right to marry and to divorce.

The purpose of this right is to provide patients with a fundamental civil right held by other citizens. The evolution of alternative lifestyles over the past two decades has reduced the requisite conditions for both marriage and divorce. The conditions for marriage are still followed in many states by many people, for example, a civil or religious ceremony, physical examination, license, age requirement, and so on. However, the number of alternative lifestyles now acceptable, coupled with the varying marriage conditions in states, has reduced considerably the restrictive effects of both the culture and legal system.

At a time when marriage and divorce restrictions for citizens generally are being reduced, the continuation of restrictions for patients is questionable. The process of safeguarding the right is only made procedurally difficult by the question of patient competency. Thus, to question a patient's intention to marry is really to question the patient's functional capability at the time of the proposed marriage. Since marriage is a contract, the basis for rejection of the marriage or divorce would be a finding that the patient is not capable of effecting a contract. It would follow that patients adjudicated incompetent are not able to marry or to divorce since they are incompetent to make or change contracts.

Brakel and Rock have clear statements on both marriage and divorce:

"The law should not attempt to prohibit the mentally disabled from marrying, since the premise that mentally disabled persons as a group are less fit for the marriage relationship than any other groups of persons is scientifically tenuous and therefore legally arbitrary, while the eugenic arguments advanced to support such prohibition are similarly unsound. . .

Mental disability shall be a ground for divorce or annulment provided that the statutes adequately protect the mentally disabled by substantive and procedural rules."[52]

Although states do prohibit marriage and do make divorce difficult, it is not likely to remain the trend since there is a lack of substantive support.

Staff could use four questions as a protection:

1. Is the patient being taken advantage of because of his or her mental disability?
2. Have family, friends, or significant others been included to provide advice on the decision?
3. Is the patient in receipt of legal advice, if money and property issues are involved?
4. Is the patient who is to marry or divorce adjudicated incompetent?

Staff are expected to provide advice on the decision with regard to the patient's treatment plan. But the right to marry and divorce prevails unless incompetency is formally found. State laws may differ currently, but staff behavior should reflect the individual decision-making for each case in each state.

The outcomes of this right are these: (1) marriages and divorces are not prevented because staff feel patients are temporarily influenced due to the condition of their disability; and (2) other persons with inappropriate motives are not allowed the opportunity to take advantage of patients. The latter is achieved by the competency test for the marriage contract.

Case 1. Boggs v. *Boggs* is an appeal by Mrs. Boggs from a lower court order denying her support from her estranged husband.[53] Her husband had filed for divorce on grounds of indignities, which generally involved conduct directed at the offended spouse in a spirit of hate, estrangement, and malevolence.

If the husband's divorce action were granted on those grounds, support would generally be denied the wife. If, however, the conduct which otherwise would constitute indignities was caused by a mental or emotional disturbance and the husband was aware of such mental illness prior to the marriage, then the trial court must give proper consideration to all these factors in resolving the issue of support. The mental illness need not be psychotic in nature but can be "a hysterical and neurotic" condition.

In this particular case, the wife's behavior was terrible. She maintained a campaign of severe harassment against Dr. Boggs and his daughter because he was unable to honeymoon with her immediately after the marriage and later could not take her to Europe as she desired. The lower court found the conduct inexcusable and denied support, but the appellate court sent the case back for further findings on the relationship between the wife's conduct and her mental condition.

Note. The issue here is whether the husband knew of the mental instability prior to marriage. If so, the marriage contract was entered into with that foreknowledge. The divorce could be granted, but the support for such action would rest on the question of the husband's informed understanding of the condition prior to the marriage.

PRIVACY

Definition. Patients have the right to privacy of their person and of their personal possessions.

The general purpose of this right is to guarantee a fundamental freedom that precedes the Bill of Rights as noted in *Griswold* v. *Connecticut.*[54, 55] In the view of Justice Douglas it is as basic or more so than the Bill of Rights provision. However, as the Barkers have noted it is to some an open question:

> "The right of privacy is yet another right defined by the 'right's revolution' and recent events indicate that we may expect many battles over the scope and nature of this newly enshrined constitutional right. . . .Technological advances and other pressures on privacy have given rise to a recognition in our public law of the importance of safeguarding the right of privacy over against competing interests."[56]

The derivation then is historical. With the aid of technologies such as computerized information and videotapes, it is of current concern.

Privacy relates to the mental health system primarily through a deprivation of personal privacy. The crowding on wards and the group sharing mean individual "aloneness" is a rare happening. Additionally, the intensive and extensive sharing of highly personal information during treatment enhances the potential for violation if that information is passed beyond the boundaries of the treatment system. As in many of the other rights areas, the *Wyatt* v. *Stickney* decision was one of the first to recognize this important protection.

The right is protected by no special organizational mechanism. The provision of personal private spaces, such as cabinets that lock and/or individual rooms, is in part a question of physical plant resources. However, exclusion of these physical supports for privacy because of the lack of resources has not been sufficient justification for the court. It is, therefore, incumbent on clinical and administrative staff to ensure that the necessary prerequisites to privacy are present. Two illustrative requirements are patient cabinets which lock and doors on toilet stalls.

The concept of privacy also concerns invasion by other means such as photographs and videotapes. These are reviewed in Chapter 6, "Confidentiality," since they become "records" of a sort.

The protection method is again a matching of the situation within the treatment setting with a general sense of what is normal outside a treatment system. Staff might ask the following questions for review:

1. Does each patient have a private space for safekeeping of personal possessions?
2. Does each patient have privacy in meeting his or her personal care needs such as showers, toilets, etc.?
3. Does each patient retain some psychological privacy if he or she so desires?

The latter question connects with the right to refuse treatment discussed elsewhere.

The outcome of the right is protection of what some consider to be a dehumanizing effect, particularly in large treatment institutions. Privacy is best protected by the development of a social system which provides the physical prerequisites to privacy and behaviors which do not generate a psychological invasion.

Case 1. In *Griswold et al.* v. *Connecticut,* the appellants, the Executive Director of the Planned Parenthood League of Connecticut (Griswold), and its medical director (a professor at the Yale Medical School) were convicted as accessories for giving married persons information and medical advice on how to prevent conception and, following examination, prescribing a contraceptive device for the wife's use.[57] A Connecticut statute makes it a crime for any person to use any drug or article to prevent conception.

An intermediate appellate court and the state's highest court affirmed the judgment. The U.S. Supreme Court, however, declared that the statute violated the right of marital privacy which is within the penumbra of specific guarantees of the Bill of Rights. Penumbras surrounding specific guarantees of the Bill of Rights help give them life and substance. Without reading certain guarantees into the Bill of Rights, the specific guarantees would be mere skeletons. So the right of marital privacy protects the specific guarantee of the fourth and first amendments (the right to be secure in the home and freedom of association).

Notes. Here the issue is privacy for the person to decide whether they will use a contraceptive. The decision is based on information which was supplied by the staff. The court supported the privacy of person against an existing statute. The case is useful in illustrating the extent to which privacy exists as documented by court rulings. The activities that potentially constitute invasion of privacy within an institution are large in number. Rights to privacy taken for granted on the "outside" are taken for granted *not* to exist on the inside.

RELIGION

Definition. Patients have the right to freedom of religion.

The purpose of the right is to ensure that patients have rights as other citizens to practice their religion. As a fundamental constitutional right, there is little debate about whether patients should have the right. The problems have only developed when the practice of the right has created an administrative inconvenience, or when the patient did not have adequate support such as the availability of priests.

The process of protecting the right is not separate from the rights protection as a whole. There are no specific procedures for insuring that patients are free to worship as they choose. If the "Bill of Rights for Patients" is placed in the open where patients can see it and the freedom of religious liberty is cited, that is probably adequate organizational preparation.

Additional steps might include mention in patient orientations about the opportunities for worship, the place, times, etc. Any restrictions on worship imposed by virtue of the patient's confinement must be managed on a case-by-case basis. That confinement then must meet the standards for denial of freedom of movement and must include provisions for worship within the restrictions of the confinement.

The outcome of the right is the protection for patients of a fundamental civil right. The right ensures that administrative processes are established to support religious practice as desired by patients.

Case 1.   *Cruz* v. *Beto* involves a case in which a prison inmate was denied the use of the prison chapel to practice his Buddhist religion.[58] He also claimed that he was not permitted to write to his religious advisor and that he was placed in solitary confinement for distributing his religious materials to other prisoners. The lower court first rejected a hearing of the case because they felt it was within the discretion of the prison administration to limit the prisoner's religious practices. The Supreme Court, however, felt that the prisoner was denied an opportunity to pursue his faith.

Notes.   The court rejected the prison administration's contention that retaining religious advisors, scheduling the use of facilities and timing the activities of prisoners would be burdensome. They may not hold that way if the administration can document significant burdens. This case was less clear in its position of denying religious practice than other cases; e.g., in *Cooper* v. *Pate* a prisoner was not allowed to receive religious mail.[59]

SEXUALITY

Definition.   Patients have the right to engage in sexual practices of their own choosing.

The purpose of this right is to ensure that patients are allowed the freedom to choose their own sexual practices and to exercise them when that choice is free of coercion. The absolute protection of the right is mediated by the need to address certain sexual-practice issues which are a contributing cause of treatment or which are "the" cause for treatment. Additionally, there is the debated question of who is responsible for protecting patients when patients are unable to do so.

Sexual practices are protected by no special organizational procedures. There is no need for encouragement to engage in sex while in the treatment setting. Nor is there support for an abolition of sex. Certainly, the administration of the center is free to control the time and place; for example, "there will be no cohabitation within the center," or "only in the privacy of rooms," etc. The center is not free, for example, to ban homosexual practice if that practice occurs outside the treatment setting and is consistent with the patient's treatment plan, i.e., the plan does not attempt to free the patient of a conflict with his/her homosexuality.

This topic is, of course, loaded with value judgments about what practices are appropriate. Rights positions are based on freedom to choose and do not advocate a position of control of specific sexual practice. Those centers which take only voluntary patients and whose patients are informed of restrictive rules regarding sex at the pre-admission hearing may have support for denial of practice. The key is whether patients have sufficient understanding of the restriction and whether they have an option to choose an alternative treatment center. If so, they are free to choose *no* treatment in the center with restrictive rules.

The outcome of this right is that sexual freedom, which all have outside a treatment setting, is protected.

Case 1. Mary Doe and John Smith were patients in a state mental hospital.* Mary was divorced; John was married. Both had been hospitalized on several occasions with this admission being over 6 months for each. They were both doing well and were eligible for weekend leave. They decided to take their weekend together at a local hotel. On return, they were asked by the staff about the weekend. When they explained what they did, the staff rescinded the leaves of both for the next weekend. Staff stated that leaves were not to be given for those purposes.

The patients objected, stating that they were adults engaging in practices of their own choice. Both had been involuntarily committed but not declared incompetent.

Notes. Unless the patients had difficulty with sexuality and were undergoing treatment for that issue, staff were in the wrong. It is not staff's role to enforce their view of morality.

VOTING

Definition. Patients have the right to vote.

The purpose of this right is to ensure that patients are not denied the right to vote on the sole basis of their status as mental patients. Denial of voting rights does happen and indeed the movement to increase patient voting identifies patients as "The Last Suffrage Frontier"[60, 61]

As a core civil liberty, voting is a strong value that has been supported by litigation along with other civil liberties such as freedom from discrimination and the rights to marriage, divorce, contracts, and wills, as addressed elsewhere in this chapter.[62] The right to vote is protected by virtue of the fact that voting is a

---

*Fictitious Case.

constitutional right. It can be disallowed if the patient has been found to be financially and functionally incompetent and has been formally adjudicated so by a court of law. But this process limits voting by incompetents in only some states, and a reading of the constitutional law finds it ill-advised with little legal support.[63] It is considered by some to be a violation of the equal protection clause of the Constitution.

The problem is that limited attention has been paid to the patient's involvement in voting. The right has been protected in one hospital by the development of a voting project.[64] The project helped patients to register, educated them about the election, and assisted them in the actual voting.[65] Voting patterns of patients and those in other groups do not differ significantly from the country-at-large.[66-68]

For those who can vote, the staff have some obligation to protect the right by assisting patients through the process. One commentator suggested the following activities to support patient voting:[69]

1. establish patients' residency
2. publicize the upcoming election
3. assist with patient registration through postcard registration or a request for a traveling registrar
4. determination of whether absentee or vote-in-person method is to be used
5. invitations to politicians to speak
6. instruction sessions on the actual voting
7. transportation on election day.

Staff action on the above list will ensure that the voting right is protected.

The outcome of the protection is that a fundamental civil liberty is protected. A secondary outcome is the promotion of a normal environment. Citizens outside the treatment system do vote—patients should continue and/or learn to do so.

Case 1. In *O'Brien* v. *Skinner* a group of inmates filed suit because they were denied the right to register and vote. The denial extended to mobile registrations, absentee voting and other procedures.[70] The inmates challenged the constitutionality of the New York election laws. Although the inmates could not register and vote in person, they felt they could do so as other citizens by absentee ballot.

The Supreme Court on review found in favor of the inmates, stating that to disallow voting because of their physical confinement was not a sufficient rationale for denial.

Notes. The case reinforces the idea that confinement in an institution does not automatically disenfranchise patients. They are not denied voting rights because of confinement but have open to them the same protections as other citizens, such as being able to vote by absentee ballot.

CUSTODY

Definition. Patients have the right to retain custody of their children.

This right is to ensure that patients do not lose custody of their children solely because of their mental disability. That is, the right recognizes that some patients while disabled may yet be able to remain good parents. The law is strong on not breaking the parent-child linkage with the justification that even poorly qualified parents can offer a stronger base of support than the trauma associated with the loss of the parents.

The question also arises as to who is most fit to determine custody—the law through an adversary process or the human services systems through an assessment process? Several commentators feel the court is the appropriate place of review and decision because of the core civil rights issues.[71,72] Others feel the court is incapable of making a fair assessment of the complex issues involved in the case and the activities supporting the welfare of the children.[73]

The right is protected by a general assumption that patients will retain custody. In order for custody to be taken away from patients, due process requirements must be met, including:

1. notice to patient of an intent to hold a custody hearing
2. patient participation at the hearing, with attorney representation
3. explanation of procedure and possible outcome to patient
4. opportunity for patient to provide a rationale for rejecting the loss of custody
5. establishment of times of custody loss, procedures for periodic review, and reversal.

These formal steps indicate that the loss of child custody is a significant event that is *not* carried out informally without the safeguards of a judicial procedure.

The outcome of the right is that patients retain custody of their children unless a formal hearing indicates that they are not adequately able to provide for them.

Case 1.   Pointer v. *Bannister* is a habeas corpus action, brought by the father to regain custody of his son Mark, who had been entrusted to his maternal grandparents after the mother's death two years before.[74] Mark's grandparents are "perfect examples" of the American ideal of stability and conventional, middle class, midwest background who could provide an opportunity for a college education if he so desired. Mark's father, although not morally unfit, was less stable and tended toward a Bohemian lifestyle that would be more intellectually stimulating to Mark than his grandparent's style of living. Mark's father wants to be a freelance writer and photographer. Thus, there was a choice between two alternative lifestyles.

The court opted for the grandparent's stability over the father's uncertain future. When the boy's grandparents took Mark, he was unruly, had trouble distinguishing fact from fiction, was aggressive toward smaller children, was cruel to animals and was unpopular in school. Now he appears to be well adjusted, well disciplined, happy, and popular with his classmates. The court held that returning Mark to his father would not be in Mark's best interests.

Notes. Here the court decided custody based on the facts of the situation. There was no mental disability, only an "alternative behavioral" style. But that was sufficient to place the child in custody of the grandparents who had demonstrated child rearing ability with the child in question.

CONTRACTS

Definition.   Patients have the right to make contracts.

The purpose of this right is to ensure that patients are able to continue their personal affairs which may involve the execution of contracts. Since the elimination of this ability significantly affects the patient's capacity to conduct his personal affairs, it is of major significance to him. In general:

> "The present trend has been toward expanding the contractual rights of patients, and toward examining how the mental characteristics of an individual affect his/her contractual ability rather than concluding that an entire class of persons is incompetent. A contract may be voided, of course, if the other party has used undue influence or fraud."[75]

Thus, the notion that a mental patient cannot execute contracts including accepting responsibility for both those beneficial and those harmful to him is no longer the case in legal terms.

It is not just a philosophical direction. Consider the following comment:

> "In short, we favor doing away with the legal recognition of mental incompetency as a ground of avoiding contracts (or making the criteria for such avoidance operational not psychiatric, and precise in the extreme), because we believe that this policy is most consistent with the traditional moral aims of Anglo-Saxon law, and especially contract law—namely, the expansion of the scope of individual self-determination and the protection of personal dignity; and because we cherish and support these values and rank them, on our own scale, higher than security or "mental health."[76]

If patients bear responsibility for contracts, they have both self-determination and the sense of actually being responsible for their actions, because they are.

The protection of this right concerns the staff's knowledge of the change in the legal trend, and it involves some specific aids when staff are aware of the patient's future involvement in a contract, namely:

1. assist the patient in understanding both the contract terms and the implications of the contract
2. secure attorney assistance for the patient
3. have a third party assist and/or witness both the review and the actual signing.

The above does not guarantee that patients will be free from fraud and bad business decisions, only that they are given every opportunity to fully comprehend their actions with regard to the contract.

The outcome of the right is insurance that the patient is able to continue his personal affairs without the interruptions generated by the inability to contract.

Case 1. Faber v. *Sweet Style Manufacturing Corp.* This is an action by the purchaser for voiding a land purchase contract.[77] At the time of the contract, the purchaser was suffering from a manic depressive psychosis which compelled the purchaser to enter into the contract. Since the status quo was restorable, the court invalidated the contract.

Prior to the purchaser's illness, he had been frugal and cautious. Gradually, however, he became less cautious. For a period of a month and a half before the contract, the Plaintiff began to drive at high speeds, to take his wife out to dinner, to be more sexually active, and to discuss his prowess with others. Then he purchased three expensive cars for himself, his son and his daughter; began to discuss converting his Long Beach bathhouse and garage property into a 12-story cooperative; and put up a sign to that effect. This flurry of compulsive activity finally culminated in the land purchase contract in question.

The general rule of thumb is that the contract of a mental incompetent is voided at the election of the incompetent and if the other party can be restored to the status quo.

Notes. In this case, the court found in favor of violating the contract and returning to the status quo. But as Alexander and Szasz note, this further weakens the patient's sense of responsibility. In this case, it in effect made clear to the patient that when he is manic he can do what he wants contract-wise, for the court will overturn it later. This reinforcement for irresponsibility is not helpful to the patient's treatment.

SUMMARY

Patients should have civil rights protections similar to those provided in the criminal justice system. The purposes of protecting civil rights are as follow: 1) maintaining patient equality with other citizens; 2) decreasing the belief in the difference of mental patients; 3) insuring the basic civil rights of patients; and 4) maintaining the normality of existence in mental health treatment centers. Methods vary from state to state, but there is common acceptance of the protection and maintenance of civil rights. This is not a legal analysis but a proposal of generic responses to be used within each state's view and individual clinical situations.

Competency decisions involve both financial and functional aspects of the patient's life. Competency assessments require adequate notice of a hearing, a hearing with patient participation, representation for the patient, exploration of alternatives, explanation of the patient's assessment, the purpose and procedure of the ruling, and the patient's right to a review of status at a time in the future. The outcome of competency hearings has serious effects for patients, including the handling of their money and property, personal life decisions, and ability to refuse treatment.

Patients may not be discriminated against in the areas of jobs, housing, memberships, etc. Their protection from discrimination lies primarily in the confidentiality of their treatment and records, as covered in Chapter 4.

Patients have a right to maintain their drivers' licenses until they are adjudicated functionally incompetent or are shown physically incapable of driving. Otherwise, they are being denied a right without due process.

The right to education is especially important for patients under 18 years of age who have been excluded from regular schools on the basis of their disability. The mental health system must provide education on the unit or secure education from other providers.

Patients have the right to work as soon as they are able to do so and to receive fair compensation for their labor. The purpose of this right is to prevent exploitation of patients, help them move toward economic self-sufficiency, and to ensure the treatment-relatedness of work.

Patients are allowed to marry and divorce while undergoing treatment. To deny this right would be to question the patients' ability to make contracts which can only be done in the cases of adjudicated incompetency.

Patients have the right to privacy of their person and their possessions. This right also covers personal information given in treatment. The institution must physically provide for privacy, for example patient cabinets with locks. Other aspects of this right include psychological privacy considered under the right to refuse treatment, and public exposure limitations through photographs and films, considered under confidentiality.

While there are no specific procedures to protect religious freedom, staff can let patients know of their freedom to worship and the schedules of services. Sexual freedom can only be mediated when it is part of the cause for treatment, although the institution is able to control time and place through rules.

Patients have the right to vote. Staff are encouraged to help them through the process such as registering and transportation to polling place or obtaining absentee ballots.

Patients should retain custody of their children while they are able to remain "good" parents. The problem here is who determines this—the law or human services. To deny custody, the institution must follow the due process procedure.

There is currently a change in the legal trend concerning mental patients and their ability to make contracts. Mental disability does not automatically negate contracts. Staff should help patients understand the contract, secure the assistance of an attorney if warranted, and have a third party assist in explanations and/or in witnessing the contract.

REFERENCES

1. Curran, W., "Hospitalization of the Mentally Ill," 31 *N.C.L. Rev.,* 274, 1953.
2. Kittrie, N., "Compulsory mental treatment and the requirements of due process," 21 *Ohio St. L.J.,* 21 (1960).
3. "Due process deficiencies in Iowa's civil commitment procedure," 64 *Iowa L. Rev.,* 65 (October, 1978).
4. Ferleger, D., "Loosing the chains: In-hospital civil liberties of mental patients," 13 *Santa Clara Lawyer,* 447 (1973).
5. Furmar, Marian Schwalm and Conners, James A., "The Pennsylvania experiment in due process," 8 *Duq. L. Rev.,* 1 (Winter, 1969–70).
6. Bassiouni, M.C., "The right of the mentally ill to cure and treatment: medical due process," 15 *De Paul L. Rev.* 291 (1966).
7. Curran, W., "Community mental health and the commitment laws: A radical new approach is needed," *Am. J. Pub. Health,* 57:1565 (1967).
8. Laves, R., Cohen, A., "A preliminary investigation into the knowledge of and attitudes toward the legal rights of mental patients," *J. of Psychiatry and Law,* Spring, 1973.
9. Ziegenfuss, J.T., "Drug and alcohol addiction personnel: An exploratory study of attitudes and knowledge of legal rights of patients," Dauphin County Executive Commission on Drugs & Alcohol, Harrisburg, Pa. 1976 and Penn State University.
10. Lasky, David I., & Ziegenfuss, James T., "Organizational Development as a Means of Implementing Patients' Rights," presented at the *First International Conference on Psycho-Social Rehabilitation, 1975.*
11. Kahle, L.R., Sales, B.D., "Attitudes of clinical psychologists toward involuntary civil commitment law," *Professional Psychology,* 9(3), Aug. 1978.
12. Swoboda, J.S., et al., "Knowledge of and compliance with privileged communication and child-abuse reporting laws," *Professional Psychology,* 9(3), Aug. 1978.
13. Ziegenfuss, J.T., *Rights and Organizational Models: Sociotechnical Systems Research on Mental Health Programs,* in book publication, Washington, D.C.: Univ. Press of America, 1982.
14. Brakel, S.J., Rock, R.S., *The Mentally Disabled and the Law,* Chicago: Univ. of Chicago Press, 1971.
15. Schwitzgebel, R.L., Schwitzgebel, R.K., *Law and Psychological Practice,* New York: John Wiley & Sons, 1980.

16. Brakel, S.J., Rock, P.S., op. cit., (item no. 14).
17. Davis, K.C., *Discretionary Justice,* Chicago: Univ. Illinois Press, 1980.
18. Brakel, S.J. & Rock, R.S., op. cit., (item no. 14).
19. Brooks, A.D., *Law, Psychiatry & the Mental Health System, 1980 Supplement,* Boston: Little, Brown & Co., 1980.
20. Burra P., Kimberley R, Miura C., "Mental competence and consent to treatment," *Can J Psychiatry,* **25**:251-253, 1980.
21. Roth, L.H., Meisel, A., Lidz, C.W., "Tests of competency to consent to treatment," *Am. J. Psychiatry,* **134**:279-284, 1977.
21a. Perr, I.N., "Incompetence and consent to psychiatric treatment and hospitalization," *Journal of Legal Medicine,* **5**(1):16H–16K.
22. *Romeo* v. *Youngberg,* 644 F. 2d 147 (1980).
23. Appelbaum, P.S., Bateman, A.L., "Competency to consent to voluntary psychiatric hospitalization: A theoretical approach," *Bull Am Acad. Psychiatry Law,* **7**:390-399, 1980.
24. Appelbaum, P.S., Mirkin, S.A., Bateman, A.L., "An empirical assessment of competency to consent to psychiatric hospitalization," *Am. J. Psychiatry,* **138**:1170-1176, 1981.
25. Hoffman, B.F., "Assessing competence to consent to treatment," *Can. J. Psychiatry,* **25**:354-355, 1980.
26. Roesch, R., Golding, S.L., *Competency to Stand Trial,* Chicago: Univ. Illinois Press, 1980.
27. "In re Horvath: Release from an incompetency commitment—the need for procedural safeguards," 3 *Ohio N.U.L. Rev.* 198 (1975).
28. *Wieter* v. *Settle,* 193 F. Supp. 318 (W.D. No. 1961).
29. Altrocchi, J., Eisdorfer C., "Changes in attitudes toward mental illness," *Mental Hygiene,* **(45)**, 1961, 563-570.
30. Edgerton, J.W., Bentz, W.K., "Attitudes and opinions of rural people about mental illness and program services," *Am. J. Public Health,* **59,** 1969.
31. Crocetti, G., Spiro, H.R., Siassi, I., "Are the ranks closed? Attitudinal social distance and mental illness," *Amer. J. of Psychiatry,* **127,** 1971.
32. Nunnally, M., Weintrob, R.H., "Emergency commitment: A transcultural study," *Amer. J. of Psychiatry,* **131,** 1974.
33. Rabkin, J.G., "Opinions about mental illness: A review of the literature," *Psychological Bulletin,* **77,** 1972.
34. *Hurley* v. *Allied Chemical Corporation,* 262 S.E. 2d 757 (W. Va. Sup. Ct. App 1980) as reported in *Mental Disability Law Reporter,* IV, 1973.
35. Leblang, T., "Epilepsy, motor vehicle licensure and the law: The physician's rights and responsibilities in Illinois," **10** *Loyola University Law Journal* (Chicago), 203 (Winter 1979).
36. Brakel, S.J., Rock, R.S., op. cit., (item no. 14), p. 308.
37. *Rodriquez* v. *Miera,* No. 78-194 p (D.N.M. April 11, 1978). reported in *Mental Disability Law Reporter.*
38. *Brown* v. *Bd. of Education,* 349 U.S. 294, 1955.
39. "State's requirement of compulsory education and the individual's right of access to education," **74** *Michigan Law Review* 1383 (June 1976).
40. *Mills* v. *Board of Education of District of Columbia,* 348 F. Supp. 866 D.D.C. 1972.
41. Kapp, M., "Residents of state mental institutions and their money (or, the state giveth and the state taketh away)," 6 *Psychiatry & Law,* (3) 287, Fall 1978.
42. Kapp, M.B., "Resident labor in public and private institutions: A disparity in the law," *Hosp. Community Psychiatry* **30**(6), p. 414-415, 1979.

43. Lebar, A., "Worker-patients: Receiving therapy or suffering peonage?" **62** *American Bar Association Journal* 219 (1976), (516, 1207).
44. Bartlett, T.L., "Institutional Peonage," *Atlantic* **214**(1):116 (1964).
45. *National League of Cities* v. *Usery*, 426 U.S. 833 (1976).
46. Editors, "Programs for Patient-Workers: Approaches, Problems in Four Institutions," *Hosp. & Community Psychiatry*, **27**(2) Feb. 1976, p. 93.
47. "Patient-worker regulations: Revisions on the way." **27** *Hospital & Community Psychiatry* (2) 103 (1976), (516, 1207).
48. Pyle, K.S., *Institutional peonage: A study in mental health policy.* Unpublished dissertation, University of Pennsylvania, 1978, 157 p.
49. Safier, D., "Patient Work Under Fair Labor Standards: the Issue in Perspective," *Hosp. & Community Psychiatry*, **27**(2), 1976, 89.
50. Safier, D., Barnum, R., "Patient Rehabilitation through Hospital Work Under Fair Labor Standards," *Hosp. & Community Psychiatry*, **26**, 1975, p. 299.
51. *Downs* v. *Dept. Public Welfare*, 368 F. Supp. 454 (E.D. Pa. 1973).
52. Brakel, S.J., Rock, R.S., op. cit., (item no. 14, p. 273).
53. *Boggs* v. *Boggs*, 221 Pa. Super. 22, 289 A 2d. 479 (1972).
54. *Griswold* v. *Connecticut*, 381 U.S. 479 (1965).
55. Westin, A., *Privacy and Freedom*, New York: Atheneum, 1967.
56. Barker, L.J., Barker, T.W., *Civil Liberties and the Constitution.* Englewood Cliffs, N.J.: Prentice-Hall, 1975, p. 392.
57. *Griswold* v. *Connecticut*, 381 U.S. 479 (1965).
58. *Cruz* v. *Beto*, 405 U.S. 319 (1972).
59. *Cooper* v. *Pate*, 378 U.S. 546 (1964).
60. Pennsylvania Advisory Committee to the U.S. Commission on Civil Rights, *The Last Suffrage Frontier: Enfranchising Mental Hospital Residents*, Washington, D.C.: U.S. Government Printing Office, 1978.
61. U.S. Commission on Civil Rights, *The Last Suffrage Frontier: Enfranchising Mental Hospital Residents.* Washington, D.C.: U.S. Government Printing Office, 1978.
62. *Wyatt* v. *Stickney*, 344 F. Supp. 373 (M.D. Ala. 1972).
63. Feldman, B., ed., "Mental disability and the right to vote," **88** *Yale Law Journal*, 1644 (July 1979).
64. Howard, G. & Anthony, R., "The right to vote and voting patterns of hospitalized psychiatric patients," **49** *Psychiatric Quarterly* (2) 124 (Spring 1977).
65. Anthony, R., *Voting Project: Creedmoor State Hospital*, Creedmoor State Hospital, N.Y., unpublished manuscript, 1972.
66. Howard, G., Anthony, R., op. cit., (item no. 64).
67. Klein, M.M., Grossman, S.A., "Voting competence and mental illness," Proceedings of the 76th Annual Convention of the American Psychological Association, vol. **3**, 1968, pp. 701-702.
68. Wellner and Gaines, "Patients' Right to Vote," *Hosp. & Community Psychiatry*, **21**, 1970, pp. 164-164.
69. Lee, W., "Helping patients to vote," *MH* (Mental Hygiene) (2) 14 (Summer/Fall 1977).
70. *O'Brien* v. *Skinner*, 414 U.S. 524 (1974).
71. Tuchler, M.L., "The Adversary System: Role of the Psychiatrist," *J. Forensic Sci.*, XVIII (1973), 193-196.
72. Bazelon, D.L. "Psychiatrists and the Adversary Process," *Scient. Amer.*, CCXXX, No. 6 (June 1974), 18-23.
73. Solow, R.A., Adams, P.L., "Custody by agreement: Child psychiatrist as child advocate," *J. Psychiatry Law*, Spring 1977, p. 77.

74. *Painter* v. *Bannister,* 258 Iowa 1390, 140 N.W. 2d.
75. Schwitzgebel, R.L., Schwitzgebel, R.K., op. cit., (item no. 15, p. 173).
76. Alexander, G. and Szasz, T., "From contract to status via psychiatry," **13** *Santa Clara Lawyer* 537 (1973).
77. *Faber* v. *Sweet Style Manufacturing,* 40 Misc. 2d. 212, 242 N.Y.S. 2d. 763 (1963).

12
Discharge

Discharge is the final point of interaction between the patient's rights and the treatment system and is formally defined as "the point at which the patient's active involvement with the program is terminated and the program no longer maintains active responsibility for the patient."[1] It is the final outcome of a process involving multiple phases for each patient. Previous chapters have demonstrated that rights must be safeguarded as the patient moves through the phases of treatment. In addition, rights also must be protected during the process of severing relations between the treatment system and the individual patient.

Patients are discharged in two ways.[2] First, they are regularly discharged when the clinical team and the patient feel the patient is ready, i.e., when there is agreement. Second, patients are irregularly discharged "against medical advice" or through an "absence without leave." It is in this second category of discharge that the patient's rights conflict emerges when there is no agreement about readiness to leave or about the actual leaving (in the case of absent without leave).

Unless involuntarily committed, patients have the right to be discharged; they are endangered by unlimited deprivation of liberty based on potential dangerousness or some other rationale.[3] Some clinicians express grave concern that the right encourages patients to leave when they are not "ready." Yet the data comparing the success of regularly and irregularly discharged patients is currently uncertain in its findings. Apparently, irregularly discharged patients do as well or nearly as well after leaving the unit.[5-9] "On balance, the literature suggests little difference between irregularly and regularly discharged patients."[10] Although researchers did find some differences in the study, the question is currently an open one, since both regularly and irregularly discharged patients appear to obtain further care.[11] Furthermore, there is little consensus as yet on a profile of the patient discharged against medical advice.[12-18]

What are the implications of the work for rights regarding discharge? One implication is that large groups of patients discharged irregularly are not becoming casualties of premature release, although some may be. This suggests that those leaving against advice are nearly as good at identifying their need for continued treatment as are the treatment teams. Patient requests for discharge are thus better grounded in accuracy than some suspect *and* at the least they should be actively involved in discharge decision-making, perhaps with an equal vote. That is the primary issue and purpose of the right—the degree of involvement and influence of the patient in the decision.

The discharge process itself involves a series of steps which normally include but are not limited to the following:

- notice of the intent to discharge provided to patient, family, and relevant others
- review of accumulated treatment progress information and an analysis of the current status of the patient;
- a hearing to secure the patient's version of his current status;
- a review of the discharge plan developed with patient participation;
- settlement of all administrative and court issues related to the release of the patient;
- the actual release of the patient.

Of course, depending on a range of individual circumstances, several of these steps may occur simultaneously.

For example, notice may be given with the review, the hearing, settlement of administrative issues, and the final decision coming the next day. Or, all steps can be completed within several days, with release to follow shortly thereafter. A critical point in the treatment care issue is that the patient be involved in each of the steps and that he receive ample opportunity to present his view of both the process of discharge and the intended outcome of this phase—leaving the unit.

The outcome of the discharge procedure should be patient freedom from the system, exclusive of any further entanglement. Entanglements are meant to include follow-ups, evaluations, research, and other mechanisms which may be used by the unit to further its knowledge of the system. The patient has often automatically been a part of this knowledge-gathering process. It is important that these "further entanglements" be voluntarily agreed to by the patient.

A troublesome aspect of obtaining this agreement is that the patient often does not feel free to reject these continuing arrangements while still a part of the system. A sincere informing of the patient of the voluntary nature of this continuing activity is the basic requirement, but even that may be difficult.

Staff become very invested in their patient's welfare, often to the point of losing recognition of the patient's real independence and right to determine his own fate. One commentator views the protectiveness of staff as one of the mechanisms by which patients' rights to discharge are violated.[19] Quite different from the nature of a right violation through neglect or abuse, this violation occurs through too much staffing—perhaps an over enthusiastic service commitment which overcomes the patient-independence balance. There are other troublesome issues regarding discharge.

In general, the discharge rights issue involves the following topics:

- the patient's right to dignity at his point of exit from the program, i.e., his transition from care to independence, or at the least quasi-independence;
- the patient's right to know what is happening, i.e., to understand the process and the outcome of the discharge decision-making, whether the decision is ultimately positive or negative;
- the patient's right to equity in cases which attempt to match clinical decisions in favor of release with the hospital's needs for beds and the court's approval of release.

In the latter case, it is recognized that coordination is time consuming and difficult, particularly when agendas conflict. Patients do have the right to appropriate discharge despite competing administrative concerns, and the patient's rights to knowledge about the decision process and the outcome override any conflicts in agendas by administrative, judicial, or clinical groups.

This chapter will review the patient's rights to a fair and professional discharge by separating discharge into three components, clinical, administrative, and judicial discharge.[20, 21]

CLINICAL

Definition. Patients have the right to be discharged from clinical services.

Clinical discharge is the point at which the patient's active involvement with the clinical program ends. The program no longer maintains an active clinical responsibility for the patient. Patients have the right to be free from clinical care when that care is no longer needed by the patient, as jointly determined by clinician and patient.

The purpose of discharge is to exit the system. The patient has an investment in being able to say he is no longer in need of care. It is necessary for the clinician to make a determination that the care and treatment received by the patient was sufficient to place the disability in control. Daily care can be reduced to a minimum, or it can be eliminated altogether. Patients have a right to have this determination made no sooner nor later than required, a vague judgmental process based on "reasonableness" developed from good clinical rationale.

As clinical work now is multidisciplinary, so is the decision to terminate it. There is increasing use of a discharge process based on a team determination with multiple sources of information for each individual case situation.[22] For example, the team would initiate a discharge discussion by including opinions of the patient, psychiatrist, nurse, social worker, aides, and physicians. Each contributes information regarding the status of the patient at that time and an assessment of readiness for release from the program. This process is more or less formalized depending upon individual unit programs. Some units may use results of psychological employment tests and reports of family, friends, and significant others. Other teams would form the judgment themselves based on the best thinking at the time of the meeting. Most discharge decisions are made in collaboration with the patient.

This patients' right is to a clinical discharge process which includes:

- notice of the coming decision
- patient involvement in the discussions
- multiple clinical team inputs
- outside opinions as necessary
- creation of a discharge plan outlining continuing care needs
- documentation of the process and the decision.

Although straightforward and relatively simple, the elements are sometimes not present as indicated by cases that result in litigation and by research on the needs and success of discharged patients living in the community.[23-31]

The patients' right to clinical discharge provides both one of the bases for the pressure to end clinical care and one of the bases for being involved in the critical decisions of treatment. Importantly, this is where the rights of the patient are significant. Patients have a right *to know* about the process which will lead to the decision and *to play* an active role in that process. The decision determines whether they will remain in care, or in the case of some patients, gain liberty.

Two cases will provide examples of the right with regard to the discharge process.

Case 1. Mrs. Roberts was arrested, convicted of child abuse, and subsequently admitted to a hospital because of mental illness.* The first admission began 22 years ago with a series of admissions and releases occurring during that period. Her request for release and child custody has come up for review. She was apparently quite good as a mother but was concerned that the neighbor's children were the "devil's agents."

She was first released from the state hospital after an initial stay of 12 years. Subsequently, she was readmitted 7 times for varying periods over the next 10 years. She had not been released in the past 3 years.

Diagnosed as a chronic schizophrenic, she was aggressive and at times assaultive, although not in the past 2 years. When admitted for the last time,

---

*Fictitious case.

the reason was due to an inability to function independently because of hallucinations and complete lack of attention to personal hygiene. There were no aggression or assault problems.

She was making steady progress over the past 3 years, progressing from a ward unit designed for the chronic long-term disabled to progressively more open units. She began working days in the patient work center and was regular in her attendance. The clinical team gave her steadily stronger positive assessments in their clinical notes. They felt she was ready to move to a community program affiliated with the local mental health association. The association maintained a policy of prior visitation and ample discussion before a patient moved from the hospital to a community residential center.

The patient visited her new home which seemed to her to be warm and comfortable. She was interviewed by a committee of two staff and two residents. The staff and residents were convinced she could adjust. Although they were given a summary of her case, they did not inquire at the interview as to the nature of her problem and her history. No one raised a question concerning the location of the elementary school at the end of the block.

On return to the hospital, her clinician and social worker secured a general consensus from her team that she was ready for discharge. A plan and schedule were developed.

The week before the patient was to be discharged, her clinician and social worker were reassigned to another unit under a general hospital reorganization. She was assigned to a new treatment team with only a psychiatric aide as a remaining member of her old group. The day before discharge, the team reviewed her case and found her not ready for discharge, although her behavior had not significantly changed from the date of her previous team's approval. They cited as rationale the location of the school to her new residence and the child abuse history. They did not note the absence of aggression in the past 10 years.

The patient filed a rights complaint claiming her right to be discharged was violated. The denial of her discharge caused depression and decompensation. However, her functioning did not become aggressive.

Notes. The new treatment team was exercising their responsibility for the decision-making. However, they ignored the preponderance of evidence which accumulated over the past 3 years. The first team monitored closely and planned the exit. They did overlook the school's close proximity and the resultant possible problems. However, given the patient's lack of aggression over the last years, the risk would appear to be minimal.

The hospital did not consider, or could not allow for, the effect on patients of staff reassignment. Although the clinician and social service worker did express concern for the disengagement from their roles in treating patients, they were not allowed sufficient time before or after reassignment to help the transition.

The patient's decompensation produced support for the denial decision, but no one was sure how much of the decompensation was caused by the actions of the hospital and the treatment team changes. The change of team denied the patient freedom.

Staff must constantly monitor the discharge decision-making process and the outcome to ensure that the patient's right to both involvement and a fair outcome are provided. Here, the team transition was not accounted for, undercutting patient involvement and fairness.

Case 2. In *Cameron* v. *State,* Dennis Butting was found unconscious in the street and arrested for disorderly conduct.[32] He was admitted to a state hospital for examination. Following a series of tests, the staff concluded that Butting was "without mental disorder, psychopathic personality, asocial and amoral trends," and he was ultimately discharged. Five days later, Butting attacked the claimant with a butcher knife and meat cleaver, severely injuring her. The lower court absolved the state from any liability for making an erroneous discharge decision with regard to Butting's mental condition. This was a matter of professional judgment, and hospitals are not guarantors of their diagnoses. However, the court found the state liable for negligence for not taking precautions to observe and monitor Butting upon his release.

On appeal, the court reversed its decision and found the state to be free from all liability to Ms. Cameron. The law does not impose upon a hospital a continuing duty to exercise a monitoring role over discharged patients.

Notes. The patient's right to be free from entanglements with the treatment unit following his or her release works both ways. If patients are completely free of obligations to the treatment unit, the treatment unit is in turn free of obligations to them. Therefore, inappropriate behaviors which may occur following the patient's formal discharge from the hospital do not reflect back on the treatment unit itself. The only time in which that reflection can be possible is if there is a trial discharge or some continuing significant involvement on the part of the treatment or administrative staff of the unit.

ADMINISTRATIVE DISCHARGE

Definition. Patients have the right to administrative discharge.

Patients have the right to notice of hearings prior to administrative alteration of their situation and to separation from administrative entanglements with the care system. This part of the discharge process concerns the completeness of the release from the treatment unit. It includes the settlement of all billings, forms, and release statements linking the patient to the treatment unit. The second part concerns transfers, changes, and alterations of the patient's status in the treatment unit which may affect discharge, as noted in *Cameron* vs. *State.*

The first purpose of this right is to ensure that the patient can be fully separated from the system. This separation should include follow-ups stemming from administrative and financial encumbrance and other possible intrusions into the patient's privacy when he or she is no longer a patient. Second, there is a concern for administrative changes that result in discharge from one unit or hospital with subsequent admission to a related unit or linked organization. Rights to care become a concern if discharges are made for the convenience and efficiency of the hospital and do not take into account the patient's needs.

Conversely, the treatment unit cannot retain a patient if the evidence at the time of a discharge does not warrant and/or if the patient is against it. The position here is quite clear:

"A patient of sound mind may leave the hospital at any time he chooses, and the hospital may not prevent it. If the hospital restricts this freedom to leave, it can be sued for false imprisonment, which involves the intentional confinement of the patient by threat or physical barriers against the patient's will. No actual damages need be proved since the law assumes harm to the patient from this conduct."[33]

The exposure to this type of liability is quite serious, underscoring the need for special care when a judgment to deny discharge deviates from the record indicating discharge as a next step.

The treatment-unit administration is responsible for the coordination of the patient's flow through the service system. It is ultimately the administration's responsibility to ensure that clinical, administrative, and legal requirements are satisfied whether discharge is approved or not. The process is one of coordinating: the notice; patient involvement; multiple team inputs; outside opinions; planning and documentation, including signed patient consent for continuing contact in follow-ups.

The primary outcomes of rights protection in this area are in ensuring that any continuing entanglements with the care system are voluntarily approved by the patient, and that the patient has a full opportunity to be heard regarding significant changes in the location of his care, whether the care is within the current treatment setting or involves a new one. The outcomes are enhanced timeliness and accuracy of discharge decision-making, as well as liberty in some cases.

Case 1. Montague v. *George J. London Memorial Hospital* concerns a patient who became a voluntary admission at the Fox River Hospital.[34] The patient was voluntarily admitted to the hospital. Approximately 6 days later, he properly executed and delivered a 5-day notice of his intention to leave following the requirements of that state's Mental Health Code. The code is as follows:

> "Each voluntary admittee shall be allowed to leave the hospital within 5 days excluding Saturdays, Sundays and holidays after he gives any professional staff person written notice of his desire to leave, unless prior to leaving the patient withdraws such notice by written withdrawal, or unless within said 5 days as petitioned and certificates of 2 examining physicians at least one of whom shall be a psychiatrist, are filed with the court, and the court shall order a hearing pursuant to such an 8-8, patient may continue to be hospitalized pending a final order of the court in the court proceedings."

The patient claims that the defendants both failed and refused to allow him to leave within 5 days after the receipt of the notice. Furthermore, they did not secure a petition and two certificates from examining physicians to be filed with the court in order to sustain his hospitalization on involuntary status. The patient claimed that he was held against his will for approximately 4 months after submission of his 5-day notice.

As a result of the hospital's refusal to discharge him, the patient claimed that "he was wrongfully and improperly deprived of his freedom and liberty for the indicated time periods; was caused to be subjected to unnecessary, painful, discomforting and harmful treatment and medications; was prevented from conducting his business and professional affairs; and suffered considerable loss of income; incurred substantial medical bills and obligations; sustained great pain and suffering; suffered great mental and emotional anguish and trauma; and otherwise suffered and sustained great damages and injury. Plaintiff further alleged that defendants acted in the foregoing respects in willful, wanton, malicious and wicked disregard of his rights."

The patient, therefore, claimed that the hospital was in violation of a code which purports to define the policies and procedures relating to discharge from the system. The patient documented that he had in fact fully followed those procedures. Upon doing so, he was entitled to be released, or the hospital was to have followed their own procedures defining the follow-up steps to legally retaining him in the hospital.

Notes. This case is an illustration of discharge problems developing from administrative policies and procedures. The code does define what is to happen when a voluntary patient submits a request to be discharged. Staff refused to follow this stated policy and procedure, and thus were in violation of the patient's rights as stated by the staff's own code of procedures. The case does not center on a clinical decision-making conflict. It solely identifies staff disregard of standing policies and procedures defining the patient's status as a voluntary participant in the system.

The case also illustrates the substantial list of damages that can be inflicted when this type of right is violated. The patient's personal damages are identified in terms of denial of liberty, loss of income, substantial medical bills, and psychological anguish and trauma. Obviously, not all discharge conflicts produce such a list, but this is certainly significant damage.

Finally, the case serves as a notice of the importance of following procedures which define the very nature of the voluntary concept. Ignoring those procedures makes a mockery of the concept of voluntary admission. *Without discharge* as provided for in the laws and regulations, there is in reality no such thing as a voluntary admission. There is *no exit* from the system—a frightening prospect.

Case 2. In *St. George* v. *State,* suit was brought against the State of New York by the wife of a victim of a stabbing attack by a former inmate at a state hospital for the mentally insane.[35] William Jones, the attacker, had been previously convicted of assault and attempted robbery. He was transferred from prison to a state hospital. The prison psychiatrist found him to be suffering from a persecution complex and diagnosed him as a "psychotic with psychopathic personality and paranoid episodes."

The hospital records show that Jones repeatedly assaulted other inmates with little and/or no provocation. His attacks were based on the feeling that people were giving him the evil eye and laughing at him. He insisted that other inmates were calling him names and trying to "bug him." In one three-month period, he was confined to camisoles for assaulting an attendant, threatening and accusing officials of stealing his underwear and pen and pencils, assaulting other inmates, and fighting.

The circumstances surrounding these incidents were not recorded in the hospital records, although officials admit that it is vital to determine if the attacks were of a "delusional" nature. The only entries made were by attendants in the work book, which was not viewed by psychiatrists or available at their diagnostic staff meetings.

The diagnosis was based solely on the report of an administrative psychiatrist and an interview of Jones conducted at the staff meeting. An example of this process illustrates that from May through August, Jones was confined to the camisole on 4 separate occasions and yet the administrative psychiatrist reported that the "patient was pleasant and agreeable."

The hospital reviewed Jones' case and classified him as recovered despite his numerous assaults and aggressive behavior. On 3-1-50 he was released. On 3-5-50, four days, later, he brutally stabbed 7 people, killing 4, none of whom he had ever seen before.

The court found that the hospital was grossly understaffed and over-crowded. Incidents were not investigated, simply because there were no resources to spare for an investigation.

The court found the hospital to be derelict in its duties to protect the public from dangerous psychotics. It awarded $40,000 to the wife of one of the stabbing victims.

Notes. At issue here is the failure of the administrative process at several points. The prediction of dangerousness is currently not possible—reliable and valid technologies are not available. But the primary breakdown in the obviously incorrect decision to discharge the patient was due to the administrative difficulties in developing an information system connecting daily reports of patient behavior (made by the aides) with the brief and intermittent observations of the psychiatrist. While a team meeting was held to discuss the patient's situation, the depth of the evidence collected and the review conducted was not sufficient to detect the inconsistencies in the finding of approval for discharge.

Although it was in the end a mistaken clinical judgment that the patient was ready for discharge, it was in fact the management of the discharge process which led to the inappropriate clinical judgment. This assumes that a definition of the administrative component of the discharge is the *management* of that process: (1) to ensure that the patient's rights are considered and (2) to ensure that the process leading to that decision is both *thorough* and *fair.* Here the lack of thoroughness because of poor information was a serious error indeed.

Case 3. In *Hiatt* v. *Soucek,* the plaintiff was serving a life sentence in the men's reformatory when he was found to be insane upon examination by a board of physicians. He was subsequently transferred to the department for the criminally insane. The finding of the plaintiff's insanity conformed to the procedures spelled out in the Iowa Statute. The statute essentially stipulates that even if a prisoner is about to be released after serving his term, he can be transferred to a facility for the insane upon such a finding. The plaintiff challenged the statute on the grounds that it denied him due process of law in that there was no judicial hearing or finding of insanity prior to transferral.

The court, however, viewed the Iowa statutory scheme in its totality. They found the procedure to be constitutionally sufficient because a related statute provided for a judicial hearing after the plaintiff's transfer to an insane ward. The hearing would not only encompass the question of whether the transfer was valid but also the question of the plaintiff's insanity.

Notes. In this case, the discharge from the prison involved a subsequent admission to a mental hospital unit. The question was not a clinical-decision issue as to whether or not the patient was ready. Instead, it concerned the timing of the hearing to determine the patient's status.

Administratively, it was more efficient for the organization to provide the hearing after transfer. The question arose, however, as to whether transfer prior to review was allowable according to the patient's right to due process. Due process involves the provision of appropriate opportunities to be heard through a hearing process prior to transfer and/or discharge. In this case, there was a hearing simultaneous to transfer, i.e., at the time of arrival at the new unit which satisfied the patient's right to a hearing.

JUDICIAL DISCHARGE

Definition. Patients have the right to a judicial discharge.

Judicial discharge is the point at which the patient's involvement with the court is terminated and the court no longer maintains an active responsibility for the patient. As noted previously, the judicial discharge may or may not correspond to the clinical and administrative discharge. For those patients who are undergoing treatment as a result of a court process, there is a continuing need to coordinate the clinical, administrative, and judicial processes of discharge. Unfortunately, it is often the case that clinicians will determine that a patient is ready for discharge when in fact the hospital administration and/or the courts have an alternative opinion.

The right to judicial discharge asserts that the patient does have a right to be free from never-ending involvement with the court. Once the reasons for hospitalization have been satisfied, i.e., treatment is rendered—patient change is achieved, the patient should be free to leave. It is of course necessary for the treating team to build a case for the decision to discharge. The right is protected by the clinical staff's support in clearly documenting and presenting their "evidence" that the patient met the criteria defined by the court as necessary for judicial satisfaction.

Patients can in some states petition the court for release at varying intervals.[38] They can also petition the court for a writ of habeus corpus. The habeus corpus proceeding may consider only legal issues (constitutionality of process), any factual issues (mental state of the patient), or it can consider both.[39] Thus the patient has a means for helping himself to protect his right to judicial discharge.

Importantly, patients can use the petition process to effect their discharge from treatment provided against their will. The court will then review the process by which they were admitted. The review will focus on whether the admission included:

- notice
- a hearing

- patient participation in the hearing
- attorney and/or family, friends representation on patient behalf
- second opinions
- documentation of the assessments and the steps of the total process

If one or more of these were absent, the patient may be discharged on due process grounds. That is, the patient's liberty was denied without proper legal safeguards.

The outcome of this right is ensuring the patient's ability to free himself from the control of the courts. Again, for those patients who are court committed, the treatment is a denial of liberty. To allow the patient to have his liberty denied without continuing mechanisms for review is to undercut a fundamental constitutional right to freedom. The judicial discharge right depends on a strong clinical process to make the case for the patient's release, *and* it provides a way for patients themselves to secure their own release through petitions. Both processes lead to an outcome of freedom if the court is shown that the presenting conditions of the patient have changed or were wrong to start with.

Case 1. In *In re Klepper*, a patient used the judicial system to secure discharge from treatment that was forced upon her.[40] A habeus corpus petition was filed challenging the patient's commitment to a private mental hospital. The patient claimed that her federal constitutional rights were violated by her commitment. Specifically, she cited the restraint of liberty as guaranteed by the 14th Amendment to the U.S. Constitution.

Notes. Since she was denied due process, substantive and procedural, the patient was ordered released by the court. Although the opinion did not identify the details of this particular case, the court did uphold the patient's right to use habeus corpus to secure judicial discharge from the mental hospital. It can be inferred from the outcome of the case that appropriate notice, opportunity to be heard, and/or opportunity to be represented by counsel were not followed at her original admission. The case illustrates that there is a mechanism for patients to correct the violation of their right to freedom, i.e., their admission and subsequent holding in the hospital.

Case 2. In *Davis* v. *Page*, Hillary Davis, the mother of a 14-month-old baby, left her husband because he beat the baby.[41] His repeated beatings eventually broke the baby's arm. She spent the night in the hospital while the boy was cared for, then asked the state for help as she had no resources to pay either hospital bills or support.

An initial hearing of the State Juvenile and Family Division took place after which the child was to be placed in the custody of the Florida Department of

Health and Rehabilitation Services. Mrs. Davis attended the hearing without counsel. The state received custody of the child pending a formal adjudicatory hearing. Mrs. Davis was unable to obtain counsel for the adjudicatory hearing because of a lack of financial resources. Although she attempted to secure legal aid services, she was not successful and subsequently attended the hearing without counsel.

The court reacted to this lack of counsel stating that "without benefit of counsel, Hillary Davis was little more than a spectator in the adjudicatory hearing proceeding. She was ignorant of the law of evidence, and of the substantive law governing dependency proceedings. She sat silently through most of the hearing fearful of antagonizing the social workers and reluctantly consented to what she believed would be the placement of her child with the state for a few weeks." She subsequently lost the custody of her child for almost one year.

Notes. The case illustrates the judicial discharge of a child from the state's treatment and custody because of the absence of appropriate due process. Due process in this case should have included legal representation for the client. Without that representation, the process by which the hospital discharged the child to the state's custody was a violation of the patient's right. Treatment units must consider to whom they discharge, when they are discharging and, importantly, whether every discharge meets due process even if the recipient agent is a state agency.

SUMMARY

Discharge is the patient's final release from clinical, administrative, and judicial responsibility. It is also the point at which continued care planning and sound clinical judgment are to be exercised. From the severance of service to the next point, whether it is outpatient care or independent living, the discharge process may affect the way in which patients progress and how they ultimately adjust to independent living.

Above all, staff must remember that during the discharge process, a decision is being made which either stops or continues the kind of care the patient is accustomed to and may continue to require. That decision demands careful consideration, whether the outcome favors discharge or not.

Three points are most helpful. If followed, they ensure the patient's right to fairness in discharge decision-making:

1. Decision-making requires an accumulation of facts/opinions and a sifting to determine the direction that these facts and opinions support. The material must be thoroughly accumulated and reviewed at a level which would satisfy an outside group if necessary.

2. The facts and opinions must be sifted in a setting which allows patients the right to be heard, for patients are the subject of the decision—their views must be considered.

3. The discharge decision should be developed in the context of a plan. Why are staff deciding what about the patient? What will the patient do next, when, and where? Discharge decision-making requires a planned approach.

The patient's right is to be discharged as soon as care is no longer necessary. If the decision either to release or not to release is fully documented, given patient review, and presented in the context of planned care, the right is fully protected. Lack of documentation, no patient opportunity to be heard, and/or no plan for the future is insufficient, leaving the question of substandard service and the violation of the right to discharge by virtue of either prolonged treatment or premature release.

The rights requirement for discharge decision-making is a standard for quality of care. For discharge, staff should review patient status regarding the following five steps:

1. Review of history and current situation.
2. Accumulation of evidence in support of the discharge decision.
3. Opportunity for the patient to be heard regarding his pending release from care.
4. No compelling reason to retain the patient, including continuing mental illness or dangerousness to self or others.
5. A plan for discharge: What will happen next and what is the proposed outcome?

With this process, the patient is protected by a well-reviewed decision which incorporates the consumer's viewpoint.

REFERENCES

1. Joint Commission on Accreditation of Hospitals, *Consolidated Standards for Child, Adolescent and Adult Psychiatric Alcoholism and Drug Abuse Programs,* Chicago: JCAH, 1979.
2. Glick, I.D., et al., "Outcome of Irregularly Discharged Psychiatric Patients," *Amer. J. Psychiatry,* **138**:11 Nov. 1981, p. 1473.
3. Goldstein, J., Latz, J., "Dangerousness and Mental Illness: Some Observations on the Decisions to Release Persons Acquitted by Reason of Insanity," **70** *Yale L.J.,* 225 (1960).
4. Glick, et al., op. cit., (item no. 2).
5. Meyer, G.G., Margolis, P.M., Daniels, R.S., "Hospital Discharges Against Medical Advice, II: Outcome," *Arch. Gen. Psychiatry,* 8:131–137, 1963.

6. Fabrick, A.L., Ruffin, W.C., Denman, S.B., "Characteristics of Patients Discharged Against Medical Advice," *Mental Hygiene* 52:124–128, 1968.
7. Schorer, C.E., "Deviance and Healing," *Comprehensive Psychiatry*, 6:184–190, 1965.
8. Tuckman, J., Lavell, M., "Psychiatric Patients Discharged with or Against Medical Advice," *J. Clin. Psychol.*, 18:177–180, 1962.
9. Scheer, N., Barton, G.M., "A Comparison of Patients Discharged Against Medical Advice with a Matched Control Group," *Am. J. Psychiatry* 131:1217–1220, 1974.
10. Glick, et al., op. cit., (item no. 2).
11. Singer, J.E., Grob, M.C., "Patients Discharged Against Medical Advice: A Follow-up Study," *Massachusetts Journal of Mental Health* 5:57–67, 1974.
12. Daniels, R.S., Margolis, P.M., and Carson, R.C., "Hospital Discharges Against Medical Advice: I. Origin and Prevention," *Archives of General Psychiatry*, vol. 8, Feb. 1963, pp. 120–130.
13. Raynes, A.E. and Patch, V.D., "Distinguishing Features of Patients Who Discharge Themselves From Psychiatric Ward," *Comprehensive Psychiatry*, vol. 12, September 1971, pp. 473–479.
14. Altman, H., Angle, H.V., Brown, M.L., et al., "Prediction of Unauthorized Absence," *American Journal of Psychiatry*, vol. 128, May 1972, pp. 1460–1463.
15. Miles, J., Adlersberg, M., Reith, G., et al., "Discharges Against Medical Advice From Voluntary Psychiatric Units," *Hospital & Community Psychiatry*, vol. 27, December 1976, pp. 859–864.
16. Planansky, K. and Johnston, R., "A Survey of Patients Leaving a Mental Hospital Against Medical Advice," *Hospital & Community Psychiatry*, vol. 27, December 1976, pp. 865–868.
17. Tukey, J.W., *Exploratory Data Analysis*, Reading, Massachusetts: Addison-Wesley, 1977.
18. LaWall, J.S., Jones, R., "Discharges from A Ward Against Medical Advice: Search for A Profile," *Hospital and Community Psychiatry*, 31 (6), June 1980, p. 415.
19. Darcy, P.T., "Psychiatric Nursing Today 1. Protecting the Patients," *Nursing Mirror and Midwives J.*, 147 (2):31, 1978.
20. Lindman, F.T., McIntyre, D.M., eds., *The Mentally Disabled and the Law,* Chicago: Univ. of Chicago Press, 1961.
21. Brakel, S.J., Rock, R.S., eds., *The Mentally Disabled and the Law,* Chicago: Univ. of Chicago Press, 1971.
22. Batey, S.R., Dees, A.C., Ledbetter, J.E., "Using A Resource Group to Coordinate Services in Discharge Planning," *Hosp. & Community Psychiatry* 31 (6), June 1980, p. 417.
23. Bene-Kociemba, A., Cotton, P.G., Frank, A., "Predictors of Community Tenure of Discharged State Hospital Patients," *Am. J. Psychiatry* 136:12, Dec. 1979, p. 1556.
24. Rosenblatt, A., Mayer, J., "The Recidivism of Mental Patients: A Review of Past Studies," *Am J. Orthopsychiatry* 44:697–706, 1974.
25. Fontana, A.F., Dowds, B.N., "Assessing Treatment Outcome: II. The Prediction of Rehospitalization," *J. Nerv. Ment. Dis.*, 161:231–238, 1975.
26. Viesselman, J.O., Spalt, L.H., Tuason, V.B., "Psychiatric Disorders in A Community Mental Health Center: Who Gets Readmitted?" *Comprehensive Psychiatry*, 16:485–494, 1975.
27. Franklin, J.L., Kittredge, L.D., Thrasher, J.H., "A Survey of Factors Related to Mental Hospital Readmission," *Hosp. Community Psychiatry* 26:749–751, 1975.
28. Anthony, W.A., Buell, G.J., "Psychiatric Aftercare Clinic Effectiveness as a Function of Patients Demographic Characteristics," *J. Consult. Clin. Psychol.*, 41:116–119, 1973.
29. Winston, A., Parades, H., Papernik, D.S., et al., "Aftercare of Psychiatric Patients and its Relation to Rehospitalization," *Hosp. Community Psychiatry*, 28:118–121, 1977.

30. Raskin, M.O., Dyson, W.L., "Treatment Problems Leading to Readmission of Schizo-phrenic Patients," *Arch. Gen. Psychiatry,* **19**:356–360, 1969.
31. Erickson, R.C., "Outcome Studies in Mental Hospitals," *Psychol. Bull.,* **82**:519–540, 1975.
32. *Cameron* v. *State,* 37 A.D. 2d 46, 322 N.Y.S. 2d. 562 (4th Dep. 1971).
33. Annas, G.J., Glantz, L.H., Katz, B.F., *The Rights of Doctors, Nurses and Allied Health Professionals,* Cambridge, Mass.: Ballinger, 1981.
34. *Montague* v. *George J. London Memorial Hospital,* 78 Ill, Apr. 3d 295, 396, N.E. 2nd 1289 (1979).
35. *St. George* v. *State,* 203 Misc. 340, 118 N.Y.S. 2d 596 (Ct. Cl. 1953).
36. Stone, A.A., *Mental Health and Law: A System in Transition,* Rockville, Md.: NIMLT, 1975.
37. *Hiatt* v. *Soucek,* 240 Iowa 300, 36 N.W. 2d 432 (1949).
38. Ennis, B., Siegal, L., *The Rights of Mental Patients,* New York: Avon, 1973, p. 45.
39. Ibid.
40. *In re Klepper,* 49 Ohio St. 2d 211, 361 N.E. 2d 427 (1977).
41. *Davis* v. *Page,* 442 F. Supp. 258 (S.D., Fla. 1977).

Index